CHESAPEAKE ALMANAC

Father & Mother,
Thank you for Oyster Cove
And your kind support And
Thoughts.
Enjoy the nice Fall
season on the Bay.
With Love.

Steven + Susan
XO

October, 1997

CHESAPEAKE ALMANAC

Following the Bay through the Seasons

BY

JOHN PAGE WILLIAMS, JR.

Illustrations by Alice Jane Lippson

TIDEWATER PUBLISHERS

Centreville, Maryland

Library of Congress Cataloging-in-Publication Data

Williams, John Page
    Chesapeake almanac : following the bay through the seasons / by John Page Williams, Jr. ; illustrations by Alice Jane Lippson. — 1st ed.
       p.   cm.
    Includes bibliographical references (p.   ) and index.
    ISBN 0-87033-449-2 (paper)
    1. Natural history—Chesapeake Bay Region (Md. and Va.)
    2. Seasons—Chesapeake Bay Region (Md. and Va.)   I. Title.
QH104.5.C45W477 1993
508.3163′47—dc20   93-11631

Manufactured in the United States of America

First edition, 1993; second printing, 1994

CONTENTS

CONTENTS

CONTENTS

WINTER : 181

FOREWORD

Every once in a while a book comes along that is *precisely* titled. This is one. In keeping with all good almanacs, it is filled with information, wrapped in local lore, and based on seat-of-the-pants experiences. It is written for one audience—those of us who love the Chesapeake Bay.

In my sixteen years of working for the Chesapeake Bay Foundation I have met many field instructors in our education program, all of whom I admire. One, however, stands out above the others—he is John Page Williams, the author of *Chesapeake Almanac*, an edited collection of his "Naturalist's Almanac" columns from *Chesapeake Bay Magazine.* John Page lives, breathes, and, I imagine, dreams nature—almost always through the window of the Chesapeake Bay. My admiration for him extends beyond respect to outright envy of his encyclopedic knowledge of the great outdoors.

I love the natural world, and especially the Chesapeake, with a passion that sometimes startles me. But being a naturalist on the Bay means more than just having a love of nature. It requires a familiarity, an understanding, even a deep knowledge of the intricacies throughout the seasons that make our Bay so remarkable.

John Page Williams has that kind of knowledge. He has run hundreds of field trips on the Chesapeake and all its tributaries, in every month of the year. His long experience is what makes him so well qualified to put his name on *Chesapeake Almanac.* For almost anyone else, the title would be presumptuous. John Page is a teaching naturalist, and, like all good instructors, he cannot help but teach—all of the time. And so, as you read the pages that follow, you will learn a great deal, often without even realizing it.

Glance at the titles of the essays listed in the Contents. You may want to read them sequentially, by season, or selectively, as the mood strikes. Some of my favorites are "Loons in Breeding Plumage"; "Currents: Mass Transit for Bay Creatures"; "Eelgrass: Carpet of Life"; "Fall is for Rockfish"; "How Oysters Eat, and What They Mean to the Bay"; and "Cold Water Brings a Quiet Season."

For those readers who have followed John Page's writings in *Chesapeake Bay Magazine* over the years, reacquaint yourself with some old friends, and delight in some new passages that even the most assiduous *Bay Magazine* reader misses from time to time. The introductions to each section, of course, are totally new, filled with rich prose, reverence for the Chesapeake, and abundant information.

Chesapeake Almanac does not dwell on the problems facing this magnificent body of water. Rather, it celebrates all that remains in the Bay. The collection of essays makes clear, however, that the Bay's fecundity has greatly diminished over the last several decades. Oysters, for instance, are at a mere one percent of their historic levels, and their population continues to decline. Not only have we nearly lost a valuable species and an important food source, but thousands of jobs related to oystering, packing, processing, retailing, etc., have fallen prey to the decline. Even worse for the Chesapeake, oysters are no longer available to perform their vital role of filtering the water and converting overabundant algae into tasty oyster meat. It has been estimated that the nineteenth-century population of Chesapeake oysters could filter the entire volume of the Bay every four days; today it would take over one year.

Clearly, the Chesapeake needs more John Page Williamses. It needs people who have his love and knowledge of the Bay, *and* his determination to expose others to its wonders. *You* can help. By reading *Chesapeake Almanac*, you will enhance your affection for and understanding of the Bay. Thus, you will be better equipped to help "Save the Bay." If you do not yet rate the distinction of true Bay naturalist status, this book will help you get there.

William C. Baker
President, Chesapeake Bay Foundation

ACKNOWLEDGMENTS

First of all, my deepest thanks to the people at *Chesapeake Bay Magazine* who have encouraged me to write my column, "Naturalist's Almanac," month after month and year after year. The list includes especially Publisher Dick Royer, former Editor Betty Rigoli, current Editor Jean Waller, Senior Editor Barbara Goyette, and Art Director Chris Gill. The discipline of getting out a monthly column has forced me to learn a tremendous amount about the Chesapeake.

Second, thanks to the Chesapeake Bay Foundation. My various jobs there over the past 20 years have given me great access to the Bay and its people. At CBF, thanks especially to President Will Baker for his foreword and to Senior Science Advisor Mike Hirshfield for his review of the manuscript, with helpful suggestions.

Third, thanks to A. J. Lippson, the best illustrator of Chesapeake Bay creatures I know of, and a fine writer as well. I'm honored to have her sketches grace this book.

Finally, thanks to my family, especially my uncle, Dr. John L. Patterson, Jr., who has encouraged me for years to pull these columns together into a book about the seasons. Thanks also to my mother and father, my wife Louise, and my daughter Kelly for their support during the writing and editing, and to Ellen Thorson of Annapolis Word Works for a mountain of typing.

*To all the friends named in this book,
and to the many others who have helped me understand
how the Chesapeake responds to the seasons of its year.*

CHESAPEAKE ALMANAC

INTRODUCTION

Tuning In to the Rhythms of the Chesapeake's Seasons

In September each year, the weather changes. Cold front systems sweeping down through the Chesapeake Bay country become stronger, pushing stormy weather ahead and drawing beautiful, bell-clear days with northwest winds behind. By the latter part of the month, there is a cool nip in the air.

The fronts also bring one of the most stirring events of the year—the return of our migratory Canada geese. Watch the weather maps and the moon phases. Almost without fail, after September 20, if there is a strong cold front with a waxing or full moon, the first geese of the season will ride the northwest winds down from their summering grounds on the eastern side of Hudson Bay.

Some years, all the factors work just right. The front blows through, the wind hauls around, the moon shines down through a clear sky, and suddenly one night, there is that magic honking of goose flocks high overhead.

Other years, the front stalls, the weather stays stormy for several days, and it is easy to imagine the geese stacked up behind it like commuter planes waiting for their clearance to land. I remember one year in the mid-1970s when the delay was particularly long, nearly a week. The weather was fitful, calm enough to run several school field trips on protected waters with what was then the Chesapeake Bay Foundation's only canoe fleet, but not clear enough to put away the rain gear.

I spent a damp weekend with a group of CBF members exploring some of the marshes along the Patuxent, but we had to watch the weather closely. Our sense of anticipation grew each day as the forecasters optimistically predicted that the weather would clear. Finally, on Sunday afternoon, as we were loading the canoes onto the trailer beside the river, the front moved through, and the clouds began to break up. The geese literally poured in, loudly proclaiming their excitement and busily directing their young into traditional haunts.

The fact that we had been waiting for them made the event even more memorable than if their return had been routine. Being in a good place at the right time gave us the pure joy of being witnesses to this age-old annual event and made us part—in a profound way—of the Chesapeake Bay system.

At a time when it is all too easy in our society to lose touch with the earth of which we are so much a part, and specifically with the Bay country in which we live, learning how to embrace the seasons puts us in touch with the rhythms of life and gives us new insights into our place on the planet. Doing so can mean delight at the return of long-range migrants like geese and ospreys, fascination with intricate, secret processes like the sloughing (shedding) of a crab, or even enjoyment of tasty food on the table after a visit to a yellow perch spawning river. It can mean new respect for hitherto unknown or unloved creatures like oyster toads as they go about rearing their young.

Remember that most of the Bay system's creatures, both animals and plants, are cold-blooded, so they respond profoundly to the temperature changes of the seasons and the physical processes that the changes cause in the Bay and its tributaries. Those of us that are warm-blooded (birds and mammals) respond in turn to them, generally because they serve as food for us, either directly or indirectly. Migrants that come from great distances (mostly birds) use photoperiod (the length of daylight) as an index of temperature trends here. Add other physical influences like rainfall and moon phases, and the result is a rich weave that reveals some of its secrets to anyone careful enough to watch but has enough complexity to keep even the most dedicated observer busy for a lifetime.

Even if you can't spend a hundred days afield each year, you can learn to make the most of the time you have. I hope that this book will help you become more aware of life around the Bay. What I have done is pull together a selection of the "Naturalist's Almanac" columns that I have written over the past 14 years for *Chesapeake Bay Magazine* into a picture of the Bay's year. The selection includes happenings that occur all over the Bay, and even occurrences out on the continental shelf in the Atlantic that affect Bay creatures.

Some of the best-known and best-loved of the Bay's creatures, like blue crabs and great blue herons, are around for much or all of the year, so I have included sketches of their activities in several seasons. Migratory fish and birds appear at peak seasons, and a few—like ospreys, whose presence spans more than one season— make multiple appearances. River otters are year-round residents, but they are most visible in winter, so that is the best time for learning to look for them. However, what is also worth thinking about is what they and other creatures, like oysters, are doing in the off-season.

The truth is that the Chesapeake does not have an off-season. Every month of the year plays a role in how it works, and anyone who would understand it does well to follow the ebb and flow of life as the air and water temperatures change from spring to summer to fall to winter and back to spring again. I have tried to tie these happenings together whenever possible, to get you thinking about how different parts of the Bay system affect one another as the seasons progress.

Even so, the picture is far from complete. This is a big piece of fabric with lots of open spaces. I hope that *Chesapeake Almanac* will give you a start on watching the seasons, and I hope even more that you will enjoy filling in the open spaces for yourself.

I should add a quick note about the health of the Chesapeake. This book is not about the problems of the Bay, though they are serious. It is designed instead to help you focus on all that is still beautiful and fascinating and remarkable about this wonderful resource.

But it is impossible to discuss eelgrass beds, or fresh and salt marshes, or rockfish, or waterfowl, or crabs, or especially oysters without alluding to the fact that we have changed the Chesapeake system a great deal in the last 400 years. Those changes will continue, and even accelerate, as the human population in the Bay watershed continues to grow. The Chesapeake is far from dead, and as this book is written in 1993, there are some early signs of progress in restoring its health, like the recovering population of our beloved rockfish. At the same time, major challenges remain, and anyone who enjoys spending time on the Bay (I assume that that category includes you, if you are reading this book) has a responsibility to participate in the restoration effort. If you want to learn more about the Chesapeake's problems, read *Turning the Tide: Saving the Chesapeake Bay* (see Bibliography). To find out how you can get involved, write the Grassroots Department, Chesapeake Bay Foundation, 162 Prince George Street, Annapolis, MD 21401. Help us ensure that all our children and grandchildren have a healthy Bay to enjoy as much as we do.

SPRING

IT WAS A COLD GRAY DAY spitting snow as a friend and I eased our skiff into a cove on the Wye River. The weather didn't feel like spring, and the new season was still officially a week off, but there in front of us was a clear sign of the change. A pair of ospreys were repairing a nest on top of a duck blind.

Nearby, a family of tundra swans talked in agitated tones. They were winter Bay inhabitants getting ready to head back to the Arctic coast for summer, and they would be gone within the week. The ospreys had probably returned a couple of days ago from Central or South America. Mid-March is the only time that these two species are together on the Chesapeake. We watched them and felt privileged. Somehow the day wasn't cold anymore.

Two factors make spring come for the Bay's plants and animals: increasing photoperiod (longer daylight) and rising water temperatures. The longer photoperiod means more sunlight for green plants to convert to food energy by photosynthesis. It affects algae in the water (phytoplankton), submerged grasses, marsh plants, and trees on shore alike. It is also the stimulus for migratory birds like ospreys and swans. Increasing water temperature affects virtually all the Bay's creatures, triggering everything from the end of crab hibernation to rockfish spawning.

Two other physical characteristics play key roles with increasing water temperature in bringing spring to the Bay. First, water has a high specific heat value. It takes a great deal of heat to make it change its temperature. Large, deep bodies warm very slowly on spring days. Small, shallow areas, on the other hand, do so much more quickly, though they cool down to lower temperatures at night. Thus spring comes to creeks and coves sooner than to the big rivers and the open Bay. (See "Some River Geography" to get a general sense of the whole system.)

The other factor results from spring's typically clear water, which sunlight penetrates readily. Dark bottoms absorb the sunlight and radiate heat. In early spring, shallow coves with southern exposure and black mud bottoms are the warmest places of all.

Things start to happen early in the upper tidal ends of the Bay's rivers. When the water temperature reaches 5° to 6°C (41° to 43°F) in early March, yellow perch make their spawning run. The perch have experienced serious water quality problems on a number of the Chesapeake's rivers in the past 10 years, but in waterways that still have strong runs, the fish are plentiful and beautiful.

By the time of the yellow perch run, other fish are beginning to move around and feed actively. Knowledgeable anglers trying to cure cabin fever carry thermometers to raise the odds of finding largemouth bass and white perch, which forage around sun-warmed banks. Channel catfish feed in the deep holes. (See "Early Spring Fish" for more details.)

March is a good month for birders, too (and for fishermen perceptive enough to appreciate birds and other features of their favorite waters). As noted, ospreys and swans are up and about, as are a number of ducks and other waterfowl, plus shorebirds like snipe. Variety is as high as it is at any time of year. (See "Cormorants Migrating" and "Loons in Breeding Plumage.")

Longer photoperiod and warmer water cause phytoplankton to begin blooming in the creeks and rivers. Spring rains carry detritus (decayed plant material) out of the marshes. There is lots of food for zooplankton like barnacle larvae and especially copepods, the tiny shrimplike crustaceans that are among the most numerous animals in the Bay system. Their numbers explode, so that a short tow with a plankton net, even a crude, homemade one, produces water that looks like copepod stew. Numbers reach tens of thousands per cubic meter of water. The copepods will serve as food for small fish all spring, playing an especially important role in the diets of larval perch (both yellow and white) and rockfish. (See "Copepods: Keystones of Spring" and "Barnacles and Springtime.")

The marsh plants also respond to longer days. In March, everything is drab brown stubble, with only a little green showing at the bases of stalks. By April, though, longer green shoots start to appear, and broad-leaved plants like arrow arum and yellow pond lily begin to take shape. They will grow out fully in May, and by then the wild rice shoots will have begun to look like a grass lawn (no accident—wild rice *is* a grass).

Perhaps best of all for us humans who explore these creeks in the spring, bankside trees begin to flower: shadbush and wild cherries in April, sweetbay magnolia in May. Though they do not play significant roles in the creek waters, they are delights to our eyes.

Mammals become more active. Otters, who have been working hard for few fish all winter, find their food much more abundant, as do raccoons, who have been picking at anything they can find. Tender shoots of marsh plants mean new food for muskrats, and new growth on creekside shrubs provides the same for beavers.

As spring progresses, other animals move into the upper rivers. In April, white perch make their spawning runs, and their cousins the rockfish follow them, as do shad and herring. (See "Springtime Silver in the Rivers.") Like the yellow perch, all these species have been experiencing spawning difficulties, so Bay scientists and state fishery personnel watch them closely each year.

April also brings out reptiles: snapping turtles (see "Snapping Turtles up the Rivers"), painted turtles, redbelly turtles, and water snakes (see "Water Snakes and Mistaken Identity"). Downriver, diamondback terrapin begin to stir. None of these will be obvious at first, but by May, the painted turtles will be sunning themselves on fallen trees, and the diamondbacks will be mating on the shores of saltmarsh coves. (See "Diamondback Terrapin Mating.")

The open rivers and the main Bay will still look barren in March, with gulls, sea ducks, cormorants, and loons still the only obvious inhabitants. By April, however, more birds will be in evidence. (See "Little Birds, Long Trips" and "Kingfishers: Quick, Sturdy, and Loud.") In the main Bay and the lower rivers, there is more going on than meets the eye. Copepods begin to bloom for the same reasons they do in the rivers and creeks. As they increase, smaller fish begin to feed on them. Forage species like silversides and anchovies that have wintered in deep holes move into shallows to feed on the abundant plankton. Juvenile spot begin making their way into and up the Bay from their birthplaces on the continental shelf. (See "Currents: Mass Transit for Bay Creatures" for the transportation system that helps them make this journey.) Menhaden begin to do the same.

The arrival of these forage fish is a boon to hungry predators. Loons that have returned to the Bay after wintering in the ocean find more food with less effort than they have for months. They will be around till late April or early May, feeding and gathering strength for their migrations to North Country lakes. Bluefish will follow the menhaden up the Bay in late April, with the run peaking in May. The big rockfish that spawn up the rivers in April will feed in the open Bay afterwards to gain strength for their coastal migrations to New England.

In April, too, the Bay's beloved blue crabs begin moving to shallower water. Commercial crabbers start potting in deep lower Bay waters and follow them up. By the first full moon in May (unless spring is very late), the crabs are ready to make their first molt of the season. Soft-crabbers work around the clock catching peelers and sloughing them out (holding them in floats or tanks while they shed their shells). (See "For Soft-Crabbers, Summer Is a Busy Season" in June for more on the sloughing process.)

By mid-May, it is obvious that the Bay is alive again, and everyone on the water rejoices in the fact. (See "Eelgrass: Carpet of Life," "Horseshoe Crabs: A Timeless Design," "Swallows: Barn, Bank, and Tree," "Cattails: Springtime Treats from the Marshes," and "Efficient Fish Shapes" for details of the month's rich fabric of life in the Bay and up the rivers. See also "Tides Do Strange Things" for some thoughts about the tidal currents that are the framework for the daily routines of all those creatures.)

Remember, though, that the process of seasonal change actually began more than two months before. Spring is a great time of year to be out prowling around the Bay's tributaries, looking closely at the details, watching the season mature. But even into May, the water is still cold enough that hypothermia is a serious threat, so caution and good sense are essential. However, the satisfaction of watching, figuring out, and being a part of what is going on is immense. Enjoy it.

MARCH

Some River Geography

March is a good time of year to think about rivers. They warm up faster than the main Bay. Animals in them are already stirring around. By the end of the month, the first of the river herring will be coming up from the Bay and the ocean.

This is also a wet month. Spring rains begin. The rivers and the rainwater they carry off are the lifeblood of the Chesapeake. At the same time, however, research over the past 20 years has diagnosed the problems that the rivers bring to the estuary, especially overenrichment from the nutrients nitrogen and phosphorus, which causes excessive algae growth and a host of related problems.

It is important to remember that the problems are serious precisely because the rivers are so valuable in the first place. There is no other estuary in the world with a network of rivers like the one that feeds the Chesapeake. Nutrients cause problems only at excessive concentrations. They are the essential building blocks of the biological community, and the rivers are where they come from.

The Chesapeake itself is a river, after all. It is the drowned valley of the Susquehanna. During the last ice age, or 20,000 years ago, sea level was about 100 meters (328 feet) lower than it is today, because much of the earth's water was tied up in the polar ice caps. One glacier extended, in fact, all the way down to what today is north-central Pennsylvania. The Susquehanna began at the edge of that glacier and ran southeast to the Atlantic, gathering tributaries as it flowed to its mouth on the edge of the continental shelf, well to the east of where the Virginia Capes are today.

As the earth began to warm up, sea level rose, and the Atlantic's dense salty water flooded into the river's mouth, flowing in on the tides underneath the fresh water coming downstream. Eventually, the tidal water worked its way up the Susquehanna to Smith's Falls, just above Port Deposit, creating a 200-mile-long tidal river mouth which the Indians named Chesapeake.

The point here is that the Chesapeake has its origins in the Susquehanna and its tributaries. Thus every square inch in the drainage basins of those rivers is connected directly to the Bay. It is worth looking at their geography.

The Susquehanna is the largest river on the Atlantic Coast of the United States. It stretches all the way up through central Pennsylvania and into south-central New York, where it cradles the southern end of the Finger Lakes watershed. Those lakes flow north into Lake Ontario, but the land immediately to the east and south of them drains to the Chesapeake. Binghamton, Corning, and Elmira are on the Susquehanna and so belong to the Chesapeake. In fact, until the river was dammed in the 1840s, spawning herring ran far enough up the Susquehanna from the Bay and the ocean that Binghamton had a commercial fishery in the spring. That distance is a full 500 hundred miles (200 of Bay and 300 of river) from the Atlantic.

The Susquehanna's average discharge of fresh water is about 35,000 cubic feet per second (cfs), larger than the Connecticut (16,500 cfs) and the Hudson (14,500 cfs) combined. In fact, it contributes half the fresh water that enters the Chesapeake.

That statistic looks grossly inaccurate if one examines a map of the Bay. The Susquehanna's mouth, between Havre de Grace and Perryville, is only a half-mile across, much smaller than the mouths of the Potomac (over 5 miles), the James (nearly 4 miles), and a dozen others. Even the relatively small Chester has a mouth wider than the Susquehanna's. But look at the map again. The Potomac's mouth is the mouth of its 100-mile-long tidal section. The Susquehanna's mouth, as maps define it, is just below the point where it becomes tidal.

In fact, the tidal section of the Susquehanna has a different name. It is called Chesapeake Bay. Now look at the map again and compare the upper Bay with the lower Potomac. That comparison will give a sense of how big the Susquehanna is.

Mind, though, that the Potomac is no small river either. It is, in fact, the eighth-largest river on the Atlantic Coast (11,200 cfs). Its branches come down all the way from West Virginia, the Shenandoah Valley of Virginia, western Maryland, and even south-central Pennsylvania. The James is also a major coastal river, at about 7,000 cfs. It rises in Highland County, Virginia, out on the eastern slopes of the Appalachians. Together, these three rivers contribute just over 75 percent of the Bay's fresh water.

The next three rivers, the Rappahannock, the York, and the Patuxent, are grouped together but are much smaller, at 1,500-3,000 cfs. But all three, and the even smaller ones too, are important to the system. Ask anyone who lives on the Choptank, the Pocomoke, the Piankatank, the Sassafras, the Severn, or any of the others how valuable their rivers are. Ask any Bay scientist. Yes, the Chesapeake is rich in rivers, a happy fact for all of us who live by it.

Early Spring Fish

Cold weather is losing its grip on the Chesapeake, but even a mild winter cools the Bay's waters down far enough for most cold-blooded creatures like fish to go dormant. March looks dull and bare and brown, but there are more of these cold-blooded animals stirring than meets the eye, at least at first glance. Look closely. There are already several signs of spring in the water.

That water is still cold, hovering around 4°C (39.2°F), but Norfolk spot (*Leiostomus xanthurus*) have been spawning since December out in the Atlantic on the continental shelf. The earliest-born juveniles will be entering the Bay this month, riding the deep currents up to rich summering grounds in almost all the tributaries and marsh guts. Right now, they are hard for the layman to find; tiny and transparent, they are deep in the cold waters of the open Bay. But they are there, and their presence is just as much a benchmark of the change of seasons as the first crocuses and daffodils on land.

Winter flounder (*Pseudopleuronectes americanus*), as their name implies, also are active in the lower Bay now. In fact, this month is the peak of their spawning season, at temperatures of 2° to 5°C (35.6° to 41°F). After they finish spawning, they will move to shallower waters. There they will make up part of the early catch of pound net fishermen along the Virginia Bayshore and so will find their way to fish markets.

The pound-netters will see other evidence of spring this month. As rains flush detritus (decayed plant material) out of the winter marshes, the zooplankton populations will begin to build, and members of the herring family (Clupeidae) will come into the Bay to browse on them. Labrador herring (*Clupea harengus*) are the first to arrive. Unlike their relatives, these fish are ocean spawners. They enter the Chesapeake only as opportunists to take advantage of a rich early-season food supply before going back to sea.

Shortly thereafter, the alewives, or river herring (*Alosa pseudoharengus*), enter. They may feed briefly, but they are on their way up the Bay and its rivers to spawn. The plankton will benefit them most on their way back down to the Atlantic. Again it will be net fishermen who will see them first. Those that are caught will be salted for eating or frozen for crab bait. (The Atlantic menhaden, *Brevoortia tyrannus*, is often called "alewife" or "elwye" in the upper Bay. It is a different species, though closely related to the herring.)

The rivers and creeks are lower in volume of water, so they will warm faster than the main Bay. As a result, there will be more early activity in them. These smaller bodies also tend to be more sheltered (and therefore somewhat safer for boatmen), so they will be the areas where recreational anglers open their season.

The yellow perch (*Perca flavescens*) is not large, reaching a maximum length of 15 inches in the Chesapeake's tributaries. It is, however, a sporting fish on light tackle, and very good to eat, particularly if taken from cold water. In a mild winter, yellow perch will be moderately active even in January and February, especially the females with roe developing in their bellies. Unlike the herring, yellow perch feed heavily during their spawning runs.

Their numbers declined in Maryland in the 1980s because of water quality problems in the spawning streams, probably exacerbated by historically heavy fishing pressure. Tight fishing restrictions and habitat improvements have since helped them, and stocks on some rivers are growing, albeit slowly.

Small increases in water temperature, say from 3° to 5°C (37.4° to 41°F), will start the perch schooling in rivers like the Bush at the head of the Bay and in small creeks like Mount Landing on the Rappahannock. Optimum spawning temperature is 8° to 11°C (46.4° to 51.8°F). The perch move up to the head of tidal influence on the creek (often a beaver dam), and the females lay their long ribbons of eggs. The males fertilize them immediately, and the skeins drift down with the current until they catch on submerged vegetation or the branches of fallen trees. There they wave in the current, changing direction with the tide, hatching in about a month.

Yellow perch runs can be frustrating to anglers, though. A bluebird day in March is something to treasure, and the warming trend that comes with it can trigger spawning. But March is fickle, and a cold, cloudy day with rain can shut the run right off. Because of changes in the weather, the peak of the run in any one creek will often be short, lasting perhaps only a day or two. Then the fish head back downstream and disperse, leaving the ribbons of eggs behind.

There are other fish moving in the freshwater creeks in March. The white suckers *(Catostomus commersoni)* are spawning too, leaving eggs singly or in small groups on the bottom. Just as the yellow perch had begun to school in the creeks a week or so before spawning, so now the white perch *(Morone americanus)* are doing the same. They will begin laying eggs shortly after the yellows finish, and will reach their peak a week or two later, when the water temperature is at about 15°C (59°F). The silvery minnow *(Hybognathus nuchalis)*, a common forage fish in the creeks, also will be spawning then.

Throughout the month, on sunny days, largemouth bass *(Micropterus salmoides)* and chain pickerel *(Esox niger)* will be foraging in the warmest shallows. They too have roe developing and need food to keep the process going. April will see them spawning, along with the alewives and the first of the blueback herring *(Alosa aestivalis)*.

But April is another story, officially part of spring, with green leaves coming out and shadbush blooming. The signs of new life are more subtle in March, hinging on small changes in temperature and occurring against a backdrop of winter drabness. Because of that contrast, they are all the more exciting.

Cormorants Migrating

It was Cape May Point in Delaware Bay, not the Chesapeake, and it was early October, not March, so the birds were headed south. Up high and out in the distance, a long V of large, dark birds appeared, flapping their wings steadily. Canada geese, of course. They were the right size, the wing beat had the right cadence, and the time was right. Except that these birds were entirely dark, with long, square tails, and necks that were crooked in the middle and a little too short. Besides, they weren't honking; they were silent. When they came directly overhead, it was easy to get a good look at them. They were double-crested cormorants *(Phalacrocorax auritus)*.

Most of us, if we think of cormorants at all, think of pictures we have seen of oriental watermen using birds with rings around their necks to catch fish. Maybe so, but for most of the year, double-crested cormorants are very much a part of our world here on the Chesapeake.

This bird is the only cormorant species that appears commonly on the Bay (there are several others around the world, including the one used in the Orient), and it comes in large numbers as a transient in both spring and fall. The birds flying over Cape May Point could easily have been headed for a stopover of several weeks here on their way to wintering grounds farther south. Now, in the early spring, the same birds will be working their way back north, and flocks of them will pause here to fish. They will be largely unnoticed by humans, though, mostly because there are relatively few people out on the water to see them.

All resemblance to geese ends quickly on close examination. The basic design of cormorants has not changed much in millions of years, primarily because it is an effective one for a fish-eating migratory bird that dives and swims underwater to catch its prey. The cormorants are related to two other successful fishing designs, the pelicans and the gannets. They are, however, the only ones of the group that swim extensively underwater, so they do not use the dive-bombing tactics of their more spectacular kin.

The Virginia Society of Ornithology lists the double-crested cormorant as an "abundant transient" from March 5 to May 30 and from August 10 to November 20. It is an "irregular and locally common winter resident and summer visitor," with one breeding record from the south bank of the James. More generally, the birds winter in a long band along the southern coast of the United States and breed in summer along the rocky coast of New England, the Canadian Maritime Provinces, and Newfoundland. With the Chesapeake a good source of fish squarely on the route between their wintering and breeding areas, it is no wonder that large numbers of them stop off here in migration.

The birds do not all breed at the same time, but stagger their nesting over a couple of months in the summer. Thus the young of a breeding colony will be at various stages of development at any given time, and the families will not migrate all together. Hence the protracted migration periods in both fall and spring.

March is an especially good month for early migrants. The Bay's resident fish populations are beginning to stir, and a few fish are coming in from the Atlantic. In past years, stake gill nets and pound nets set for the first herring runs acted as cormorant magnets. A line of 40 stakes would have 40 big black birds perched and resting, drying their wings. But herring runs have fallen off in recent years, fewer watermen set pound nets, and stake nets are heavily regulated. Even so, there will be plenty of cormorants around, resting on channel markers and feeding on anchovies and silversides, as well as whatever herring they can find.

On the water, cormorants have a distinctive profile. They float very low, with their backs nearly awash, necks erect, and long, hooked bills pointing skyward. Their feet and short legs, set far back on the body, are awkward on land but provide powerful propulsion on dives. The birds use their wings underwater as well, and the long beaks become efficient fish catchers. Underwater feeding is always a tricky balance between energy expended in diving and energy acquired from food eaten.

Cormorants' feathers are dense, and they have no oil glands for preening their feathers for buoyancy, which would hinder diving. In exchange for underwater efficiency, they have to put up with the inconvenience of drying their feathers before they can fly. On a line of net stakes, cormorants are almost comical, standing nearly erect on the tops of the stakes with their wings spread in the breeze.

Comical maybe, but the cormorant design is a good one, and it continues to stand the test of time. For anyone who watches the

Bay closely, they are a most interesting group of birds, adding yet another dimension to the Chesapeake's year.

Loons in Breeding Plumage

By March, it is easy to have cabin fever and a real urge to get outdoors. As long as you are prudent about safety, this is a good time to be on the water. The Bay country is still chilly, drab, and brown, but there is a lot to see.

Some things are obvious, like swans staging in large flocks for migration, or ospreys just returning from the south. But there are some quieter sights. The osprey-watcher may well swing the binoculars out to open water and find a large bird with a heavy bill sitting quietly and half-submerged. Suddenly the bird dives, but so unobtrusively that the observer wonders if it had ever been there at all. Then it is there again, as if it had never gone. It is a common loon *(Gavia immer)* in its dramatic breeding plumage: dark iridescent head and neck, collar of alternating black and white vertical stripes, white breast, and black and white–checked back. Like the swans, it will be heading north this spring.

Loons seem to live two lives. In summer, they live by couples on small lakes and tundra ponds all across Canada and the northern United States from Minnesota to upstate New York and northern New England. They breed also in Labrador, Greenland, and Iceland. In general, they live quietly and away from humans, but the few people close to them are always thrilled, amazed, or horrified by their eerie, ghostly cries.

The birds raise their chicks by the water's edge, carrying them on their backs till they learn to swim and dive. As cold weather comes in the fall, they join loons from other lakes and migrate to the coasts where the water stays open all winter.

In winter on the Pacific, they range from British Columbia all the way to Mexico. On the Atlantic, they can be found from Nova Scotia to Florida. Large numbers of them spend the fall on the Chesapeake feeding on menhaden, before flying over to the Atlantic to feed in the relatively warm, shallow waters over the continental shelf during their wintertime molting period, when they cannot fly.

They return to the Chesapeake in late February and March, resplendent in new breeding plumage. As the Bay wakes up, they feed on its spring bounty—herring in March and April, menhaden in May—to regain their strength for migration and breeding.

Loons are remarkable divers. Their bodies are streamlined and compact. Feathers are short and dense, efficient enough to insulate them all winter in near-freezing water, but not oily enough to create bouyancy and hinder them underwater. Their broad feet are placed far back on their bodies, just under their short tails. The feet generate tremendous power; loons have been caught in nets at depths over 150 feet. They are nearly as efficient as rockfish and blues at chasing small fish.

For underwater efficiency, the loon's wings are relatively small, so it takes effort and a sprint across the water to get aloft. Returning to the water, the bird cannot brake easily either, so it comes in low, hard, and fast. When approached on the water by man, it is more likely to dive than fly.

Once aloft, however, the bird is a strong flier. It is distinctive: about the size of a goose, with a similar wingbeat but a shorter neck and big feet trailing behind. There will be loons around the Bay from now until early May. Watermen, sailors, and anglers will see them, if they watch carefully.

Copepods: Keystones of Spring

It's a real drag to tow a plankton net behind a canoe—the fine mesh acts like a small sea anchor. Pulling one against the tide in a narrow creek is even tougher, but it is a good way to stay warm on a chilly March day. Besides, at the end of five minutes, the bottle at the bottom of the net will be full of tiny crustaceans called copepods, true harbingers of spring. Their population explosions at this time of year produce important fuel for the Bay's new life as the water warms.

Copepods are among the most abundant multicellular animals on earth. They are generally regarded as the most numerous in the Chesapeake system, with numbers going routinely as high as 30,000 per cubic meter of water in certain areas each spring. A five-minute tow behind the canoe means catching well over 100,000, each just barely visible to the naked eye. A 3× hand lens brings them clearly into view, and a 10× dissecting microscope gives a detailed look.

The general shape of copepods gives away their ancestry. They are closely related to shrimp, lobsters, and crabs. Like shrimp and lobsters (and crabs, though we're usually not aware of it), they have two pairs of antennae and large thoraxes (body trunks) that hold vital organs. Behind the animal's thorax is a segmented tail. Both the thorax and the tail have many paired legs covered with short bristles.

Copepods mature in one to three weeks, depending on water temperature, so it is common to find females carrying twin egg sacks, like saddle bags, one on each side of their tails. A springtime tow with the net will catch a mixture of mature individuals, nauplius larvae, and juveniles, called copepodites.

Like many other crustaceans, copepods are omnivores, eating both plant and animal matter. The arrangement of legs allows several of the important species in the Bay to filter small particles out of the water or to catch larger ones. The animals move some of their legs to set up water currents that bring food to them.

So much for scientific description. In plain language, what does an animal this small eat? It's hard for us to imagine, but here's the story.

The early March sun is still weak, but the days are getting longer, so there is more light available. Skim ice that forms at night thaws during the day, and the surface layer reaches water's densest temperature, 4°C (39.6°F), causing it to sink. This sinking forces up bottom water and some bottom sediments. The stirring action is increased by spring wind and rain. The result is a bloom of phytoplankton, microscopic (much smaller than copepods) single-celled plants (algae) that thrive on the sunlight and the nutrients brought to the surface with the bottom water.

Springtime concentrations of all types of phytoplankton are not as great as they will be later on, but they still run well over a million cells per liter, and there are a thousand liters in a cubic meter. It's crowded water, even if it looks clear. The phytoplankton are a major source of food for copepods, which filter them from the water.

The copepods' other major source of food comes from the marshes. Now is a good time of year to think about this phenomenon, with both salt and fresh marshes looking like nothing more than brown stubble. In the fall, perennial marsh plants (like salt-marsh cordgrass, cattails, and yellow pond lilies) die back to their root systems. The leaves and stems wither and begin to decay. At the same time, annual plants (like wild rice and smartweeds) die altogether, leaving their tons of seeds to carry on the following year.

All this withered plant material is broken up by winter weather: rain, wind, freezing, thawing, blankets of snow. Bacteria decay it further. Then spring rains and tides wash it out of the marshes into the creeks and rivers. Not very appetizing, is it? Or nutritious—at least to us. But this mix of detritus (decayed material, with its associated bacteria) is like a rich vegetable broth with "bacon bits" (the bacteria) to lots of Bay creatures, including copepods. The thaw and rains that we usually get in late February produce a veritable stewpot to fuel March's copepod blooms.

The timing is apt. Yellow perch are making their spawning runs now at the heads of many rivers and creeks. White perch will follow at the end of the month and in April; then will come rockfish. Silversides and anchovies, two important forage species for larger fish, are also getting ready to spawn. In all these cases, the larval fish hatch out with yolk sacs to nourish them for a week or so. After that time, they are on their own. For these young fish, copepodites (juvenile copepods) are perfect food. As the fish grow, they begin to feed on adult copepods. The little shellfish provide an essential link in the Bay's spring food web.

As the season progresses, the numbers of spring copepods drop. One species, *Eurytemora affinis*, is the dominant animal in early spring, followed as the water warms by another species, *Acartia tonsa*, especially in brackish and salty waters.

By now, the Bay and its rivers are full of menhaden, shoals and shoals of them. These fish, though larger, are filter feeders too. They swim along, gulping water so that it passes over specially adapted gill filaments. Copepods are a major food for them. Menhaden play many roles in the Bay, but the most important, to us anyway, are that they are primary forage for bluefish, rockfish, sea trout, and other predators, and that they furnish us with tens of millions of pounds of crab bait each year. Again we can thank copepods, at least in part.

You may have noticed earlier that no common names were given for *Eurytemora affinis* and *Acartia tonsa*. They don't have any. We tend not to give everyday names to creatures we do not see regularly or are not even aware of. (Scientists, of course, look at them regularly, and they are the ones who need the Latin termi-

nology.) Discovering that creatures as important as those two copepods do not have common names is a humbling experience for us
laymen. There is a lot out there in our Bay that we don't know
about. But all that unknown is part of the mystery that keeps us
facinated with it. It's especially exciting when pieces start to fit
together, linked by creatures like copepods, the keystones of spring.

Barnacles and Springtime

Copepods are not the only animals that an early spring plankton
tow will catch. Mixed in with them will be wedge-shaped creatures
with six legs each, sculling themselves about. They are barnacle
larvae.

Development of the tiny creatures is slow in cold water, and
they have some changes to go through, so it will be a month or
more before these early larvae settle on pilings and fallen trees and
boat bottoms. Like the copepods, they will build to a peak later in
the spring, but there are enough around now to make watching
them interesting. It seems strange that these tiny, transparent animals can cause enough trouble to support a worldwide industry of
boatyards and sophisticated paint manufacturers, as well as major
controverseries about toxic substances put into the paints to dis-
courage them.

Everyone has a least one good barnacle story. Invariably these
tales involve hands cut by sharp shells, or speed- and fuel-robbing
crust on boat bottoms. We tend to think of barnacles as rounded,
empty shells that scrape like a wood rasp and cling as though held
by Superglue. It takes a sharp eye to watch a live adult in action.

Two hundred years ago, barnacles were considered mollusks,
kin to oysters and clams. But an early microbiologist set up an
experiment to watch a few adults spawn. He raised the larvae and
was surprised to find they were actually crustaceans, kin to copepods, shrimp, and crabs. They molted, changed to a second larval
form, settled onto a firm base in the tank, and metamorphosed into
adults. The experience led him to closer examination of the adults,
which of course showed them indeed to be crustaceans.

This group of animals, like their relatives the insects and
spiders, have hard outer shells of protein and calcium combined
in a substance called chitin, with bodies and legs jointed for move-

ment. In the case of the barnacles, the outer shell, with which we are all too familiar, is made of plates of chitin locked tightly together, with two sliding hatches of shell overhead that are opened and closed by muscles inside. Look at an encrusted piling at low tide. Open, empty shells are dead, but those with closed doors are live ones. When the water returns, they will open up, and the animals will begin to feed.

There is an old saying, attributed to T. H. Huxley, that a barnacle stands on its head and kicks food into its mouth with its legs. It is a good description, except that the adult barnacle does not have much of a head, and its nervous system is relatively simple compared with that of a motile crustacean like a crab.

But the curved, feathery legs are graceful and beautifully coordinated. They sweep out of the shell and back in, picking up zooplankton (probably even including some of the barnacle's own larvae), diatoms, and other phytoplankton. The legs set up currents that sweep in smaller creatures like bacteria. The easiest way to watch barnacles is to find an encrusted chunk of wood or oyster shell and put it into a pan or a bucket of water. The barnacles will close up during the transfer, but after a few minutes, they will open and begin feeding again. Even now, in March, adult barnacles are feeding, especially on sunny, warm days.

It is all too easy for us boatowners to take a negative view of barnacles. They not only foul a boat's bottom themselves, but they offer good nooks and crannies where other creatures can attach as well. A community of algae, worms, sponges, amphipods, and other tiny animals builds up around the shells.

On a boat bottom, this creates a royal mess. But consider its value if it is growing on a piling. Sometime this summer, lie on your stomach on a dock and watch what is happening around its pilings. Crabs rest on them, but they also feed on the worms, amphipods, and grass shrimp they catch there. White perch and spot nibble at the same foods, as well as nipping and crushing some of the barnacles themselves. The fish turn and roll, flashing in the dim light as they labor to get purchase on stubborn shells. Enterprising fishermen know to work a group of bridge or pier pilings for these panfish, and sometimes for the bigger rockfish, trout, or flounder that they in turn attract. Barnacles are problems on boats, but in other places they are extremely valuable.

APRIL

Springtime Silver in the Rivers

In late April and early May, Bates Chappell catches himself staring out of his office window more often than usual. He is on the fifteenth floor of a bank tower in Richmond, and his window faces the fall line of the James River. Some days, he comes to work with an aluminum skiff on the roof of his truck, and he sneaks out of the office early to fish for the shad and herring that run up the river to spawn. Both are great sport fish, and even better food. He's been making these afternoon trips for 25 years; they are a major rite of spring.

In our civilized end-of-the-twentieth-century society, there is still a part of us that relates strongly to primordial occurrences like springtime spawning runs. Fish like shad and herring that live at sea but ascend the rivers to spawn have always been symbols of rebirth at winter's end.

The fish also provided lucrative commercial fisheries to watermen up and down the Chesapeake, from haul-seiners at Ocean View to pound-netters out of Mathews and gill-netters from Rock Hall. Combined Virginia and Maryland catches of herring (alewives and bluebacks together) ranged between 20 million and 40 million pounds each year through the first half of this century. During the same period, the fishery for American shad (*Alosa sapidissima*) had the highest dollar value of any on the Bay, despite a season of only about four months; and, from the early 1950s on, the fish supported a significant recreational fishery as well. Shad roe and fresh asparagus on a table set with a vase of daffodils is a classic Chesapeake springtime dinner.

Many of us have had some experience with the shad and herring runs, but it is surprising to look at descriptions of the runs in the late eighteenth and early nineteenth centuries, when the Bay watershed was still mostly forest and farmland. George Washington, for example, was primarily a planter, but he knew the profits to be made in fishing the springtime runs and always maintained haul seine crews for the season at Mount Vernon. The Potomac yielded him herring in such numbers that they were sold not by the pound but by the bushel.

Even more surprising is the geographic extent of the runs in those days before the rivers were dammed. Herring Run Park in northeast Baltimore, for example, is named for a time when Back River and its tributaries were far different from what they are today. On the Rappahannock, the fish swam up past the fall line at Fredericksburg and spread themselves all over the Virginia Piedmont, right up to the eastern slopes of the Blue Ridge Mountains. On the James, shad ran all the way to Lynchburg, and herring ran to Covington, on the Jackson River (a James tributary), at the edge of the Allegheny Plateau.

The greatest Bay river of all, the Susquehanna, distributed the fish throughout central Pennsylvania, on the West Branch and the Juniata as well as the main stem. Until about 1830, when the river was first dammed, there were commercial herring fisheries all the way to Binghamton, New York, over 300 miles upstream from the Chesapeake.

But times have changed. Bates talked about them while we spent an afternoon on the river, casting tiny gold spoons with light spinning rods under the shadow of Richmond's Mayo Bridge. We caught some herring and white perch, but no shad, and the herring were smaller than they had been in past years. The change is ironic, because 25 years ago when Bates began his spring trips, the James was a dirtier river. Richmond now seems to be serious about dealing with its sewage, and water quality, while still far from pristine, is improving.

Bates's sense of decline finds concrete and quantitative verification in the records of the commercial fisheries. Catches of both herring and shad have plummeted. Maryland imposed a ban on all fishing for American shad in 1979, and for its smaller cousin, the hickory shad *(Alosa mediocris)* in 1980. In Virginia, the stocks have dropped far enough that most watermen have shifted their efforts to other species, and the Virginia Marine Resources Commission is phasing in a total moratorium on fishing them in the Bay and its rivers. These once-prized fish are now almost forgotten by the public at large.

What happened? As usual, there are no easy answers, beyond the one that is always there: human activities change waterways, usually to the detriment of the creatures that live in them. Migrating shad and herring do not leap like salmon. By the 1830s, the Susquehanna, James, and Rappahannock were being dammed for water power and canal systems. On the Susquehanna and its tributaries, some 500 miles of spawning habitat were cut to 10 by the early part of this century. Herring, which spawn in small tributary creeks, found themselves cut off by blockages as apparently innocent as road culverts.

Changes in water quality have affected the stocks too. The fish apparently home in on their natal rivers by smell, and we still do not know how these characteristic river smells have changed in the Bay system over time.

Fishing pressure has also played a role. Reducing harvests is tough on watermen and recreational anglers, but it is one of the few things that we can do *now* to conserve fish while we address the problems like blockages and water quality that require longer-term solutions.

Solutions? Can these declines be turned around? There are indications that they can. A major fish lift at Philadelphia Electric Company's Conowingo Dam on the Susquehanna, plus stocking and a tagging program conducted jointly by the Pennsylvania Fish and Boat Commission, the Maryland Department of Natural Resources, and the other utility companies with dams on the river have shown that shad will still spawn in central Pennsylvania. The utility companies have entered into an agreement to provide passage around all four of the dams above Conowingo, opening the river all the way to Harrisburg.

Farther south, the City of Richmond and the Virginia Department of Game and Inland Fisheries have breached the two lowest dams on the James and are now planning to open up the next two, which will allow the fish to run to Lynchburg. Virginia is also working on plans for the Rappahannock and the Appomattox (a large James tributary).

Maryland, in addition to its work on the Susquehanna, has begun an aggressive program on the Patapsco and is attacking smaller blockages on the Elk, the Patuxent, and the Gunpowder.

The Delaware River and the Connecticut River are good models for us to follow. The Delaware is no rose, but it has no dams, and its water quality has improved over the past 20 years. It now has a strong run of both American shad and herring each spring, providing a wonderful sport fishery of great recreational and economic value to areas above Philadelphia like Bucks County. On the Connecticut, where fishery agencies have had to provide passages for both Atlantic salmon and shad around many dams left over from the early Industrial Revolution, the runs are improving. On that river in 1982, Atlantic salmon ran upriver into Vermont for the first time since 1797.

These achievements took long-term dedication from many people, which makes them all the more gratifying. Here on the Chesapeake, we *can* have shad and herring again. Shad roe, asparagus, and daffodils. Imagine how sweet it is to see a resource restored.

Snapping Turtles up the Rivers

"There he is. Look at that ugly old thing," chuckled Bill Pike affectionately as he took a break from his perch fishing. A washtub-sized boil appeared on the water as a big snapping turtle surfaced and stared at us.

It was April, and we were anchored in Bill's skiff beside a fallen tree in one of the salt ponds on the Severn River above Annapolis. The tree was on a south-facing bank, so the sun by midday had warmed the water several degrees and brought a school of perch to forage on grass shrimp among the submerged limbs. It had also brought the turtle, not so much for the perch, which the big animal was too slow to catch, but for the warmth the critter received by basking at the surface. Bill had fished the tree several times in the previous few days. He and the turtle were well acquainted with one another.

The Chesapeake region is home to a broad variety of turtles. Many brackish and high-salinity marsh areas have healthy populations of diamondback terrapins. Several species of sea turtles venture into the open waters of the lower Bay. Painted turtles and a number of other freshwater species inhabit the upper reaches of the rivers.

The most widely distributed species, however, is the common snapping turtle *(Chelydra serpentina serpentina)*. The snapper lives in an impressively large range of habitats, from farm ponds to shallow creeks to backwaters of tidal rivers, including areas like the Severn where salinities can reach up to one-third the concentration of seawater.

Archie Carr describes the snapper as big, aggressive, ubiquitous, and succulent in his excellent *Handbook of Turtles* (see Bibliography). The animals are quite large, commonly reaching weights of 20 to 30 pounds. Growth is slow, and age is difficult to determine in the wild, but snapping turtles appear able to live at least 15 years.

Snappers are known to be active occasionally even in cold water. They have been observed crawling under ice in winter, but normally they bury themselves in mud then to hibernate. Their body metabolism slows way down, and they are able to live for long periods on small quantities of oxygen. Bill Pike's turtle had probably just emerged from the mud and was basking in the sun to raise its body temperature. It spent most of an hour near us, suspended just below the surface with only its eyes and nostrils out of the water.

The snapping turtle's name describes both its disposition and its standard method of feeding. Young snappers are agile enough to chase and capture moving quarry like crayfish, but large snappers are more likely to lie in wait and strike at prey with their long necks and sharp beaks. Although slow of body, they are remarkably quick at ambush. The tactic allows them to catch fish, frogs, snakes, small birds, and mammals that come within reach. They tend to be most active at night.

In fact, snapping turtles are yet more versatile. An animal that lives in such a broad range of environments must be able to handle a very broad diet. This turtle is a true omnivore, feeding also on brackish water clams, crabs, worms, and tender parts of marsh plants. It even scavenges dead fish.

In the water, snapping turtles are not always as aggressive as might be expected, even around humans. When we Chesapeake Bay Foundation field instructors were first experimenting with fyke nets in the education program, I raised a net to the surface by hand on Occupacia Creek on the Rappahannock. As the net cleared the water, I saw that my fingers were 4 inches from the head of a 15-pound turtle, which just stared at me without making a move. The incident was a good lesson in turtle behavior, but we've found other ways to retrieve our fykes since then.

On land, a snapping turtle is on the defensive and should be treated with great caution. Remember that it cannot run fast, but it can strike quickly, and its neck can extend a surprising distance. Do not handle one if you can help it. If you must, the rough tail is a safe handhold for dragging the turtle, but it is not good for lifting, as the animal's weight can cause severe injury to its vertebrae. If possible, lift by the hind legs. Hold the turtle well away from your legs with the belly toward you. (This suggestion comes from *Turtles of the United States*, by Carl H. Ernst and Roger W. Barbor; see Bibliography.)

Snapping turtles breed from April to November. There seems to be a peak of activity in late May and June. The female will hunt for a sandy spot, often some distance from the water, dig a hole, deposit her eggs, cover the hole, and leave. It is not unusual to find one making a nest on a sandy road at the edge of a marsh. Eggs hatch in two or three months if they are undisturbed by skunks, raccoons, black snakes, and other predators. Sometimes eggs laid in the fall will not hatch till the following spring.

Snappers are not as highly regarded for food on the Bay as the diamondback, but, as Carr noted, they are succulent. There is a limited but steady market to make snapper soup, especially in central Pennsylvania. Most of the turtles are caught in wire traps baited with dead fish. An old practice of catching them with baited hooks on lines set from poles is now outlawed in tidal waters of the Bay system, though it is legal in nontidal ponds in some areas.

The only danger of harvesting them is that, since they grow slowly, it is difficult for a population to recover from heavy fishing pressure. For this reason, full-time turtle trappers are constantly on the move from place to place. At present, demand seems to be modest enough that the Chesapeake's snappers are not in any danger of extinction.

Snapping turtles appear to labor under a number of handicaps. They are slow-moving and slow-growing. They have big bodies to feed. But they represent a highly successful design. Adaptability appears to be their great strength. At first glance, they are ugly and mean, but on second look they become much more interesting. No one could call them beautiful, but they are not hard to appreciate. Bill Pike speaks to his turtle with genuine affection.

Water Snakes and Mistaken Identity

My daughter Kelly and I were sneaking along a trail in the Patuxent River Park on a raw, damp April day, trying to get a good look at a raft of ducks resting in the wild rice marshes of Jug Bay. Suddenly Kelly shrieked and jumped what seemed like 6 feet sideways. She had stepped on something she thought was a tree root, and it had moved under her foot. Considering that she was only six years old at the time, her reaction was understandable. To her credit, she went right back to look at the "root." It was a water snake *(Natrix sipedon)* caught in an embarrassing situation.

The two previous days had been warm. As best we could guess, the snake had come out of its winter burrow and begun moving around, at least enough to find a sunny spot where it could bask to get its body temperature up. But a low pressure system had swept into the area, bringing rain and cooler temperatures. The snake's metabolism had slowed down again, catching it out in the open. It could react only with a sluggish heave of its body to the insult of being stepped on. We gently moved it out of the path and left it to rouse at its own pace.

April sluggishness is a fact of life for a cold-blooded animal, but it is not otherwise a characteristic of the active, curious, and occasionally feisty water snake. By far the most common snake along the Chesapeake's rivers and marshes, the water snake belongs to a large group of nonpoisonous snakes, the family Colubridae, which also includes the very common terrestrial black, king, and garter snakes.

In general, the water snake grows to a length of $3\frac{1}{2}$ feet, with a narrow head and wide, dark-brown bands on its back. These bands are interspersed by lighter brown, and they taper to narrow markings on the sides. Bellies are white to yellow.

There are, however, some 10 subspecies of water snake in North America, so markings can vary a great deal. Some water snakes in the Chesapeake region are almost uniformly brown.

The striped individuals are sometimes mistaken for copperheads. However, the copperheads have the reverse color pattern: tan hourglass markings across the back, interspersed by narrow dark-brown bands. Their heads are broader and flatter than the water snakes' and are generally brightly colored, "like a new penny," as the saying goes. The bodies are much stockier.

Copperheads occur around the Bay and its rivers, but they are not common, and they are much more docile than water snakes. One is tempted to believe that, with their venom, they need not be as aggressive as water snakes, either in catching prey or in defending themselves. They should, of course, be treated with great caution, and any bite from one should receive immediate medical attention.

Water snakes are sometimes mistaken for another species of poisonous snake as well. Some years ago, I spent several summers running a water ski boat for Camp Whitehall on the Mattaponi River at Walkerton, about 30 miles upriver from its confluence with the York at West Point. One day, a snake swam across the river toward the boat. Apparently it felt that it had the right of way, for it opened its mouth wide, showing a lot of pinkish-white skin, and lunged at the hull. The two boys skiing behind held on for dear life as the snake dove under them. They made sure to tell their cabinmates that night that they had been attacked by a cottonmouth moccasin.

It was a good story, and similar ones are told every summer all over the Bay, but the cottonmouth is a southern species. The south bank of the James is the northern limit of its range, and the snakes seldom stray far north of the Great Dismal Swamp and Back Bay. We can take some comfort in that fact, because cottonmouths can be aggressive, and their venom is strong.

Water snakes should not be trifled with either. If cornered, caught, and handled sloppily, they will bite. The bite, though not poisonous, can lead to serious infection. They also give off a nasty odor to repel captors. The best policy for an inexperienced snake handler is to admire the animal for the interesting creature it is and let it go its own way.

Any species that can successfully spread over most of North America and diversify into so many subspecies has found a favorable niche. Water snakes can swim very well, both on the surface and underwater. Their aquatic diet attests to their swimming ability. They eat a wide variety of food, primarily fish and frogs, but also crayfish and aquatic insects. As is true for other snakes, their jaws and throats can stretch to accommodate large prey. Reputedly, they are able to swallow young catfish and digest them, even if the sharp spines pierce the walls of their stomachs and intestines.

Water snakes spend a significant part of their days on riverbank tree branches absorbing the sun's warmth, but they do not spend much of their time on land (except when caught there by cold weather). They bear their young live, in the water, a trait shared with other aquatic snakes.

Kelly is still not much of a snake handler, but she has turned into a good snake watcher. She has learned to appreciate these animals as active and graceful members of the Bay community.

Little Birds, Long Trips

It's Monday, a sunny April day on the Gunpowder, just above Joppatowne on the western shore north of Baltimore. The canoe glides around a bend, and a small brown-gray bird takes off quietly from a fallen sycamore at the water's edge. It beats its wings several times and then glides. The wings are brown, with double white stripes along the tailing edges. Its white breast is sprinkled with brown dots. The bird, lighting on another log, begins to bob its tail up and down. That's the giveway. It is a spotted sandpiper *(Actitis macularia)* and the bobbing tail is a distinctive field mark, easily observed at a distance.

A day later: Tuesday in the Patuxent wild rice marshes. On the old steam barge wreck just below Selby's Landing, there is a small brown-gray bird. As the canoe approaches, it gets up and flies to the duck blind stake at the mouth of Mattaponi Creek. Its tail bobs up and down.

Wednesday on Occupacia Creek, off the Rappanhannock between Tappahannock and Port Royal: a small brown-gray bird stands, bobbing its tail, on the trunk of an oak tree that has fallen down one of the steep banks. As the canoe approaches, it flies. Thursday in the Big Salt Marsh at Poquoson, a few miles down-Bay from the mouth of the York. The tide is out. At the head of a cove, a small brown-gray bird walks over the mud, its bill probing and its tail bobbing.

During the latter part of April, it is possible to go to a different part of the Chesapeake system each day for a couple of weeks and see spotted sandpipers. There are a lot of them migrating through now, but they always turn up by ones and twos, not by large flocks. It is as though a thin veil of birds were being drawn slowly through the Bay country. While most animals gather together in migration, the spotted sandpipers spread themselves out, with a few birds in every nook and cranny of the Chesapeake system.

The birds stay for a short time, feeding on insects, worms, crustaceans, and other invertebrates as the mud flats and marsh banks warm in the sun. Then they move on. They are on the way from wintering grounds in the southern United States and Central America to breeding grounds as far north as the Ungava Peninsula on Hudson Bay. They are unobtrusive but sure trademarks of the season.

Their larger relatives, the greater yellowlegs *(Totanus melanoleucus)*, are moving through at the same time. These birds are more conspicuous. Congregating in small flocks of six to twelve, they allow observers to come close to them, and they give clear, whistling calls of three to five notes as they take off to fly. Greater yellowlegs are relatively large shorebirds (length 15 inches, wingspread 26 inches) with brown backs, white rumps and tails, and, of course, bright yellow legs. They too are feeding on new life developing in the warm mud of the April marshes. At this time of year, they are most commonly found poking through the stubble of the upriver wild rice marshes.

The yellowlegs travel even greater distances. They are headed to the North Country tundra and muskeg, spreading themselves across Hudson Bay and all the way west to British Columbia. Some have wintered in the southern United States, but most have come from farther south. A few have flown all the way from Patagonia, at the southern tip of South America—quite a trip for a small bird. For them, the Chesapeake's rivers and marshes are good stopover areas for feeding and resting. By mid-May, most will have left the Chesapeake for their breeding grounds.

In the wooded swamps at the heads of rivers and creeks, another bird will be arriving toward the end of the month. This is the beautiful prothonotary warbler *(Prothonotaria citrea)*, bright yellow-orange with blue-gray wings. As the swamps turn green, the prothonotaries add splashes of color.

The birds nest in holes in trees anywhere from water level to 25 feet up. Occasionally, a nest even turns up in a floating log. Their eggs are also beautiful, creamy white with deep red, lavender, and purple spots.

Most of the Bay's rivers have these warblers around their headwaters. Cypress rivers like the Chickahominy, Dragon Run at the head of the Piankatank, and the Pocomoke are particularly favored areas, but the ash and maple swamps on rivers like the Pamunkey, Mattaponi, Rappahannock, Patuxent, Choptank, and Nanticoke hold some too.

These are small birds (length 5 inches, wingspread 9 inches), and they also have traveled a long way. They breed and summer through the Midwest and along the East Coast, but they have come all the way from Mexico, Nicaragua, Colombia, and Venezuela. In migration, many of them fly straight across the Gulf of Mexico from Yucatan to the United States. They are fat when they start and lean when they finish.

April is a turning point in the almanac of the Bay country, and indeed in the Western Hemisphere, so the flow of life through here is heavy. It is remarkable how many different birds make different uses of the Chesapeake system at this season.

Kingfishers: Quick, Sturdy, and Loud

"I've never been able to catch a kingfisher on film. They're too quick for me. Sorry," said Bill Portlock over the telephone. I had called him in search of a photograph for my column. Portlock is a superb field naturalist and photographer who lives near Bowling Green, between the Rappahannock and Mattaponi rivers. The fact that the Bay Country's kingfishers have stymied him is strong testimony to their speed.

The well-stocked Chesapeake is home to a lot of fishing birds. Half a dozen species of gull, three or four kinds of terns, nine species of herons and egrets, ospreys, and loons are all successful in their niches.

Creeks and coves with high, sandy, wooded banks and shallow flats are full of tasty little fish, and the dominant fisher here is the belted kingfisher *(Megaceryle alcyon)*. The banks provide nesting habitat, the trees good perches and lookouts, and the flats plenty of food.

Virtually every long river from the James to the Susquehanna has a healthy kingfisher population, especially in upriver sections where strong currents and meander curves create high banks. Shorter, brackish rivers with wooded banks like the Severn and the Wye have their share of the birds as well. Boating people who cruise out in open water are generally unaware of the bird, but gunkholers, inshore fishermen, and canoeists know this aggressive blue-and-white bombshell well. It flies out to complain about their presence in loud, chattering kingfisherese.

Compared to ospreys and herons, which average 25 to 50 inches tall, the kingfisher appears small, only 13 inches in height. The bird is nearly as large as a common tern, and much bulkier. Not only is its bill stout, but its head is large, its neck short and thick, its body stocky.

The kingfisher's unique build contributes to its food-catching skill. With some luck, a careful observer can witness the bird as it watches for prey from a high perch in a tree or, if necessary, hovers over the water. Once it spots its target—small fish, generally 2 to 5 inches in length, like silversides, killifish, anchovies, and menhaden—it dives precisely, grabbing the prey with its powerful bill. The kingfisher can swim underwater with its wings if necessary.

Once the prey is caught, the bird uses its broad wings to get aloft again, shaking itself in midair, just as ospreys and terns do. Then it flies back to a perch, bangs the fish's head on a limb to subdue it, and swallows it headfirst.

The kingfisher's heavy bill and blocky design are helpful for more than just catching fish. The male bird uses his bill to drill the nest burrow into a creek bank. With his powerful wings, he flies at the bank, chipping out dirt until the hole is large enough to create a ledge on which to perch. The big head and bull neck are well adapted for this avian battering ram operation.

Once the male can perch on the edge of the burrow, he uses his bill and feet to hollow out a burrow that is $1\frac{1}{2}$ to 3 feet in length (and sometimes longer), rising gently to a nest cavity.

Throughout their range, on rivers and creeks across the United States, kingfishers nest in risky places. Steep banks guarantee minimal interference from egg-loving predators like raccoons and blacksnakes, but the tradeoff to that protection is the threat of flooding during storms, especially on small streams.

In April, the female lays a clutch of six to eight eggs, which the male incubates for 23 days. Then the male and the female feed the young for another 23 days until they are fledged. Laying eggs is a big effort for the female. The male shoulders most of the responsibility for parental care, giving her time to recover. Then, if the first clutch were killed by a flood, she could lay a second. Kingfishers are survivors.

The aggressive behavior that we associate with kingfishers is part of the species' overall survival strategy. The birds are extremely territorial, defending both good fishing flats throughout the year and good nesting banks during breeding season. When an intruder comes into a bird's territory, it will fly out to scold and complain. It will follow the intruder to the edge of its territory and then double back, because to encroach on the next bird's territory is to risk loud confrontation and a fight. Kingfishers do not attack humans, but their bank-digging and fishing capabilities can make them vicious fighters.

It's odd to find that such an active, brightly colored, loud bird as the kingfisher is so unknown to boating people. If you don't recognize these birds, look for them this year. If you do, you're already aware of how much fun they are to watch.

Currents: Mass Transit for Bay Creatures

There is a current running upstream most of the time in the deep waters of the Bay. Watermen were the first to find it. "Tide's rising on the Bay bottom 90 percent of the time," says Captain Wallace Lewis, the dean of fishing guides in the Reedville/Smith Point area. He discovered it when setting purse seines for menhaden in the 1940s and fifties.

Then there is the celebrated story from 50 years ago of some drift-netters off Kent Island who found themselves and their boat moving down-Bay with the surface tide while their net moved up-Bay. When they went to Dr. Donald Pritchard, at the Johns Hopkins

University, and told him what was happening, Pritchard was intrigued and pursued the strange phenomenon. He found the current and figured out the forces behind it.

When the last ice age ended about 17,000 years ago and the sea level started to rise, the Atlantic flowed into the low Susquehanna valley, gradually extending tidal water up to what are now the heads of navigation on the rivers—Richmond, Fredericksburg, Washington, Baltimore, and the others. But fresh water flows down the rivers to meet this seawater.

Seawater, with all its dissolved minerals, is denser, so it stays close to the bottom, and the fresh river water flows over it. Thus, under the river water, there is a wedge of saltier water.

As the river water flows downstream, friction causes turbulence waves between it and the seawater. The fresh water picks up some of the seawater from these waves and carries it downstream, diluting it in the process. Taking the place of what is lost this way, more seawater flows into the Bay and up the rivers. To be sure, the tides retard and even reverse this flow twice a day, but individual water molecules move farther up on the flood than they move back on the ebb. The net movement of water along the bottom is up the Bay.

At the same time, water from the rivers slides inexorably down to the Atlantic. It too reverses with the tides, but the net movement of surface water is down the Bay.

The system is actually quite complex. Variations in moon-driven tidal currents; river flow powered by rainfall in upstream watersheds; winds; and the geometry of individual river basins all complicate the basic pattern. Even the Coriolis forces of the earth's rotation affect it. In summer when freshwater input is low, the dividing lines between layers of different salinity can be quite distinct. When flows are high, turbulence is greater, and there is quite a lot of mixing between layers.

The general principles, however, remain the same: Deeper water is usually saltier than surface water; the net flow of water close to the bottom is up-Bay, and the net flow at the surface is down-Bay. Of the two, the surface flow is greater, so the overall net movement of the Bay water is down to the Capes and out into the Atlantic, although this flow through the Bay is *much* slower than the flow in the upstream portions of the rivers above the tide lines.

It is a rough guess that the Bay has been working this way for 15,000 years. Over that time, many of the animals that inhabit it have learned to use these two currents.

As described in the sketches for March, warming spring temperatures bring heavy blooms of phytoplankton. Spring rains flush decayed plant material (detritus) out of the marshes. Both the phytoplankton and the detritus fuel an explosion of zooplankton in the surface layers of the Bay and its tributaries.

But these surface layers are moving down-Bay. If the zooplankton stayed in those layers, they would be swept out to sea. To remain in the Chesapeake and take advanatage of this floating lunch counter going by, they have developed a special behavior mechanism. They feed in the surface layers at night, being moved down the Bay as they do. During the day, they sink toward the bottom, and are moved back up the Bay. Thus they follow a circular path, and over the course of several tidal cycles, tend to stay in the same general area.

Fish and shellfish use the currents too. Oyster larvae, eel larvae, menhaden, herring, shad, rockfish, even bluefish will catch a ride when it is advantageous.

For the naturalist, perhaps the most striking example comes from pulling a minnow seine in April on the Wye River, or the Little Choptank, or the York. Surveys indicate that all of the Bay's Norfolk spot spawn on the continental shelf off the mouth of the Bay in winter. Female crabs spawn at the mouth of the Bay in the warmer months. Even so, that minnow seine pulled alongshore in April will turn up handsful of transparent spot $\frac{1}{2}$-inch long, and tiny crabs less than 1 inch across. Both species can swim at this stage of life, but neither can make long migrations under its own propulsion until later. These young reach their nursery grounds up the rivers and up the Bay by staying close to the bottom and riding the deep currents.

Those little spot and crabs appear fragile, but they are well traveled. They are truly miracles of spring on the Chesapeake, thanks to its mass transit system.

MAY

Diamondback Terrapin Mating

There is a cove on the Patuxent several miles below Benedict that often appears to have several black sticks poking up a couple of inches above the water's surface. If a boat approaches one of these, it disappears, only to reappear in five or ten minutes. The patient observer will discover the sticks to be the heads of diamondback terrapin.

This month, though, the observer need not be so patient. Sometimes in May there are 200 heads bobbing in the cove, which is only 60 yards across. Indeed, there are often nearly 100 terrapin on the cove's marsh banks. This is the mating season.

Early on, the American colonists began eating terrapin. They were abundant and easy to catch. Soon they were so frequently dished up that several colonies passed laws prohibiting landowners from feeding terrapin to indentured servants or slaves more than three times a week. In 1797, the legislature of the young state of Maryland passed a law restricting terrapin to one meal a week for slaves. The supply seemed endless.

During the nineteenth century, the citizenry came to appreciate the terrapin as a gourmet food, especially in a rich stew laced with cream and sherry. In 1887, during the glory years of Crisfield's railroad, a seafood dealer from Philadelphia named LaVallette came down and developed a tremendous market, buying terrapin from watermen for next to nothing, keeping them in holding pens in the marshes where he fed them scrap from the crab-picking houses, and shipping them to the finest restaurants and clubs in Baltimore, Philadelphia, and New York. LaVallette was able to control the market so tightly that he could dictate his selling price: one dollar per inch of width on the undershell (the plastron). Thus a single female cost five to eight dollars, and a male three to six dollars. A dozen big females could bring 100 dollars in 1900. (Bear in mind that these dollars were much bigger than ours today.)

Demand held up for 25 years, so watermen fished the diamondbacks hard. Other seafood dealers began to compete with LaVallette, and the inevitable happened: the harvest outran the ability of the resource to renew itself, and the supply dwindled. Laws were passed limiting the harvest, but the market was so lucrative that it continued illegally till there were so few terrapin left that packers no longer found them profitable.

Once they became difficult to obtain, terrapin dropped out of favor with all but a few. As the harvest came to a virtual standstill, the stocks began to rebuild themselves. There is still a law on the books prohibiting their capture in warmer months, and catching them in winter is a skill that few watermen possess. Though terrapin are difficult and messy to prepare, there is still a small market for them (the Maryland Club in Baltimore will always have terrapin stew on its menu). But at this point, harvest pressure is relatively light.

Thus there are more diamondbacks around now than there have been for years. These are pretty turtles, with slate-blue skin dotted with black spots. The shell is covered with distinctive, diamond-shaped concentric rings which may bear some relation to the animal's age during its first few years. Their feet are broad, flat paddles with claws, so they swim and walk well.

Terrapin prowl the Chesapeake's salt marshes, free from competition with their upriver cousins, feeding on periwinkles, fiddler crabs, worms, insects, and fish when they can catch them; they crush their food with powerful jaws. Terrapins are predators, not scavengers. They prefer unpolluted water and thus are indicators of healthy marsh systems.

The diamondback species *(Malaclemys terrapin)* ranges from the cordgrass marshes of Massachusetts to the mangrove keys of the Florida Gulf Coast and then west to southern Texas and maybe beyond. Within that range, there are seven subspecies. Our own is the northern diamondback *(Malaclemys t. terrapin)*, which lives from Cape Cod to Cape Hatteras and is considered the finest tasting of the lot.

The Chesapeake's diamondbacks winter in the mud, but as spring warms the water, they emerge. Thus May on the Patuxent finds them not only mating, but also simply absorbing spring sunlight on a warm marsh bank. Indeed, females do not necessarily mate every year. Apparently they can store sperm from one mating for up to four years, though the longer the female goes without mating, the fewer of her eggs will hatch.

The eggs will be laid later this month, in nests dug into sandy beaches. In some parts of the Eastern Shore low country, one occasionally finds a nest dug into a sand road next to a marsh. Serious egg-lovers like raccoons and blacksnakes will be busy from now through the summer, looking for nests to rob. A depression in the sand filled with leathery, dried-up little white tubes signals a succcess for them. By late August, however, such a crater may well mean a new litter of 1-inch terrapin.

They will then face another predator, the great blue heron. Fortunately for the species, there are plenty of other tasty morsels to compete for the heron's attention. Some will be lost to its stalking skill, but most will survive.

The terrapin's major threats are loss of habitat and exploitation by man. As long as laws regulate destruction and alteration of coastal wetlands, and, perhaps more important, as long as people object to the mess involved in cleaning these turtles, they will be around, unobtrusively going about their business. Look for them bobbing in the Bay's marsh coves this month.

Eelgrass: Carpet of Life

We felt as if we were floating on air as the skiff carried us over the shallow flats in the northwest corner of Pocomoke Sound. The water was crystal clear, and the bottom was a green carpet much of the way from Broad Creek to the Chesapeake Bay Foundation's lodge on Great Fox Island. Since it was the end of April and the water temperature was in the midfifties (F), we knew that the green was all eelgrass *(Zostera marina)*. It was the thickest stand around

Fox Island in years, and we cheered when we saw it. Eelgrass is a very valuable resource.

To understand that statement, it is helpful to know a little about the plant. Eelgrass lives in a harsh environment. It is one of only a handful of flowering plants that can live submerged full-time in salt water. Salt causes severe water balance problems that kill most higher plants, but eelgrass has developed the capability to excrete it. (So, for that matter, can the plants like saltmarsh cordgrass, *Spartina alterniflora*, that live on the banks around the eelgrass beds; but eelgrass can also live fully submerged, which the cordgrass cannot. Eelgrass has also developed the capability to take oxygen out of solution in the water and transport it throughout leaves, stems, and roots.)

Finally, the plant has developed the ability to disperse pollen without the aid of insects or wind, which most other flowering plants rely on for that task. Instead, it uses water currents to broadcast its threadlike pollen grains. When a grain washes up next to the female stigma of another plant, it winds around the stigma so that the two can fuse and form a seed, which also will be dispersed by currents. These adaptations permit eelgrass to grow in areas where it has only minimal competition from other species.

Eelgrass thrives in a broad range of water temperatures, so it is widely distributed around the world. In North America, it is found from northern Florida all the way up to the Arctic Circle, including parts of Hudson Bay. On the Pacific Coast, it grows from Southern California to southwestern Alaska, including Prince William Sound.

The ability to grow in cool temperatures gives it an important advantage in the Chesapeake, because it can begin in early spring while the water is clear and have its seeds made by the time phytoplankton growth reduces light penetration in June. Remember that a submerged flowering plant needs a great deal of sunlight energy to reproduce. The heavy plankton growth that most of the Bay now experiences in summer (as a result of excessive nitrogen and phosphorus) reduces underwater light to below the level that most submerged flowering plants need to reproduce.

The early start benefits more than the eelgrass alone. We were about to have a firsthand look at the ecological value of a lush eelgrass bed in early spring.

As preparation for the trip, we had all read "Summer and Scraping" from William W. Warner's classic *Beautiful Swimmers*, in which Warner describes spending a day with an expert Smith Island soft-crabber pulling a specialized dredge (a "scrape") through the eelgrass beds in the area. Now we stowed our gear in the Fox Island lodge and put a scrape aboard the skiff to go see for ourselves.

Liz McKnight, on her first trip to Fox, was "flabbergasted at the amount and variety of life in the grass." We all watched with great pleasure as her children, Philip (then aged nine) and Anna (then six) pawed through the bales of grass that the scrape brought up. Hidden inside were grass shrimp and sand shrimp, oyster toads, juvenile sea trout, baby spot and croakers, young flounder, little hogchokers (our only native sole), tiny shrimplike amphipods, long green pipefish, mud crabs, and, of course, lots of blue crabs, of all sizes from tiny juveniles to big, mature jimmies.

For Anna, sorting through the grass was like a treasure hunt, with all kinds of new creatures to discover. Philip, a little older, could understand for the first time "how everything is connected to everything," about how functional a patch of submerged grass can be. Suddenly he understood why his father, Turney McKnight, likes to hang around the edges of eelgrass beds, casting bucktails and plugs to the trout (and in the fall, rockfish) that cruise those edges looking for small fish that stray out of them. Turney grinned when he saw the light go on in his son's eyes.

He also smiled as he watched Liz figure out the critical role that eelgrass plays in the lives of the crabs and the crabbers of Pocomoke and Tangier sounds. She had seen a couple of the low-slung "Jenkins Creekers," or scraping boats, being readied for the season in Crisfield. Now she realized that the water was almost warm enough for the crabs to slough, or shed their shells, for the first time in the year.

A few crabs had already done so, and the first of the scrapers had been out making exploratory "licks" to see what was happening. The main run would begin some 10 days later, on the strong tides of the new moon, but the crabs were already in the grass, getting ready to hide from predators during this very vulnerable stage of their lives. The fact that eelgrass begins growing early in the season is of tremendous value to the crabs.

Our object lesson with eelgrass was a spring one, but if we had been at Fox in summer, we would have seen even more life in the beds; and in late fall, we would have seen waterfowl feeding on it. All of the Chesapeake's submerged grasses are valuable to the system, but eelgrass is one of the best. It suffered from a disease early in this century, which caused much concern around Tangier and Smith islands. Then it came back strongly, only to be affected like the other Bay grasses by the excessive algae growth that has plagued our Chesapeake for the past three decades. Planktonic algae drifting in the water block light from the plants below, and other species of algae attach themselves to the leaves of the grass, fouling them like a boat bottom and blocking out even more light.

Now eelgrass is returning in much of the Bay from the Potomac and Smith Island south. The best places are broad, shallow flats that are protected from high wave energy, like the upper end of Pocomoke Sound, the Virginia Eastern Shore creeks, Mobjack Bay, and the Poquoson River.

Even so, eelgrass is growing in only about 20 percent of the areas where it used to be abundant. It suffers especially around slow-flushing creeks and coves where algae growth is high because of heavy runoff from farms and discharges from towns and cities.

Eelgrass is a good indicator of our success in cleaning up the Bay. We should cheer any time we see a thick stand like the one that so fascinated Philip and Anna, but we do well not to pat ourselves on the back until widespread distribution signals major progress.

Horseshoe Crabs: A Timeless Design

May is the beginning of horseshoe crab spawning season on the Chesapeake. For much of the year, the animals live in the deeper channels of the Bay and lower rivers, but this month they come into the shallows by the thousands, to breed and lay their eggs.

Breeding time can be spectacular—big brown crabs everywhere in the shallows, along sandy shores and marsh banks. The careful observer will note that much of the activity centers around especially high tides ("spring tides") coinciding with the full and new moons. The females, each dragging at least one male mounted on her back, crawl up to the water's edge, dig shallow nests, and deposit their eggs, which the males fertilize.

While the tide is high, a female and her mate will produce several nests, but if the tide falls before the female has deposited all her eggs (about a quart), the pair will retreat to deeper water and try again on the next high tide. Their aim is to deposit the eggs as high on the beach as possible without leaving the water.

A large number of eggs are eaten almost immediately, as killifish, eels, and other fish dart around and even under the mating crabs. But they must work at their feeding, for the water is very shallow, and they too must retreat as the tide falls. Gulls and shorebirds feed on the newly laid eggs as well, and they sometimes uncover nests later.

But the horseshoe crabs apparently lay enough eggs to compensate for the appetite of these predators, and the species survives. The eggs stay buried in the sand, which becomes a moist incubator in the warming spring sun. In two weeks when the next spring tide brings high water again, the eggs will have developed enough for the young horseshoe crabs to hatch and move out into the shallows.

The strategy of working around the tides seems sensible enough to us, but there is more to think about here than just an animal's adaptation to the lunar cycle, interesting though that is. What is remarkable is that the horseshoe crab's behavior was probably developed at a time when there were no fish to prey on the eggs when they were laid, and no birds or land animals to feed on them after the tides receded. The horseshoe crab came into being before any of them. We actually have no assurance that those ancestral crabs followed the same strategy of laying eggs in the uppermost reaches of spring tides, but they may well have done so. If they did, the scheme was a good one, for there were very few predators to disturb the eggs after they were laid.

All this was about 400 million years ago, a time so far in the past that it is hard for us to comprehend. When we beach our fiberglass skiffs and aluminum canoes to watch the horseshoe crabs spawning, the time warp is staggering. Even the primitive plants that produced the fossil fuel gasoline for the skiffs' outboards came 100 million years after the first horseshoe crabs. They predate the origin of the Atlantic Ocean itself, which apparently was born from a rift in the great supercontinent of Pangea some 250 million years ago.

Down through the ages, the horseshoe crabs have survived great changes in the earth and its community of living things. They are, in fact, so old that they cannot be classified as crabs at all. Our beloved blue crab is a much more recent development. The horseshoe crabs are certainly related to the ancestors of the blue crab, but they are classified in a group off by themselves, more closely related to spiders than to anything else.

What allows an animal's design to survive so much change in its environment over so long a time? The question cannot be answered definitely, but it is interesting to work out some educated guesses. The horseshoe crab is simple and unspecialized. For much of the year, it probes the bottom in the channels, feeling its way along to pick up worms, small clams, and other bottom-dwellers. Its diet is broad, allowing it to take advantage of whatever is available.

Most of the time, the shell offers excellent protection. It protects the crab from attack from almost any direction, and it appears to be stable enough to hold bottom in turbulent currents.

There are no big claws, legs, or tails holding large quantities of meat to make the horseshoe crabs attractive prey. They do have predators, even including man, but the level of predation is relatively low.

The horseshoe crabs go their way, slowly, methodically, with little complex behavior. They are the oldest animal design with which we have contact here on the Chesapeake.

Swallows: Barn, Bank, and Tree

Dan and Babs Bellinger live in a house that overlooks a cove and a marsh of the Severn River several miles above Annapolis. Their dock in the cove has a pretty fishing skiff tied up to it most of the year, and seagulls usually roost on the pilings. But from now on through the summer, the gulls find other places to stand. In this season, the dock belongs to the barn swallows.

To anyone used to looking at gulls, great blue herons, and ospreys, the swallows look small: little bullet-shaped birds with steel-blue backs, chestnut masks, and buff-tan breasts. Their bills are small and their tails are deeply forked. It is easy enough to ignore them. But watch them fly and one's point of view changes. They are powerful, quick, and graceful. Those tiny beaks are quite adequate for catching the insects that live in the Bellingers' marsh and along the river shore.

The birds' flying abilities are amazing. They catch mosquitoes, houseflies, horseflies, and greenheads on the wing by the hundred. Certainly they are welcome warm weather residents.

Barn swallows are not normally thought of as Bay birds, and indeed they are quite widespread inland, but they are especially common around bodies of water and marshes because of the abundance of insects in both kinds of habitat. Thus they flock to the Chesapeake from May into September. They come to us from Central and South America, with flocks spending our winter in similar habitats from Mexico to Argentina and Chile. Powerful fliers indeed, many migrate north across the Caribbean, with stops in the West Indies and the Bahamas. They are warm weather birds strong enough to follow the summer back and forth across the equator.

Tagging studies indicate that the birds return faithfully to the same place each summer, so the tenants of the Bellinger dock represent an ongoing community. With an abundance of insects available nearby, there is little need to compete for territory, so several families roost on and nest under the pier. They seem particularly fond of perching on the skiff's dock lines, sometimes three or four in a row.

Besides flying, the birds have another skill: they are excellent masons. The underside of the dock offers rough timbers upon which nests can be built. In those tiny beaks, they carry mud, scraps of grass, and feathers back to the dock to build their round nests, each with an entry hole. Underneath the decking and over 4 to 8 feet of water, the young birds are safe from raccoons, possums, dogs, gulls, hawks, and all but the most stubborn blacksnakes. Even so, predators are ill-advised to approach the nests too closely. The feisty parents will drive them away.

The swallows mate early, and the young develop quickly, usually being fledged and able to feed themselves at three weeks of age. It is quite remarkable that the young can grow so fast. Thus the parent birds can raise a second and sometimes even a third brood each summer. They stay busy feeding their offspring, and sometimes young swallows from the first hatch will help feed their later siblings.

By late August the birds leave, heading to the coast and joining other groups of barn swallows for their long flight to the south. Their innate powers of navigation and place recognition seem magical to us, though the birds are quite matter-of-fact about them.

Worldwide, swallows are a successful group of birds. There are several other species common around the Chesapeake. If the barn swallow is a good mason, the bank swallow is a champion digger. A striking feature of the Severn River is its high banks of red sand and clay. Around the corner from the Bellingers' dock is a bank that shows several rows of these cliff dwellers' houses—their 3-inch-wide caves dug into particularly firm strata that they have picked out from the looser soils. These birds' beaks are no larger than those of the barn swallows, but they are as good for digging sand as their relatives' are for carrying mud, and they certainly are as good for catching insects. Often in the evening, mixed flocks will hunt the shore by the cliff, with the blues and tans of the barn swallows contrasting with the browns and whites of the smaller bank swallows.

Also mixed in will be a few tree swallows. Between the other two species in size, these birds have iridescent green backs over white bodies. In general, tree swallows nest in trees along the shore, raise only one brood a summer, and eat some plant foods along with insects.

It is interesting to consider how the niche of each of the three species differs slightly from the others. Thus, the birds can avoid competing directly with each other, which would usually result in one species being driven away.

Watching a group of swallows flying and feeding at dusk on a warm evening is one of the pleasures we can look forward to in the coming months. Bank and tree swallows are certainly attractive enough, and we are grateful for their diet of mosquitoes and flies. But there is something special about the barn swallows that live under our docks and perch on our boats' lines summer after summer. Dan and Babs can be understood if they begin to feel a personal relationship with their birds.

Cattails: Springtime Treats from the Marshes

Grace Ann Gray teaches biology at Southern Senior High School in Anne Arundel County, down below Annapolis. Generally each year she sets up a spring field trip with the Chesapeake Bay Foundation. She and her students meet a CBF trip leader in Galesville, where they put the canoes over into the West River to paddle around the corner at the Hartge Yacht Yard and up Lerch Creek.

People on the creek may find it strange to see two dozen high school students sloshing around a marsh on a Wednesday morning, pulling cattail heads over into plastic bags and shaking them. But the students are learning two profound lessons. The first is that Lerch Creek is getting fresher, which says something about the way estuaries work. The second is that there are some unorthodox but tasty and nutritious foods along the margins of the Bay.

Euell Gibbons ate a lot of cattails in his time, many of them from the Chesapeake. He called the plants "supermarkets of the swamps" and gave them a chapter in *Stalking the Wild Asparagus* (see Bibliography). His particular joy in them, as in all his wild food foraging, was the relationship between the forager and the natural community around him or her. The Southern High students come back from Lerch Creek with an understanding of Gibbons and his writings that goes far beyond his old cereal commercials.

There are two species of cattail common to the Bay country: narrowleaf *(Typha angustifolia)* and broadleaf *(T. latifolia)*. The narrowleaf is more widespread, occurring in the tidal fresh portions of all the rivers and at the back edges of upper Bay salt marshes. Each of its leaves is about an inch wide. This is basically a freshwater species, but it can tolerate low salt concentrations. Thus it is a good indicator of freshwater input to brackish waterways like Lerch Creek. Broadleaf cattails are strictly freshwater plants, so they grow in rivulets, streams, branches, and roadside ditches. Their leaves are about 2 inches wide.

Cattails are perennial, growing each year from rootstocks in the mud. The narrowleaf begins sprouting earlier, generally in mid-April. The broadleaf comes a couple of weeks later. From then on until mid-June, the stalk hearts are good additions to a salad. Grasp a stalk near its base and pull it gently but firmly from the mud. Peel the leaves back to the tender white heart. Wash it and eat it. It is crunchy and mild, with a flavor somewhat like cucumber.

Toward mid-May, the narrowleaf bloom spikes begin to emerge on the plants' central stalks. The stalk hearts of such plants will no longer be tender, but the tips of the spikes make a good cooked vegetable. The top is the male part of the bloom, 6 to 8 inches long, growing an inch or so above the familiar furry female cattail on the stalk. Cut off firm male spikes from several plants. Steam them in salted water for 10 minutes, add a little melted butter, and eat them down to the central stalks, as you would corn on the cob.

By late May, the male spikes swell and soften as they begin to release their bright yellow pollen to the wind. Now is the time for those not allergic to pollen to emulate the Southern High students. Put a small bag over the bloom spike, bend the stalk over, and shake hard. Some of the pollen will fall into the bag. Fifteen or 20 minutes' work will yield a cup or so. Mix the pollen with flour in any standard pancake or waffle recipe. (Substitute pollen for one-fourth of the flour called for in the recipe.) The result is golden yellow cakes with good quality protein and a distinctive, pleasant flavor.

After the pollen flies, the male spike disintegrates. The female spike, now fertilized, swells and begins the long business of developing its fluffy seeds. The astute forager then shifts attention to broadleaf cattails, which will just be blooming. They will be good for another three weeks or so. The real die-hard forager can wrap surplus spikes in a bag and freeze them to eat in the winter at a table with an arrangement of dried cattails on it.

It would be a great mistake, though, to suggest that cattails have value only as food and table decoration for humans. The plants are important to the river communities as both food and habitat for a variety of birds, mammals, insects, and even fish. Even so, during this month, they offer us a great opportunity to be part of the food web, partners in the intimate relationships of the Chesapeake's biotic (living) community.

Efficient Fish Shapes

Bob Dornin teaches science at the Hill School in Middleburg, Virginia, when he isn't busy being retired. Every spring, he takes his eighth-grade class on a three-day field trip with the Chesapeake Bay Foundation. Using one of CBF's canoe fleets, they explore Occupacia Creek, a tidal tributary of the Rappahannock, and Rosier Creek, a lower Potomac tributary. The students are bright and well prepared, and Bob is good company, so CBF's field instructors fight over who gets to run the trip.

Bob has chosen his trip sites well. Occupacia is long and deep, with heavy freshwater inflow. Over the space of 6 miles, the salinity increases from 0 parts per thousand (ppt) to about 5 ppt (about 15 percent the salinity of seawater). There is enough creek there for two full days of studying hardwood swamp, marsh plant communities, sediment transport, water chemistry, zooplankton, birds, and fish. Rosier Creek offers a good contrast. Only 2 miles long, its head too is fresh, but its mouth has a salinity of 15 to 18 ppt (about 50 percent the salinity of seawater). Between them, the two creeks offer a broad slice of estuarine habitat, with a variety of plants and animals.

Spring is a good time to be on the two creeks. Both have large populations of freshwater fish. In addition, Occupacia has a run of alewives (river herring) in April and a run of blueback herring in early May. By that time, juvenile spot and menhaden have worked their way up to Rosier Creek from the mouth of the Bay. Big bluefish come up the Potomac to the mouth of Rosier on an early-season feeding binge. The range of lifestyles is wide.

"Form follows function," is one of the grand old themes of classical biology. It holds that the structure of an animal's or plant's body is closely related to its ecological niche, to its habitat and lifestyle. Thus a heron has long legs and large feet for wading shallow flats, and an osprey has sharp talons for catching fish on the fly.

Last year, this theme was set the first day of the trip, on the upper section of Occupacia. A marsh cove beside a beaver lodge produced a 3-pound largemouth bass. The bass was stocky, with a broad, fanlike tail and, of course, a wide mouth. The mouth marked the fish as a general predator, capable of eating anything as large as a bullfrog or as small as a 1-inch shiner minnow. The bass's body shape is not hydrodynamically efficient, but it does not have to be. This particular fish had lived all of its life in the creek and the nearby sections of the river, never migrating more than 5 or so miles at a time and not going even that far very often. The bass did, however, have to be quick and maneuverable to hide in tight places under stumps and logs and to lunge at passing baitfish. The compact body and the powerful tail suited it well.

A mile above the beaver lodge, in the narrow, wooded headwaters of the creek, the students came upon a young man standing waist-deep in a pool with a long-handled dip net in his hands. He was holding it in the current for a minute or more, then picking it up. Several bright, silvery herring about 12 inches long came up each time. They were bluebacks, on their annual spawning run. Two months before, they had been in the Atlantic, at least 150 salty miles to the south and east. The adults that survived the run would be back at sea by late July. These travelers formed a stark contrast with the bass. They had slender, thin, fusiform (bullet-shaped) bodies with deeply forked tails, a structure well suited to long migrations.

This body shape also fits well with the blueback's feeding method. These fish are plankton feeders. Their mouths are smooth funnels, with soft gill filaments for catching copepods, barnacle larvae, fish eggs, crab larvae, and anything else they swim through that has nutritional value. To filter enough water to feed themselves, they swim constantly, with their mouths and gill covers working all the time. The blueback's low-drag body shape is as important for efficient feeding as it is for migration.

Given the basic principles from the first day on Occupacia, the students found several more examples of the relationship between body form and ecological niche on Rosier Creek. At our put-in site near the mouth, a waterman was docking a skiff with his morning's catch. A typical river fisherman, he had caught all sorts of creatures in his pots and fykes, from crabs to a snapping turtle.

He also had two dozen big bluefish, 12 to 15 pounds each, from a gill net. Again the students had a migratory species to examine. The blues too were fusiform, with powerful shoulders tapering to deeply forked tails—a shape well suited to predators that roam constantly through open waters. These fish travel from the ocean off North Carolina to the Outer Banks beaches; then up through the Chesapeake and the C & D Canal and out to the Gulf Stream to spawn; then back to the Bay and down to Carolina again, all in one year. I filleted off a palm-sized cheek muscle from one of the blues, and the students discussed how that muscle had articulated the powerful jaws and the sharp, interlocking teeth with which the fish attacked schools of baitfish.

On the beach at Rosier's mouth, the minnow seine caught young spot and menhaden, both ocean spawners that spend much of their first year in the Bay country's upper nursery grounds. Spot are bottom feeders; even though these were less than an inch long, their underslung mouths marked them as nibblers of worms, barnacles, and amphipods on the river's oyster bars. The menhaden, like their herring cousins, were fusiform, with funnel-shaped mouths for filter-feeding. They are even more widely traveled than the herrings, so hydrodynamic body shape is critical for them too.

As they wrote up their trip log, the students talked about other fish body shapes they knew, like catfish, rays, and oyster toads. And they talked about other examples of form following function, in birds' wings and trees' leaves and dogs' ears. A theme from a textbook had taken on firsthand meaning in the outdoors. They had learned something about science, and something about education too.

Tides Do Strange Things

Walkerton is a sleepy little town on the Mattaponi River in King and Queen County, Virginia. Up through the early part of this century, it was a river port for steamboats and lumber schooners, but the highways took over, and the boats quit calling at the town. Walkerton is 30 miles above West Point, where the Mattaponi runs into the York, and it is another 28 miles down the York to the Bay, so the water at Walkerton is completely fresh, with lily pads and wild rice growing in the nearby marshes. It is easy to forget that the town has any connection with the Bay at all. But Walkerton has a major claim to fame. In the tide tables published each year by the National Oceanic and Atmospheric Administration, it has the highest average daily tide change of any location on the Chesapeake—3.9 feet— more, even, than the 3.0-foot average at the mouth of the Bay.

It is hard enough to understand how a river can be fresh and still tidal, but for a freshwater town to have such a strong tide is startling. The river's narrow, deep channel seems to accentuate it. In summer, the boys just upriver at Camp Whitehall have to plan their day's schedule around it, waterskiing and swimming on high water, exploring the marsh guts by canoe on low, and always trying not to have to paddle against the powerful current, whichever way it is flowing. Anyone around Walkerton who remembers the schooners has great admiration for the captains who could negotiate that tide in such a narrow channel under sail. (See pp. 83-84 of Snediker and Jensen's *Chesapeake Bay Schooners* for an account of what it was like getting a lumber schooner into Walkerton.)

The double phenomenon of strong tide in fresh water is the same on all of the Chesapeake's other big rivers, though the tide changes are not as great as on the Mattaponi. Anyone who spends any time on these waters puzzles over it. We all start off thinking of tide as water flowing in from the ocean and then back out. But when a river's own freshwater flow from its watershed gets into the picture, things start to get confusing.

Tides are waves, moving bulges in the surface of the water. All boaters are familiar with the waves that come from wind and the wake that forms as a hull moves through the water. These are short-period waves. They come every few seconds, and we are usually aware of the times when one set of waves gets superimposed onto another.

By contrast, tides are long-period waves, traveling about 12 hours, 25 minutes apart on the Chesapeake. They develop primarily as the moon moves around the earth. It literally pulls a bulge of high water as it goes and trails a following trough of low water. We can visualize the bulge and its following trough moving across the ocean, but once this pair starts to move through confined and semiconfined waterways like the Bay and its rivers, the pattern gets more complicated.

In the Bay, the tide will affect any waterway whose surface is at sea level; that means that it will reach up to the heads of navigation on the rivers. But the rivers are carrying great quantities of fresh water downhill out of their watersheds. When the fresh water reaches sea level, it pushes the salt water in the rivers' lower basins downstream. The distance varies with the power of the individual river and with rainfall.

The fresh water is now at or below sea level, so it is affected by the tide's moving bulge and trough, hence the tidal fresh sections of the rivers. When it reaches the denser salt water, it flows up over it and mixes with it, at the same time continuing to move downstream and thereby creating the Bay's two-layered system. The tidal current will push it back upstream for a time, but the net movement is down, so it does flow all the way to the ocean.

Thus Walkerton has a tide, but why is it so strong? Helping to answer that question is another familiar phenomenon: short-pe-

riod waves coming into shallow water become steeper before breaking on the shore. Apply that concept to tides as long-period waves.
As a tide wave travels up the Mattaponi, it becomes more and more
confined by the narrowing channel and by the riverbed, which is
gradually becoming shallower, so it gets steeper and steeper. If the
channel is just the right length from one wave's peak to the next,
each wave will be able to develop fully without interference from
the next one coming up and may even be reinforced by it. If not,
the two will get into each other's way and damp themselves down.
The shape and length of the Mattaponi together lend themselves
well to tide wave development, giving Walkerton its place in the
tide tables. Remember, though, that most of the Bay's rivers have
strong tides.

The long-period wave concept explains another puzzling
characteristic of the rivers: slack water does not necessarily corre-
spond to the time of highest or lowest water level. As a tide wave
travels upriver, the crest produces high water at successive locations, but the wave continues moving, so the current continues
upriver even as the water level starts to drop. As the trough approaches, the water from the upriver crest begins to run back
downhill, assisted by the river's downstream flow from its watershed. This flow may continue after the wave's trough passes, at low
water.

Thinking about tide as a twice-a-day wave answers a lot of
questions. Some are casual, the kind that form in the mind while
sitting on a dock, just looking at the water. Others are more directly
useful, whether to the river fisherman trying to decide which side
of a wharf piling his or her quarry will be on, or the racing skipper
playing the complex of currents around the Bay Bridge, or the boys
and counselors at Camp Whitehall. Most of the Bay's creatures have
developed specific behaviors to take advantage of the tides. We do
well to follow their examples.

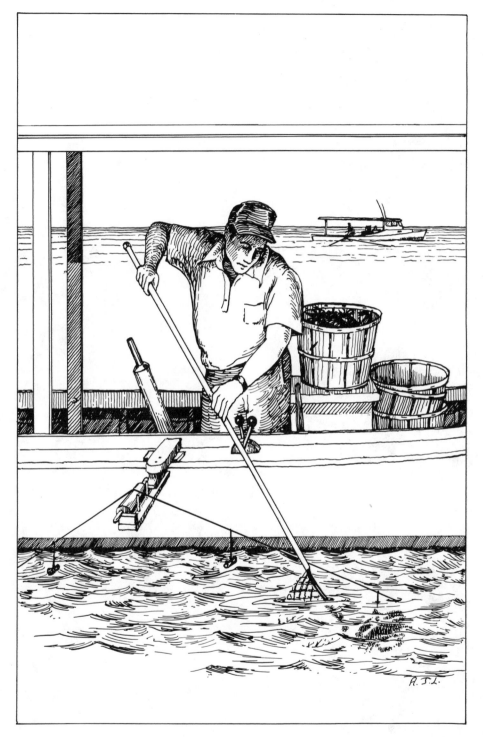

SUMMER

WHEN SUMMER COMES, Dr. Jonathan Sutton relaxes. He is a busy Annapolis pediatrician, but at this time of year, he spends a lot of time on his big sloop *Wahoo*, and the Bay soaks up the tensions of his tight schedule. Some years, he and his wife Mary lead the Sailing Club of the Chesapeake on a cruise down to the East River, on Mobjack Bay in Mathews County, where he spent his summers growing up. For short cruises, he likes to head for the Wye River, with its rolling, pastoral shoreline. He always trolls a line behind, so as to have a fresh bluefish for dinner. (One year he caught a blue a bit too large for dinner—14 pounds—but it won the annual contest sponsored by *Chesapeake Bay Magazine* for sailboat-caught bluefish.)

Jon Sutton is a summertime Everyman. He's a good example of someone who loves the Chesapeake and spends a lot of time on it, especially in this season of the year. But we could find thousands of other people like him for whom the Bay is summer playground and soother of spirits. For most of us, this is the high season. Whatever we do, whether fishing or crabbing or cruising, or all of the above, this is our favorite time on the water.

In any season, what we choose to do *on* the Bay is a strong reflection of what is happening *in* the Bay. In summer, the air is warm, if not downright hot. Rainfall is often sparse. The weather is generally stable, with morning calms and afternoon southerly breezes, punctuated by occasional and generally brief thunderstorms, which, as any Chesapeake skipper knows, can sometimes be violent. But the overall pattern is one of less wind than in spring and fall.

The summer weather pattern has a number of effects. The high water temperature generally raises the activity level of cold-blooded animals like fish and crabs, whose body temperatures are dependent on it. These animals have optimum activity ranges, and summer water temperatures sometimes get too high for them, especially in the shallows during midday. At those times, they seek cooler areas.

Because rainfall is less and high air temperatures increase evaporation, salinity begins to rise. Fresh water coming down the rivers floats over the salt water coming in on the tides, as it always does; but because the river flow is diminished, there is less turbulence and mixing between the layers than in the spring. Thus, the bottom water may be half again as salty as the surface water, and its greater density reinforces the effect of separation. Under these conditions there will be little exchange between the two layers. Hence the main Bay and the lower tributaries become stratified, with cool, salty water at the bottom and warmer, fresher water above.

Remember that the deep layer of salty water tends to move up the Bay and into the rivers, while the net movement of fresher surface water is down the Bay and out into the Atlantic. This phenomenon works all year, but its effects are perhaps most easily observed in summer, when many of the Bay's animals use the two currents as up and down escalators.

Perhaps the best example of this use is by blue crabs. All of the Bay's crabs are spawned at high salinities near the Bay's mouth. As larvae, they are swept out into the Atlantic, onto the continental shelf, returning in a short time to be swept up the Bay. (See "Traveling Crabs" in July.) As they go, they metamorphose from larvae to tiny but recognizable juvenile crabs. (See *Beautiful Swimmers* for a good description.) The currents and the crabs' increasingly strong swimming ability carry them up the rivers into coves, creeks, and marshes where we see them and wish them speedy growth to catchable size. Once on their summer grounds, the young crabs find plenty to eat, and warm water temperatures keep their activity levels high, so they grow quickly. Thus we find plenty of their sloughs (cast-off shells) when we walk the shores at low tide. (See June's "For Soft Crabbers, Summer Is a Busy Season" for details of the sloughing process.)

Spot, the favorite panfish of the lower Bay, are spawned on the continental shelf, and they too are swept into and up the Bay. Juvenile spot, in fact, travel farther up than do adults, so it is not unusual to catch them in minnow seines north of Baltimore in May, even though they are only 1 inch long then. Food for them is abundant in summer, so they grow fast, reaching 2 to 3 inches in July and 4 to 5 inches by September.

Spot belong to a large family of fish, the Scianidae, that also includes croakers (hardheads), sea trout, and drum. All members of the family follow the same life cycle pattern to some extent. In addition to spot, it is common to find small trout and croakers spread all over the system. Besides the Scianidae, bluefish and flounder also use the Bay as juveniles, especially later in the summer.

As if these well-known species weren't enough, the summertime Bay is also full of forage fish: anchovies, silversides, and menhaden. These are the most numerous fish in the system. Only menhaden are fished commercially—for industrial oil, animal feeds, and crab bait. Around 500 million pounds of them are caught each year. Probably just as many are eaten by fish, birds, and other creatures. (See "The Essential Menhaden" in June.) Yet enough are left over to make more menhaden for the following year, so their total weight might be something over 1 billion pounds, at an average of maybe three fish to the pound. Those numbers are the roughest sort of estimates, but they give a ballpark idea of the fishes' abundance. Recent research suggests that there are even more anchovies than menhaden in the Bay.

All three forage species feed on plankton, the only food base abundant enough to sustain such huge fish populations. The menhaden, which may be anywhere from 1 to 10 inches in length in the Bay, filter food from the water as they swim. Anchovies and silversides, which grow to 4 inches, are small enough to prey on large individual members of the plankton community, like copepods.

Like bluefish, flounder, and the *Scianidae,* most menhaden winter on the continental shelf, coming into the Bay to feed in the summer. Menhaden shoals are familiar sights on the surface on slick calm summer days. Anchovies and silversides winter in deep holes in the rivers and the Bay, like the 70-foot trench along the Kent Island shore near the Bay Bridge. In summer, however, they are everywhere. The little fish make patterns like raindrops on the surface.

With young spot, young trout, young croakers, anchovies, menhaden, and silversides, the Chesapeake is full of small fish in the summer. Down the Bay, there are even more that we do not normally think of as Chesapeake fish. (See "Jumping Mullet" in July.) There are also a lot of small shellfish available. (See "Grass Shrimp Don't Have Many Friends.") Thus our waters are also full of predators. Bluefish, like Jon Sutton's big one, grow fat. They seem to be especially partial to menhaden and spot. Young bluefish eat anything moving that they can get their mouths around, especially anchovies. But even the young blues have their predators, especially big gray trout. There are other well-known predators too, like rockfish, and, in recent years, Spanish mackerel, plus others of which we are generally less aware. (See "Cownose Rays Are Really Graceful" in June, "Needlefish: Fierce but Delicate" in July, and "Sea Turtles in the Bay" in August.) Finally, upriver predators are active now too, especially the familiar largemouth bass and channel catfish. Here also there are less well known but interesting fish-eaters. (See "Garfish: Another Successful Old Design" in July.)

Great blue herons and ospreys catch their share. (See "The Stalkers: Great Blue Herons and Their Kin" in June and "A Challenging Month for Osprey Chicks" in August.) We are fortunate to have so many of each species on the Bay each summer. Two of the season's real pleasures are watching a heron stalk the edge of a marsh, spearing small spot and silversides as it goes, and seeing an osprey hover, then dive on a school of menhaden.

The Chesapeake's gulls are much in evidence during summer, but many of them are immature birds. Early in the summer, a large number of the adults are preoccupied with laying eggs and rearing young on the Chesapeake's most remote islands and along the barrier islands across the Eastern Shore on the Atlantic Coast. (See "Gulls Nesting" in June.)

We must count in other fishermen as well, like the river otters that forage mostly at night. The most obvious ones, of course, are ourselves, whether we be cruising sailors trolling a line for dinner, or hard-core anglers jigging trout or bottom fishing for spot.

Most of us tend to focus on the larger creatures of the Bay community, but there is a vast array of smaller creatures as well. While ospreys, herons, and gulls draw the greatest portion of our attention, the male red-winged blackbird does his best to claim a share. (See "The Proud Red Badge" in July.) In the water, several fascinating animals escape our notice unless we look for them. (See "Secret Inhabitants: Seahorses and Pipefish" in June and "Cold Fire in the Water" in August.) There is, however, at least one animal of summer that we would just as soon overlook, if we could. (See "What Good Are Sea Nettles?" in August.)

Finally, with all of this life in the Bay, there must be fish and shellfish dying, and thus scraps for scavengers to clean up. Blue crabs stay busy at this task, as do a host of mud crabs, worms, barnacles, anemones, and other small creatures. They in turn furnish more food for fish and blue crabs, making the system ever richer and more diverse.

As summer unfolds, inevitably signs of seasonal change begin to herald the fall, and it is always a good game to try to spot the first of them, like a leaf or two on a black gum tree turning red at the end of July. One of the most intriguing is the movement of monarch butterflies through the Bay region in August. (See "Monarch Butterflies in Migration.") At the same time, the salt marshes and the upriver brackish and fresh marshes reach their peaks in an explosion of green growth and, especially in fresh waters, showy wildflowers. (See "A Nice Gestalt: Bay Marshes at Summer's End.")

All of this activity under and around the water invites us to join in. This is the high season. Enjoy it.

JUNE

For Soft-Crabbers, Summer Is a Busy Season

Louis Whittaker's life is just getting back to normal, if a soft-crabber's life can ever be said to be normal during the season. The first big run of peelers comes on the full or new moon in mid-May. It means traps that are 2 and 3 feet deep in crabs, shedding tanks full to bursting, everybody working heavy overtime. The early season is like a sprint. Summer means settling into the rhythm of a marathon.

Louis runs Sea Products, Inc., in Reedville, an innovative soft crab operation with shallow indoor shedding tanks. From May until late September, his life and the lives of his family are dominated by crabs sloughing (shedding) their shells.

Baywide, everyone in the industry is getting into the summer routine. Whether using closed-circuit shore tanks, flow-through tanks with pumps, or traditional overboard floats, in season a soft-crabber is always busy, and sometimes extremely busy. There are crabs to be caught, certainly a major task. Then there are the floats or tanks to be cared for. "Dipping up" is a several-times-daily ritual, removing newly shed soft crabs, their sloughs (empty shells), and any peelers that have died in the process. Finally, there is the business of cleaning, packing, freezing, marketing, and shipping.

Crabs don't molt when the water is cold, so the first run in spring is a good one. There are lots of peelers, and shedding survival is high. But crabs must continue to slough as they grow.

68

Later in the summer, as the water warms, a larger percentage of crabs will "hang up" and die in the process of shedding: in conventional floats, late summer survival can be less than 50 percent. A good spring run can make the difference between profit and loss for the year, so soft-crabbers give it their best efforts, but they work hard all season to keep survival as high as possible.

Molting, or shedding an entire shell, seems like a bizarre way to grow, but it is common in the crustacean world. And it is not simply a periodic event in the life of a crab. During a 24- to 30-month life span, the animal will molt over 20 times. At first, shedding comes every five days or so. Gradually the interval lengthens to over a month as the crab matures. In the period between each shed, it must regain its strength, fill out its new and larger shell, and build up its energy reserves before the actual molting process begins anew. There is very little time in a crab's life when it is not concerned with some aspect of shedding.

The process begins when nerve receptors inside the shell signal the crab's central nervous system, which controls a system of hormones—basically chemical signals—in the blood. These cause the cells at the base of the shell to separate from the shell itself. Nerves attached to sensory receptors in the shell begin to retract. The base cells form a new shell inside the old one. It is this new shell that shows up as the white, pink, or red sign that crabbers look for on the next-to-last segment of the swimming leg on a peeler.

The shell is a complex structure with several different layers that give it strength and its characteristic colors. It is made up primarily of protein and chitin, the latter a complex fibrous carbohydrate that is the crustacean equivalent of cellulose fiber in wood. Between the old shell and the new one is a layer of mucus.

When the new shell has developed, some of the material in the old shell is reabsorbed at critical points like the bases of the limbs, to soften the potential bottlenecks in the molting process. By this time, the crab has ceased feeding, hidden itself as best it can, and begun to drink large quantities of water. The water causes the animal to swell and split its shell along the back line between upper and lower sections. Hence the nickname "buster" for this stage. Now the animal begins to back out of its old shell, with the mucous layer providing lubrication.

This is a critical time for a crab, especially a big one in warm water. It is wriggling out of everything, even its old gills, mouth parts, and antennae. The new gills cannot function for a time, but once they begin to work, they must supply the crab with plenty of oxygen so it can complete the process. And since warm water holds less oxygen than cool water, summer molts are especially risky, both in the wild and in the crabbers' tanks and floats. A major advantage of the shore tanks at Sea Products is their ability to keep the water well oxygenated even in late summer.

Once the crab is free of its old shell (assuming it is not caught and eaten by an eel, a raccoon, a rockfish, a human, or any of the other animals that appreciate it), the cells at the base of the new shell go to work again. They extract calcium from the blood and secrete it to the outer shell. Within a matter of several hours, the calcium mineralizes the chitin-protein structure, giving it the consistency of parchment, hence the nicknames "papershell" and "buckram" given to this stage. Within 48 hours, the shell is hardened. The crab begins filling out its new shell and getting ready for its next molt.

Vertebrate growth processes are complex, and it is always exciting to watch babies and puppies and ospreys and rockfish grow up. But there is a special drama to walking a marsh at dawn after a full moon and finding the bank littered with sloughs, or catching a buster, putting it into a bucket, and watching it shed. And even a veteran soft-crabber like Louis Whittaker smiles whenever he has a chance to watch it.

The Essential Menhaden

Some years, John Hall sets a little pound net on the Potomac at the mouth of the Yeocomico River, on Virginia's Northern Neck. A fellow from up the beach happened by one morning early and asked what the net caught. "Bunkers mostly . . . mostly bunkers," said John.

If the visitor had been from the other side of the river, he might not have understood. Most Marylanders call them "alewives," though that term refers properly to their cousins, the river herring. But alewife or bunker, or bugfish (as they call them up the Bay in Rock Hall), or Atlantic menhaden, or *Brevoortia tyrannus*, commercial fishermen on the Chesapeake do catch a lot of them—several hundred million pounds a year.

That's an awful lot of fish. In fact, menhaden usually make Reedville, the town on the Northern Neck where most of them are landed, the largest fishing port on the Atlantic Coast in annual tonnage. Now what uses do we make of all those fish?

The eighteenth-century naturalist Mark Catesby is quoted in John Frye's *The Men All Singing* as finding the menhaden "an excellent Sweet Fish." The species appeared in Washington markets regularly until late in the nineteenth century, and some were packed for human consumption even early in this century. When absolutely fresh, they are indeed good, rich fish. But they are oily and bony, and they spoil very quickly. Tastes have changed, and bunkers never appear in markets any more. Many people are unaware of them, except as the source of stench from spring fish kills.

Because of the oil in their flesh, they are the primary bait used in commercial crab pots: by any measure, the crab pot industry goes through a million pounds of menhaden *per day* in season. The bait industry serving it involves a wide range of gear, from John Hall's little pound net to million-dollar purse-seiners with sophisticated refrigeration units that ensure good bait quality. A number of people around the Bay make a good living distributing the bait each day—getting it out to the crab-potters so they are ready to fish their pots the next morning.

Recreational anglers use some as well. At the mouth of the Potomac, there is a large fleet of charter boats carrying parties from the tip of St. Mary's County in Maryland and from the Smith Point area on the Northern Neck. They specialize in chumming—ladling ground-up bunkers overboard from an anchored boat. The oily slick drifts downtide for a mile or more, attracting bluefish and rockfish, and occasionally trout, drum, and cobia. Each boat goes through several bushels of chum a day. They add to the demand for bait.

The most visible, and the largest fishery for menhaden is in Virginia, with purse-seiners operating all over the lower Bay from their docks in Reedville. There are about 20 of these vessels, all over 100 feet long. Each uses two purse boats—diesel-powered launches—to set a 600-yard-long net some 40 feet deep into a circle around a school of bunkers located by airplane. The fishermen purse a line

running around the bottom of the net, forming it into a shallow bowl from which the big boat can pump the fish into its hold. This is how the majority of menhaden are caught in the Bay and along the Atlantic and Gulf coasts. Purse seine–caught fish are used primarily for industrial purposes.

A century ago, the fish were caught for their oil, which was cooked out in kettles. It was used for tanning leather, manufacturing paint, tempering steel, and other processes. The leftover scrap was dried in the sun and sold as fertilizer. Today, the oil is used in cosmetics, paints, and pharmaceuticals. Much of it is shipped to Europe as an ingredient in margarine. The leftover fish meal is high in protein; it finds a ready market as animal feed, especially for chickens and hogs.

New uses for menhaden products are being found every year. Though they have long since been deemed too valuable to use as fertilizer, the fish are seldom considered fit to feed to humans today, but that status may well change as a hungry world turns to widespread use of powdered fish protein concentrate.

Man is not the only animal that preys on menhaden. Most of the Bay's bluefish bulge with them. Menhaden are also preyed on by rockfish, trout, cobia, flounder, Spanish mackerel, and every other large fish that eats small fish. In the Bay's upper tidal rivers where salinity is low, the 1- to 3-inch juvenile bunkers of summer are fed on by largemouth bass, channel catfish, and chain pickerel. Gulls, terns, and ospreys dive on the schools of young. In the shallows, herons stalk and spear them.

As John Frye and others have observed, menhaden are virtually designed to be eaten. In addition to their high levels of protein and oil, they are abundant and defenseless. They travel in dense schools, making them easy to find and easy to catch in large numbers.

Even so, Atlantic menhaden are able to withstand this tremendous predation and still have sufficient brood stock to maintain the population. How can they do it? Certainly they are fecund: much remains to be learned about spawning, but estimates are that females drop from 38,000 to 600,000 eggs at a time (figures from Frye). More fundamental still is the menhaden's source of food. If there are that many fish out there, there has to be several times that much food available to them.

As one might expect, menhaden eat low on the food web. When first hatched, they feed selectively on zooplankton. But soon their gill rakers develop long feathery projections forward into the mouth, and they begin filter-feeding—swimming with their mouths open and straining water at the rate of several hundred gallons an hour. Food includes diatoms (photosynthetic plankton), copepods (tiny crustaceans), and detritus (decayed plant and animal material).

In a rich estuary like the Chesapeake, the fish are everywhere in the summer. Juveniles travel up the rivers in shoals, going all the way to the heads of tidal waters. Adults tend to stay in the lower rivers and the open Bay. They are omnivorous vacuum cleaners, eating much that is not usable by other creatures and turning it into high-quality protein.

We the public pay attention primarily to fish that are good to eat or sporting to catch. It is remarkable that such a major fishery resource could exist so unobtrusively on the Bay. Yet much of our food and sport fishery, and much of the Bay's economy, is dependent directly or indirectly on bunkers. We can be thankful for them whenever we broil a bluefish or bite into a crab cake.

Cownose Rays Are Really Graceful

Captain Jim Webb had a group of anglers aboard his charter boat, *Afternoon Delight*, trolling surgical hose lures for bluefish off the mouth of the Patuxent. Seven rods stood in the boat's holders, with lines streaming astern. Suddenly one of the rods jumped and bent over. Line poured off the reel as a heavy fish ran with the lure.

Jim smiled. It was the tenth of June, too late for a big rockfish, so he knew what they had hooked. It was a big cownose ray. He took the boat out of gear and let it idle. One angler picked up the rod and began to work on the fish while the others brought in the empty lines.

The ray was big, 30 inches across the back and 30 pounds in weight. It made four long, steady runs before the angler could lead it to boatside for Jim to gaff. "Gee," said the angler rubbing his arms, "I didn't know they were that strong."

Back at the dock, Jim cut four big fillets from the ray's wings. The angler took them home and came back the next week raving about how tasty they had been. Jim smiled again. What he likes most about charter boat fishing is helping people enjoy themselves, and if they learn something in the process, so much the better.

For Jim's clients and for most of us, rays and skates appear at first to be most peculiar and unconventional. It is hard to think of them as fish. But they form a group that includes a large number of species adapted to several different lifestyles in habitats all over the world. Diversity and wide distribution are considered two good indications of success for a biological design.

Like sharks, rays and skates have cartilage skeletons instead of bone. But unlike the sharks, their pectoral (side) fins are greatly enlarged, becoming dominant body features ("wings"). Dorsal (back) and caudal (tail) fins are very small or absent altogether. Gills are inside a series of slits on each side of the body, as they are in sharks, but instead of being above the pectorals, they are below, on the flat underside next to the mouth.

Skates belong to a family that is related to but separate from the rays. They are primarily bottom dwellers. Only a few true skates occur in the Bay, mostly down near the Virginia Capes.

A number of different ray species turn up in the Chesapeake. By far the most common is the cownose *(Rhinoptera bonasus)*. Schools enter the Bay each year in late spring and stay till fall, feeding heavily on shellfish. Sometimes a school can be located by the mud stirred up as its members work through a softshell clam bed. They beat their wings down hard on the bottom, dislodging sediments and exposing the clams.

Newborn cownose rays are about 12 inches across and 1 pound in weight. They can grow to wingspreads of 45 inches and weights of over 50 pounds. Cownoses are more agile and active than skates and most other rays, appearing to fly through the water with powerful wing strokes. They are particularly well adapted to feeding on shellfish, but in addition they eat some fish. On each jaw the teeth are fused together into a solid mass like a small paving block with a convex surface. The upper and lower jaws work together as crushers.

Rays have a remarkable system of reproduction. Unlike the skates, whose young develop in egg cases, rays are viviparous—their young are born live. The female cownose has a uterus with two chambers, each equipped with tiny fingers called villi that are richly supplied with blood vessels. The unborn young apparently develop while nestled in the villi, taking food and oxygen from them. Births occur soon after the rays come into the Bay from the ocean in early summer.

Catching and handling a ray requires some care. Almost any one caught on a hook and line will weigh over 10 pounds—a strong animal with few handholds. In addition, the cownose and almost every other species of ray in the Bay has one or more sharp, venomous, barbed, 2- to 5-inch spines at the base of its tail. The spines are dangerous weapons, and anyone struck with one needs immediate medical attention.

But a ray at boatside can be handled safely. First, gaff it by reaching underneath the head with the hook of a gaff. Feel for the mouth and teeth, then pull the hook home and raise the fish's head to the boat's gunwale. Hit it between the eyes with a billy club or similar instrument. This is an unpleasant task but certainly the most humane way to treat any fish taken for eating. Then place the ray in the cockpit and, still controlling it with the gaff, remove the spine(s) carefully with a pair of pliers. Ice it down like any other fish.

Rays are easy to clean and very good to eat, as Jim Webb's anglers discovered. The fish are standard fare at the Chesapeake Bay Foundation's Great Fox Island education center in Tangier Sound, where students and staff grill them. The students are naturally leery of the rays at first, but catching, cleaning, and eating them breeds fascination and respect. The fish deserve at least as much from the Bay community at large.

For more information on ray biology and on cooking them, see Bibliography.

The Stalkers: Great Blue Herons and Their Kin

The great blue heron *(Ardea herodias)* is one of the Chesapeake's best-loved birds. People who live on the Bay's rivers, creeks, and coves talk of "our herons" who fish the shores outside living room or kitchen windows. Many a cruising family has spent a happy hour at anchor in the Wye River or the Corrotoman watching a solitary great blue stalking the edge of the marsh. Canoeists feel their spines tingle as they round a bend in a stream to see one of the big birds taking flight with a squawk. Great blue herons are stirring sights at any time. There are large numbers of them in this region, and many stay year-round unless driven south by winter ice.

The great blue stands 50 inches tall, with a wing span of 70 inches. The species is widely distributed, breeding in spring from coast to coast across Canada and from there south and east to South Carolina and Bermuda. The birds winter from the northern United States down into Central America. The Chesapeake is in the overlap between the breeding and winter ranges.

The great blue heron's bill is a most lethal device. Six-and-a-half inches long, sharp and strong, it ranks up there with the osprey's talons and the angler's hook for tonnage of fish caught on the Chesapeake Bay each year. The osprey has powerful wings and good distance vision to go with its talons, a superb combination for catching fish on the surface of open waters. The angler has a rod and reel, and often a boat and a depth-sounder, for catching fish on the Bay bottom.

The great blue heron is at least as well equipped. That bill is attached to a long neck which can be curled up to strike like a snake. To guide its lightninglike dart, the bird has excellent close-range binocular vision with keen distance judgment. Four-toed feet 6 to 8 inches long allow the animal to walk on almost any sort of river bottom from hard sand to soft muck. Long legs allow it to hunt in water up to 18 inches deep and give it a high vantage point for locating prey. The bird coils its long neck, stands motionless, peers into the water, and then strikes quickly and powerfully. There is no predator on the Chesapeake better designed for catching fish in shallow water.

The Chesapeake provides lots of habitat for herons. The main-stem, tidal tributaries, and small feeder streams have over 8,000 miles of shoreline. Most of it offers water less than 2 feet deep, and some areas like Tangier Sound and the Poquoson River have broad expanses of shallow flats. Even the fresh and low-salinity portions of the tidal rivers, which normally have deep waters on the outsides of their sweeping meander curves, build large marshes with extensive flats on the insides of those curves.

These edges are rich, fueled by thousands of acres of fresh, brackish, or tidal marshes, and, when the Bay is healthy, thousands of acres of submerged grasses. The shallows are havens for all the small creatures that make up the heron's diet. In low-salinity parts of the Bay system, these include banded killifish, shiners, and young pickerel. In high-salinity waters, they include mummichogs (common killifish), striped killifish, silversides, bay anchovies, and juvenile menhaden. The birds feed also on crayfish, small crabs, frogs, young snakes, mice, and even grasshoppers. Like most widely distributed animals, they are opportunists.

The fact that the fish they catch are small works in the herons' favor: they are best equipped to handle prey under 6 inches long (though they do occasionally take larger food), and what the fish in the shallows give away in size, they more than make up for in numbers and overall tonnage. So the herons have a great deal of food available to them.

In the air, the heron's flight is slow (about 30 miles per hour) and deliberate, with the neck coiled up for balance and the long legs trailing behind. The coiled neck has an interesting feature. In most birds, such a curve would collapse the trachea (windpipe). The herons and their kin have S-shaped joints that allow their tracheae to be folded without collapsing. The joints are visible when the birds are wading or roosting.

The heron's large wings provide great lift. The bird may glide for short distances, but most of the time the wingbeat is steady. Apparently this system allows those herons that migrate to make their long trips successfully. It also gives them great maneuverability. They are particularly impressive coming into or taking off from the tall trees in which they often roost. They are adept at braking their flight and can climb almost vertically from one limb to another in the same tree.

Great blue herons change their habits in February and March to travel to their rookeries. Relatively tolerant of people during the rest of the year, they retire until early summer to a few well-isolated locations where they congregate in large numbers. This is the nesting season, and only unmated or subadult birds remain in their usual haunts. The rookeries are always places with mature, tall forests, generally pines or tulip poplars, and they always offer the birds some privacy. A number of the rookeries, each with 15 to 200 nests, are on the islands that stretch down the Eastern Shore, from Poplar Island in Talbot County, Maryland, to Watts Island in Accomack County, Virginia. There are also a number of rookeries in the wooded, upper tidal sections of the western shore's big rivers.

The largest rookery on the Bay, in fact, with over 700 nests, is at the head of one arm of Nanjemoy Creek, on the Potomac in

Charles County, Maryland, just above the Route 301 bridge at Morgantown. There are indications that great blues come from considerable distances outside the Bay region to join local herons here. The Maryland Chapter of The Nature Conservancy deserves a great deal of credit for preserving this invaluable piece of heron habitat.

Great blues are relatively quiet most of the year, but their rookeries are noisy with the cries of both young and old. Nests are platforms in the trees, 30 feet or more off the ground. Occasionally a young bird falls out of the nest, to get caught in a tree branch or drop to the ground. Either way, it is left to die and rot. The results of such accidents, added to decaying scraps of fish left around the nests, give these places a characteristic stench.

A rookery may seem to be a chaos of loud squawks and unpleasant smells, often surrounded by poison ivy and thorny greenbrier. But somehow, out of it come beautiful, graceful birds that disperse around the Chesapeake and to points beyond. We are fortunate to have so many of them here.

In fact, we are more than fortunate. The Chesapeake has enough habitat for stalkers that it supports eight other species of herons besides the great blue, though most of them are warm-weather residents: the great egret *(Casmerodias albus)*, the snowy egret *(Egretta thula)*, the cattle egret *(Bubulcus ibis)*, the little green heron *(Butorides striatus)*, the little blue heron *(Egretta caerulea)*, the Louisiana heron *(Egretta tricolor)*, the black-crowned night heron *(Nycticorax nycticorax)*, and the yellow-crowned night heron *(Nycticorax violacea)*.

Of these "others," the egrets are the most obvious. They are white. The great egret is nearly as large as the great blue, with black legs and a yellow bill. It is more a bird of open marsh country and higher salinities than the great blue, though there are exceptions, especially in spring and fall. (All three egrets winter south of the Chesapeake, so at times of migration, large numbers of them move through our region.)

The snowy egret is much smaller than the great egret and is distinguished by a black bill and bright yellow feet. In Victorian times, it was hunted nearly to extinction so that its white plumes could grace ladies' hats. Protection since the first part of this century has brought it back. The snowy occasionally forages in the wash along open beaches.

The cattle egret is a recent arrival, having spread across the Atlantic from Africa to Brazil and then up through Central America. This species, as its name implies, tends to stay with large herds of cattle, eating insects and field seeds. It is often seen around farms on the rivers, like Wye Plantation on Maryland's Eastern Shore.

The little green heron is the smallest of the group and has the shortest legs. It perches on fallen trees and other shoreline objects, stalking or waiting as appropriate, then making a lightning strike with its lethal bill. This strategy actually gives it an advantage over the others, because by relying on perches like tree limbs, it can fish water deeper than the others can reach by wading. Due to its dependence on trees and the like, it prefers rivers and creeks. After the great blue, it is probably the Chesapeake's most widespread heron, but because of its size, it is usually unnoticed by humans. It is a beautiful bird and a delight to watch.

The little blue and the Louisiana herons frequent the marshes of the lower Bay. They and the yellow-crowned night heron are the least common in this area, but they are well worth keeping an eye out for. The little blue, as its name implies, is half the size of a great blue, and is colored a deep cerulean sky blue, in keeping with its Latin name. The Louisiana is easily recognizable for its very slender build and its white breast under a slate-blue body. The two night herons are, as they name implies, most active from dusk till dawn. They are stockier than the others and again, are primarily birds of the open marshes.

A point worth noting about the Bay's herons is that while their niches (lifestyles) are *basically* the same, they are not *exactly* the same. This diversity allows all nine species to coexist while minimizing direct competition. The diversity lets them as a group take maximum advantage of all the stalking niches the Chesapeake offers.

Thus we have a rich community of herons here. If there is any threat to them, it is their need for isolated, protected, mature woodlands for breeding. Like the great blue, the others all require trees for their nests, and in a few stands, all nine species nest together, sorting themselves out by height of nest from the ground. Disturbance from humans drives them away, so protection of heronries is an important part of land conservation efforts. We all owe a debt of gratitude to the private and government landowners who have heron rookeries and protect them. A Bay without its stalkers would be a poor place.

Gulls Nesting

From May through September, the passenger boat *Chesapeake Breeze* runs one or two round trips a day from Fairport, at the eastern tip of the Northern Neck, across the Bay to Tangier Island and back, carrying tourists and island residents who have business on the lower western shore. As the boat enters or leaves its home cove just off Cockrell Creek and the Great Wicomico, a cloud of gulls follows. Apparently they are feasting on scraps of food thrown by tourists, but they are also preying on the small fish—mostly silversides, anchovies, and young menhaden—churned to the surface by the big boat's propellers.

Gulls may well be the most taken-for-granted group of birds on the Chesapeake. There are always some around every waterway. They appear to adapt easily to man, eating a variety of foods and not worrying about being close to crowds. Laughing gulls dive on baitfish driven to the surface by bluefish, even if there are fishermen in powerboats around them. Ring-billed gulls follow farmers in the spring, feeding on worms and insects at plowing time and seeds at planting time. Herring gulls hang around municipal dumps, especially in cities and suburban areas close to the Bay and its rivers. Great black-backed gulls, the biggest of the lot (5½-foot wingspread) hang around dumps too. They also hunt and eat young birds and small mammals, especially herons, ducks, and muskrats. They even steal from smaller gulls.

Scavengers, predators, herbivores, carnivores—gulls fit all those terms. They are opportunistic omnivores. We watch spellbound as they soar over the water, but it is all too easy to stop seeing the flocks that scatter themselves around any harbor. They become commonplace parts of the scene, greedy birds that feed on scraps from peoples' lunches, not majestic, noble creatures. They are deceptive. Their adaptability is the key—it is a hallmark of evolutionary development. Gulls may well be the most intelligent birds on the Chesapeake.

But as adaptable and tolerant of man as they are in feeding and everyday living, gulls are specific in their nesting requirements.

They breed and raise their young in isolated places. They want no interference then. Actually, they get very little of it from man, at least not directly. They are, and have been for some time, protected by law from all types of hunting at all stages of their lives, from egg to adult. But man's laws do not govern foxes, raccoons, blacksnakes, and other animals that relish eggs and chicks. To get away from these predators, gulls seek out islands, preferably small barren ones that would be of little interest to any animals other than themselves.

Little Fox Island, in Tangier Sound, was a good example. A century ago, Little Fox was 50 acres or so, with a stand of tall loblolly pines. Ten years ago, it was a half-acre of sand, cordgrass, and tidebush. The nearest tree was on Tangier, 4 miles to the west across open water. The nearest land was marshy Great Fox Island, half a mile to the north. Watts Island, 5 miles to the south, is large, with extensive stands of loblollies, hardwoods, and poison ivy. Tangier, Great Fox, and Watts all have raccoons. And Great Fox has occasional blacksnakes and, naturally, foxes that swim over from the nearby Cedar Island marsh, which is connected to the mainland. All three systems are large enough and diverse enough to support these animals. But Little Fox was neither. It was poor wildlife habitat. Thus it was no accident that, each June, it supported 40-odd great black-backed gulls' nests. Today it is just a shoal.

Now there are only a few islands on the Chesapeake suitable for gull nesting. Most are in the lower Bay. The majority of the gulls that live here nest on the seaside, either up the Delaware shore or on the Virginia barrier islands. Again, the birds in both areas favor the most isolated and barren sand spits.

A gull nest is a simple affair, often just a hollow scooped out of bare sand, lined with a few scraps of dead vegetation. It may be on the upper edge of a beach, on the high part of a marsh, or on a low dune. The birds nest in colonies, using their numbers to confuse or intimidate any predator stubborn enough to reach them.

The breeding season for all species of gulls that use the Bay is long, from late April to early September. Thus the summer populations on the Bay are shifting ones, made up of birds that have finished nesting and those that have not yet begun, augmented by immature birds and unmated adults.

"Our gulls" are ours in the same sense that "our" ospreys or "our" Canada geese belong to the Chesapeake—birds that spend part of their year here. The gulls come and go, east to west from seaside to Bayshore, north to south up and down the coast with the seasons. The patterns are complex, changeable, and opportunistic, but those characteristics are to be expected from adaptable creatures. We, the most adaptable creatures of all, should understand them.

Secret Inhabitants: Seahorses and Pipefish

One morning about 40 years ago, my father and I were crabbing out on our dock on the Potomac near Kinsale, on the Northern Neck. We always kept three crab pots tied to the dock, baited with the heads and guts of the fish we had caught the day before. When we pulled up the first pot, a seahorse *(Hippocampus erectus)* lay among the crabs.

We were amazed. In those days, there was an awful lot we didn't know about the river. We certainly had no idea seahorses lived in it. Fascinated by our catch, we put the seahorse into a bucket of river water and watched it swim around by rippling the funny little dorsal fin on its backside and the two little pectoral fins that stuck out like ear flaps behind its eyes. Unfortunately it died in the bucket, but we salted it down to preserve it, and today it still sits on the mantelpiece of our cottage.

Seahorses tend to be creatures of high-salinity waters. Our place is 20 miles up inside the mouth of the river, about as far as seahorses come in dry seasons. That summer may have been a dry one, and the Potomac a little saltier than usual. The Chesapeake Bay Foundation's field staff, who are on the water virtually every day in a dozen or more different places, encounter them occasionally in the lower Bay. Most recently, a large one (about 8 inches) turned up at our Great Fox Island education center in Tangier Sound.

The seahorse is a peculiar animal. It has bony rings around its body that are made of scales fused together. It is built to swim upright in the water, and its head is turned at a 90-degree angle to its body. The tail, which is long and curls around, is considered to be prehensile, like our hands, and the animal can reach out and wrap it around objects in the water. The caudal fin, which most fish have at the ends of their tails, is missing on the seahorse, and its other fins are tiny, allowing only limited locomotion. As my father and I learned from the seahorse at our cottage, the fish swims by rippling its small dorsal fin, and it stabilizes itself and maneuvers with the little pectoral fins on its head. Its jaws are fused together into a tube-shaped mouth.

There is method, however, in this unusual body design. The seahorse fills its niche as a patient predator that hooks itself to underwater grass stalks like a tiny piece of debris and then sucks in small crustaceans like copepods and amphipods, as well as fish larvae and even fish eggs, as they drift by. The seahorse has large, bright eyes which allow it to see its prey clearly. By pointing its mouth in the correct direction, it can bring in these tiny creatures from a distance of as much as an inch and a half, which, in relative human terms, is comparable to the distance between a plate on a dinner table and a seated person's mouth.

When we caught the seahorse on the Potomac, the river bottom just beyond our pier was covered with widgeon grass, a natural habitat for seahorses. CBF's lodge on Great Fox Island has acres of eelgrass and widgeon grass beds close by. The chapter "Summer and Scraping" in William W. Warner's *Beautiful Swimmers* describes the multitude of living things in the grass beds, including seahorses. Sea trout and bluefish are two grass bed predators that are large enough to eat a seahorse, but the animal's bony skeleton limits its food value. The biggest threat to a seahorse's existence is not being eaten but losing its grass bed habitat through man-caused changes in the Bay's water quality. The widgeon grass bed in front of our cottage has been gone for years.

The seahorse has a close relative in the Bay, the northern pipefish *(Syngnathus fuscus)*, which has the same vertical build as the seahorse but a slenderer body and no 90-degree bend at the head. Pipefish appear to be much more streamlined than seahorses, but they, too, swim upright. This long, thin, green creature can camouflage itself in an eelgrass bed by holding itself vertical in water, just like a grass blade.

The northern pipefish has a wider distribution in the Chesapeake Bay, venturing into lower-salinity brackish waters up the rivers and the mainstem of the Bay into Maryland. Pipefish spend the summer in the grass beds but winter in deeper waters, at depths of as much as 60 or 70 feet. It would be fair to guess that seahorses do the same.

Although the pipefish does not have bony rings, it has a thick chain mail–like covering of scales. It, too, has few predators. I caught a flounder once in the grass beds at Fox Island that had four pipefish in its belly. They appeared to have been an indigestible meal. Perhaps that's why the flounder was hungry enough to take my lure.

The most unusual adaptation that seahorses and pipefish exhibit is that the male carries the eggs inside his body. In the fish's belly there is a fold, the two sides of which are fused together to form a pouch called a marsupium that is somewhat similar to the pouches of kangaroos and other mammals in Australia. This is, however, a completely independent evolutionary development—obviously seahorses and pipefish have little relationship to mammals. A male seahorse matures at the age of about one year, and the pouch develops thick, spongy walls full of blood vessels. These allow for the passage back and forth of oxygen, carbon dioxide, food, and wastes as the young develop.

During mating, the female deposits the eggs into the male's pouch, where he fertilizes them. She puts in several dozen at a time and then stops, while he goes though a series of convulsive flexing movements to work them down into the pouch. Then she deposits several dozen more, and he repeats the exercise. Two to six matings of this type will give him several hundred eggs. This role reversal has given rise to at least a couple of humorous poems about innocent young seacolts being seduced by worldly, older seamares, and also to a lot of comments that there is at least some justice in the world.

The seahorse male incubates the eggs for about 10 days and then gives birth to ⅓-inch-long seacolts and seafillies by going through more contortions, with rests in between. He provides at least a short period of parental care after birth. The whole business appears to be a tiring process; but once his responsibilities are discharged, he will most likely go off and mate with another female.

The care that seahorses give to their young is, in fact, among the best in the fish world. It is very different from the broadcast spawning of thousands of eggs undertaken by most of the other fish species in the Bay. Like the adults' strange body design, though, this strategy has a reason behind it. A male seahorse is able to protect his eggs from the egg-eating practices that nourish adult seahorses and omnivorous filter feeders like menhaden, who consume at least some of their own young. There are a lot of egg-eaters in the grass beds, and parental care is a good procedure for a tiny animal that does not produce thousands of eggs.

Seahorses and pipefish aren't prominent members of the Bay community because they don't have much economic value to us. It is worth remembering, though, that they worked out their ways of life long before we started assigning economic value to any of the Bay's creatures. They have as much of a niche in the Bay's fabric of life as crabs or rockfish. The richness and variety of that fabric is part of what makes the Bay so valuable to us.

JULY

Traveling Crabs

"The Maryland crab is different," said the man in the tackle shop at Solomons. "Its meat is sweet, like a lobster's. Virginia crabs just aren't the same animal."

He said that nearly 30 years ago, when we were all more naive and more provincial about our Bay. The Atlantic blue crab grows best in the fresher waters of upper estuaries, but it spawns in late spring and summer in salty waters near the estuaries' mouths. The man in Solomons was right to the extent that "his" crabs grew fat in excellent Maryland crab-growing habitat. Even so, virtually all of them had been born in Virginia between the mouth of the Rappahannock and Hampton Roads, and they had done a surprising amount of traveling before they made it up to the Patuxent River.

Any waterman working the spring and fall migrations and any biologist looking at catch survey data could see the general pattern, and William W. Warner's *Beautiful Swimmers* has done a lot to get the message across to the general public. Our beloved blue crabs are true creatures of the estuary, and their life cycle sends them from one end of the system to the other, rivers and main Bay alike. They are not Maryland or Virginia crabs. They are Chesapeake crabs.

Because the blue crab is so valuable to the economy of the Bay country, its population fluctuations are watched closely by scientists, state fishery management biologists, watermen, and seafood packers. As much as possible, the latter two base their business strategies on the expected catch for any given season. For years, the trawl net survey conducted by Willard Van Engel at the Virginia Institute of Marine Science (VIMS) served as the foundation for predictions. The crab harvest has a history of varying widely from year to year, and there have been years when the survey did not predict the catch well at all. In June 1972 tropical storm Agnes led to just such a situation.

Before then, it was believed that a high summer river flow, especially from the James, would flush crab larvae out of the Bay and into the Atlantic, killing most of that year class of crabs. Agnes poured fresh water down the Bay's rivers, including a particularly heavy flow from the James (the river crested some 28 feet above flood stage at Richmond). According to the prevailing theory, that year's larvae would have been swept out to the ocean and lost. In 1973, however, the Bay was full of 1972 crabs. Something had happened at the mouth of the Bay that the scientists did not know about. Observations that do not fit accepted theory are opportunities. This kind of occurrence is what advances scientific knowledge.

The problem was too large for one scientist or even one laboratory to attack alone. If larvae were being swept out to sea, tracing them would require physical oceanographers who could study the currents at the Bay mouth and out on the continental shelf. But the larvae might not stay in the same position in the currents. If they swam up or down, they could find themselves traveling first one way and then another as they changed current levels. Thus the study needed biologists to study the behavior of crab larvae in detail. Lots of data had to be collected aboard research vessels in the Bay and in the ocean, and it had to be fitted in with all the observations that had already been made over the years. A team was developed that included biologists and physical oceanographers from the University of Maryland, the University of Delaware, Old Dominion University, and VIMS. Funding was supplied in large part by the Sea Grant programs in the three states.

For nearly 10 years, the team pieced the puzzle together. It appears now that larval crabs tend to swim away from the force of gravity and toward light. Thus, when they hatch on the bottom in the spawning grounds at the Bay's mouth, they migrate toward the surface. This movement puts them in the fresher water layers that move generally seaward, rather than the saltier deep layers that move generally into the Bay.

Virtually the whole year class travels out into the Atlantic over the continental shelf. This is the normal condition, not just the result of a big storm like Agnes. To some extent, the oceanographers have been able to model water temperature, wind speed and direction, and current conditions on the shelf to predict the movement of the larvae. "When it works, it's almost eerie," said one scientist. "We feed our computer some wind and current data, and it gives us Loran coordinates. We run forty miles offshore to those numbers, put down the plankton net, and there they are." It is the ultimate needle-in-the-haystack game: the larvae are microscopic in size.

Movements on the continental shelf depend on weather patterns. It is probable that some patterns send larvae into the Chesapeake, while others push them into Delaware and Chincoteague bays, and into the bays behind the Virginia barrier islands. Research at Old Dominion is concentrating especially on how the crabs move back into the Chesapeake. It seems almost certain that they develop another behavior pattern that allows them to ride some combination of deep currents to their estuarine nursery grounds in the fall. Another team, from VIMS, is working on how the young crabs use those nurseries.

The patterns are large. Concentrations of larvae at the mouth of the Bay can reach 30,000 per cubic meter. The area of water involved is huge, and the current patterns vary each year with the weather. There is plenty to intrigue scientists, and us lay crab lovers as well.

One thing is sure, though. The blue crab's behavior is much more complex than the fellow in the Solomons tackle shop ever imagined. Thirty years ago, the area of the continental shelf where the larvae that would be his Patuxent River crabs spent their first summer were international waters. Chesapeake crabs don't care anything about politics.

Jumping Mullet

July on Ragged Island Creek: hot weather, hazy sky, a big salt marsh fairly humming with life. It was a good place to solve a mystery.

The mystery went back to a different day five months before, in March, when I had been there with a Chesapeake Bay Foundation canoe fleet and a group of students who were studying the James River. Ragged Island Creek runs through a 2,700-acre salt marsh complex on the south side of the James in Isle of Wight County, opposite Newport News. The big marsh is quite a contrast to the city and the shipyard on the other side.

On the March day when the mystery began, the students had just finished pulling a minnow seine on the shore. The water was still cold, but the day was warm, and the sun had been working on the shallows. The net was full of silverside minnows, but there were also a number of 1-inch-long, bullet-shaped fish with green backs and bright silver flanks. "Bluefish," said a student, and indeed that is what they looked like at first glance. But their mouths were a little too small and their bodies a little too chunky.

This was also the wrong time and place for young bluefish. Blues spawn in early and midsummer out in the Atlantic, on the western edge of the Gulf Stream. By the time the young fish get into the Bay, they are 3 to 6 inches long, and it is late summer. These fish were something different. The students dug through their field guides but came up with nothing.

Late winter and early spring pose all sorts of mysteries. What is this little green shoot just poking up through the mud? What will this marsh look like with the full bloom of summer on it? What will this little fish in the net grow up to be? I was glad when the chance came to return to Ragged Island Creek in July with another group of students.

Midmorning of that hot, hazy day found us paddling into a cove that leads back deep into the marsh. A school of fish that looked like young menhaden dimpled the surface up ahead, so I got out of the boat with a cast net and began stalking them from the marsh bank. They were moving a lot, though. Stalking turned into slogging and running, and after 10 minutes I realized that the fish weren't behaving like menhaden. When the net finally went out and came back with 10 4-inch striped mullet (*Mugil cephalus*), things began to make sense. These were what we had caught in March, only now they were grown, if not to adulthood, at least to adolescence.

It is ironic that we had looked at the juvenile mullet in March and thought about bluefish. Both species are streamlined, powerful fish capable of quick acceleration and strong leaps into the air. The striped mullet, in fact, is known throughout much of its range as the "jumping mullet" for its free-leaping habits. But the resemblance is superficial and ends early. Bluefish are toothy carnivores. Mullet are nearly toothless prey, primarily herbivorous. With soft fins and rich flesh, they are prime targets for bluefish and other predators ranging from the tropics to Delaware Bay.

Mullet are not as well known in the northern parts of the Chesapeake as they are further south. They are most common in the lower Bay and the mouths of the Virginia rivers. The ones that do summer here are immature first- and second-year fish, reaching maximum lengths of 10 to 12 inches. These fish appear to be part of a larger coastal population that stretches south to Florida and into the Caribbean. They reach sizes over 24 inches on the southern coast, playing a major role as forage in the diets of large predatory fish like tarpon and king mackerel. They are also the objects of a major gill net fishery for bait and for food. Smoked or fried, mullet are a standard local item on Florida's Gulf Coast menus.

As they are strong, mullet would be superb sport fish if they could be caught easily on hook and line. But, as noted, their mouths are small, with tiny, bristlelike teeth. They nibble tufts of green algae and strain mud for worms, crustaceans, and even microscopic algae like diatoms.

This diet brings some special digestive requirements, as plants universally possess cell walls of indigestible cellulose that animals must break down in order to extract and absorb their food value. We humans cook our vegetables to make them easy to digest. Herbivorous mammals like muskrats have ridged molar teeth for extensive grinding. For their part, mullet have muscular, rough, gizzardlike stomachs and very long intestines for digestion and absorption of food. Several authorities verify that a 13-inch mullet may have a digestive tract 7 feet long!

Solving the mullet mystery was certainly worth the 10-minute chase on the marsh bank. The fish may be obscure to us, but they are certainly well known to the bluefish, trout, and flounder of the lower Bay.

Grass Shrimp Don't Have Many Friends

It was a case of two boys, a skiff, a tidal creek, and a summer day. John Ochsner was probably 12 years old, and I was 10. My parents and aunt were visiting his mother. John and I gravitated to the dock behind his house, on Hoskins Creek in Tappanannock, the classic river town on the Rappahannock. He had a nice little skiff and a shiny green Johnson 5-horse. The motor was a year newer than mine, I remember, so it had a neutral clutch, a big innovation.

We took two fishing rods with bobbers and hooks, and he grabbed what looked like a crab net, except that it had very fine mesh. "What's that for?" I asked. "Shrimp," he replied. My experience on the Bay was limited at that point to the Yeocomico, a big tributary near the mouth of the Potomac. Over there, we used peelers for bait. I'd never heard of shrimp, except the frozen kind we got from the market.

John dipped his net a couple of times around the dock pilings, and it came up squirming with handfuls of tiny ($\frac{1}{2}$- to $1\frac{1}{2}$-inch-long) transparent grass shrimp *(Palaemonetes pugio)*. I was fascinated. He showed me how to thread a couple on a hook headfirst, and we caught a bunch of fish, mostly ring perch (yellow perch) and bream (sunfish).

It turned out that there are plenty of shrimp in the Yeocomico too, though we still didn't use them for bait there. In fact, grass shrimp are distributed all over the Bay and its tidal tributaries, and their slightly larger cousins, the sand shrimp *(Crangon septemspinosa)*, occur throughout the lower Bay. Their value to the Bay's food web is immense, but they have no commercial market except as bait. Every predator fish over 4 inches long eats them with relish, even bluefish.

The anglers who catch their own probably know as much about shrimp as anyone in the Bay country. Let's look through their eyes, bolstered with a little information from the scientific community.

First, grass shrimp are "opportunistic omnivores," which means they eat a wide variety of foods, switching from one to another depending on availability. On their first two pairs of legs, they have tiny pincers, which they use to pick up their food. It can be algae growing on a dock piling or the surface of a mud flat, or scraps of decayed grass with its associated bacteria at the edge of a marsh, or tiny pieces of a dead fish. The food can be alive or dead.

Bearing in mind the kinds of food shrimp favor, look for them in beds of submerged Bay grasses, at the edges of marshes, and around wood. The submerged grasses offer them not only food but good hiding from predators. Marsh grasses do the same, especially at high tide. Wood cover like fallen trees also offers protection.

Mud flats, dock pilings, and bulkheads, especially old ones, don't offer much hiding space, but apparently they offer so much food that the shrimp use them anyway. Think of the fouling community—barnacles, worms, anemones, algae, and the like—on an old piling, and then think what it means to an opportunistic omnivore. It was no accident that John Ochsner could find bait right under his dock. Dick Houghland, a very fine charter captain who ran his *Mary Lou* for years out of the Rod 'n Reel Dock in Chesapeake Beach, used to catch enough shrimp from the bulkheads at the marina for a day's fishing.

Grass shrimp spend much of the year in such areas. In the spring, dark-bottomed mud flats with southern exposure warm up quickly, and the shrimp come to them once the water temperature reaches 50°F or so. From then on, right around till Christmas, they can be had in shallow water, although late in the fall it may take some looking to find them, especially big ones. Not much is known about where they go in really cold weather.

In midsummer, though, the shrimp are abundant. Any good catch will include a number of gravid (egg-bearing) females. Some will be shedding their shells, growing larger the same way crabs do. Yet the mature shells are naturally so soft that it's hard to pick out those which have just molted. One thing that is noticeable is a parasite which causes a bulge in the carapace (the front body segment) of a few individuals. The parasite is an isopod (actually a relative of the shrimp), and while it must cause the shrimp some discomfort, the host always appears otherwise healthy. Fish certainly don't seem to mind the taste.

So how do you catch grass and sand shrimp? The easiest way is for two people to pull a 15- to 25-foot fine-mesh minnow seine (available at many fishing tackle shops) along the edge of a marsh. If you can find a submerged grass bed, so much the better. You may find more shrimp than you can use. Fortunately, they are easy to release alive.

Around tight spots like pier pilings and fallen trees, a 12-inch fine-mesh dip net like John Ochsner's does good work. The only problem is that its small size doesn't cover much ground, so unless the shrimp are plentiful, it takes a long time to catch a mess for bait.

The rig that serious shrimp devotees use is a roller net. It has a rectangular frame with a wooden roller on the front edge, a long handle on the back, and a deep bag made of fine-mesh netting. The frame (and the roller) may be 18 to 30 inches long. Push the net with the roller working along the bottom. This is the best tool of all for working mud-bottomed coves, and it is big enough to work bulkheads or marsh edges at flood tide.

Finding good concentrations of shrimp may take some exploring. My friend Bill Pike, who fishes with shrimp from March through December, likes to work hard-bottomed marsh edges in tidal ponds and coves along the Severn River above Annapolis. He's 70-something years old, and he says walking through deep mud is too much work. He catches all he needs, but a younger friend who works for a local charter captain swears by mud bottoms. Try both and decide for yourself.

What do you do with shrimp? Around Annapolis, fish them on a simple two-hook bottom rig for white perch. Use fine wire hooks and thread two or three shrimp onto each. Some people like to thread a couple onto a shad dart (a small jig) and cast it around docks and fallen trees. On tidal fresh sections of rivers like the Choptank and the Rappahannock, the same rig will catch crappie, largemouth bass, and channel catfish.

Perhaps the most elegant use is to chum them around oyster bars and bridge pilings. That term means tossing out a thin but steady stream of shrimp to drift back with the tide. Then drift shrimp-baited hooks in the chum line with spinning tackle. Traditionally, this is a very effective way to catch rockfish, when they are in season. Chumming shrimp also works on other species, like perch, trout, and even flounder.

Keeping shrimp healthy in hot weather can be tricky. Direct contact with ice will kill them. Long-time shrimpers build small, stackable wooden boxes with screen bottoms. Stack the boxes in a cooler with ice on either side and keep the shrimp on the screens. Take out only a few at a time and keep a rag moistened with Bay or river water over them to keep them from drying out.

One last thing: If you don't care to fish with your shrimp, eat them yourself. Start with fresh, live shrimp. Steam them and pinch off their heads (the thoraxes, or large front body segments). Eat the tails whole. The shells are soft enough to crunch up easily. The shrimp turn pink on cooking and taste like, well, shrimp. It's hard to make a meal of them, but they make great appetizers.

It's been about 40 years since that day on Hoskins Creek. The skiff I fish from now is more sophisticated than anything John Ochsner and I would have imagined, but there's a bracket on it to hold a roller net. It's difficult to imagine getting through a fishing season without grass shrimp.

Needlefish: Fierce but Delicate

"Wow! Look at that," said a student. A streak of silver, very long and very thin, arched out of the waters of Pocomoke Sound and sliced back in with scarcely a ripple. Then I realized it was hooked on my line.

Four summer students and I were headed back to the Chesapeake Bay Foundation's lodge on Great Fox Island after an afternoon's "food habits study." The subjects were some trout, croakers, and spot that would turn into our own food (supper) later on. We had picked our fishing spot carefully by reading its bottom type on the depth-sounder, then verified our reading with a bottom grab sampler. It held sand, a little mud, a lot of tiny clams, and some oyster shells encrusted with sponges, worms, and anemones. Cleaning the fish back at the lodge would involve checking stomach contents against the material brought up by the sampler. We were all thinking a lot about bottom-feeding fish and bottom habitat.

But halfway home, we saw a school of bay anchovies dimpling the slick calm surface of the sound like so many raindrops. A large form slashed through the school. Thinking to pick up a bluefish for our mixed bag, I cut the engine and picked up a spinning rod from one of the racks in the skiff.

The strike came on the first cast, but the fish wasn't a blue. It hit the silver jig and leaped immediately, as the species is prone to

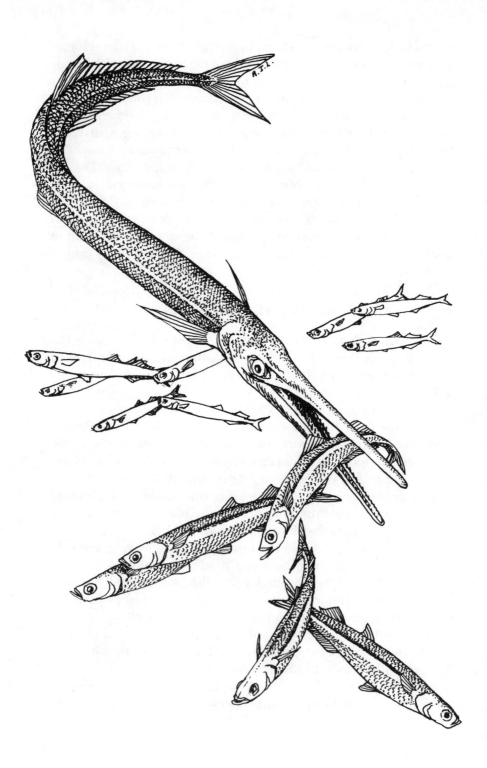

do. The reason I didn't feel the strike, even though the fish was every bit of 3 feet long, was that it weighed less than 2 pounds. Like a tall young basketball player leaping for a rebound, it didn't have much weight to throw around. It was a flat needlefish *(Ablennes hians)*.

The fish came quickly to the boat, even though the tackle was not heavy, and we could see its green-and-silver form flashing in the clear water. Then the hook pulled out. I was just as glad. Needlefish are fragile, and I had wanted to release it anyway, but was worried about bruising it or breaking its long jaws in the net. We all had a good look at it. It was a spectacular animal, much better off back chasing anchovies.

While we cleaned our catch back at the lodge, two students began throwing a cast net around the docks. In no time they had two more needlefish. These were the smaller but more common Atlantic needlefish *(Strongylura marina)*. They were young fish that had been hiding around pilings and in eelgrass beds to ambush newly hatched silversides. Unlike the basically bottom-oriented trout, croaker, and spot, needlefish are creatures of the surface— ambush feeders that depend on quick acceleration to make their living. The placement of both dorsal and ventral fins back close to the tail fin gives them a good grip on the water for a quick start.

One student saw an adult needlefish about 14 inches long cruising by, and she picked up a rod to cast to it, but with no success. After five minutes without a strike, she wanted to know what she was doing wrong. Then she went back to look at the juveniles and realized that her lure was much too big. Despite their toothy jaws, needlefish have very small mouths.

The truth is, the fish are a study in contrasts. Their appearance is fierce, but their skin is thin, their flesh is soft enough to bruise easily, and their jaws are brittle. They may terrorize small anchovies and silversides, but a bluefish of comparable size will chase down much larger and faster prey.

The Atlantic needlefish is a warm-weather resident of the Bay. Though often called a garfish, it is no relation to the primitive gars of tidal fresh water. The species ranges from Maine to the Caribbean and apparently tolerates a wide range of salinities. Individuals have been found at the head of the Bay and up near the heads of navigation in several of the major rivers.

These needlefish spawn here, along the shore in summer. It is a feature of the needlefish family as a group that their eggs are large, with radiating filaments that help them attach to weeds, dock pilings, and the like.

Although the Atlantic needlefish grows larger in other parts of its range, 2 feet is about the maximum here, and 8 to 14 inches is the average. It may be that after their first few summers in the Bay, older and larger individuals remain outside along the coast in their later years. The flat needlefish occurs here in greater lengths, as noted above, but it is much less common.

Atlantic needlefish are good to eat, but there isn't much meat on one, and most people are put off by the fact that their bones are green. Instead, as the students at Great Fox Island could attest, they offer us a different sort of opportunity. Being surface dwellers, these beautiful, graceful animals are readily visible to the careful observer. We don't often get an opportunity just to watch fish in the wild. Maybe we should appreciate them simply for that.

Garfish: Another Successful Old Design

Camp Whitehall is a summer camp for boys just above Walkerton on the Mattaponi River, one of the two major tributaries of the York. The river at Whitehall is narrow, deep, and winding, fresh but strongly tidal (just under 4 feet in average vertical range, the highest in the Bay system). Campers and counselors live by the tides, swimming and waterskiing on high water, rowing and canoeing on low.

Once the campers have picked up the basics of paddling, a favorite trip in the canoes is downriver a mile or so to a deep curve where the river has carved out a shady high bank on the outside and dropped sediment for a broad wild rice marsh on the inside. Depth in the turn is some 20 feet. Channel catfish like to lie in the deep hole and the eddies that form around it, but for the campers the action is all at the surface.

As the boys work their way through the curve, they usually find themselves surrounded by big, fierce-looking fish with long, toothy jaws, rolling on the surface. On a hot July afternoon, the water is never quiet for more than a couple of minutes at a stretch, and sometimes there will be as many as half a dozen fish on top at once. The curve is known as Gar Playground.

One look at a longnosed garfish *(Lepisosteus osseus)* might convince parents that Whitehall's staff lack good judgement and that their sons are in grave danger. The boys, of course, relish the sense of adventure and regale each other at dinner with stories of the monsters that snapped at their boats that day. After all, some of the fish are over 3 feet long, and they do have a lot of teeth. But the gars are not eyeing the campers as fresh meat; instead, they are gulping oxygen.

At first glance, garfish look like chain pickerel. They are long and skinny, with dorsal and anal fins set back almost to their broad tails, a body design that gives quick acceleration—perfect for an ambush feeder. But the gar's relationship to the pickerel is distant.

The Whitehall counselors sense that distance when they slip down to Gar Playground on their free time to try and catch a river monster. It isn't hard to get a gar to take a live minnow floated just under the surface, but hooking the fish is another story. Unlike the pickerel, the gar strikes by slicing its jaws sideways at the bait and grabbing it in its teeth. Then it must work the minnow headfirst down those long jaws to its mouth, which turns out to be incongruously small compared with the fish's overall size. If the angler tries to set the hook before the bait reaches the mouth, the hook merely pulls out. Serious gar fishermen have developed a variety of baited snares to use instead of hooks, and some even use tassels of frayed rope, which tangle in the gar's jaws.

A close comparison of the tails of pickerel and garfish reveals another fundamental difference. The pickerel's caudal (tail) fin is slightly forked and quite symmetrical. The gar's is rounded and appears symmetrical too, but its base slants diagonally upward to the rear, very much like the tails of sturgeons, to which it is more closely related than it is to pickerel.

Like the sturgeons, gars are primitive. They developed some 100 million years ago, during the Mesozoic era, the Age of Reptiles. Much of the earth was warm and swampy, full of shallow, stagnant lakes that were very low in dissolved oxygen. The only fish that thrived in these lakes were ones that developed air bladders, primitive lungs inside their body cavities.

Since then, living conditions on earth have continued to change, and nearly 20,000 species of modern fish have developed.

Most retain the air bladders, but now those organs are adapted to amplify underwater sounds for the fishes' ears and, in species like drum and croakers, to produce sounds. Some fishes also appear to use them to regulate buoyancy.

Only a small number of descendants—fewer than 20 world-wide—of the Mesozoic air-breathing species survive. But those that do seem to fare well in their own niches. Five are gars that live in the United States. They thrive in the murky, slow-moving rivers of the south and the east, gulping air even when there is plenty of oxygen in their rivers, lying quietly in wait in weedy backwaters and pouncing on their prey. Their metabolism is slow but efficient, and growth can be quite rapid, especially in the early years.

The fish have few enemies because of their size and jaws. In addition, they are covered by tough hides of diamond-shaped scales that interlock instead of overlapping, creating a sort of chain mail armor. The flesh is said to be tasty, but it is bony, and few people eat it.

Gars are widely distributed on the Bay in the upper tidal reaches of nearly all the rivers. The Rappahannock and the Nanticoke have especially active gar playgrounds of their own. The fish are big, ugly, and abundant, interesting creatures with a good story to tell. And they are the stuff of summertime adventures for boys in canoes.

The Proud Red Badge

Picture this: You're rounding a marsh point on your favorite river in your favorite small boat. An osprey on an old duck blind is coaxing its chicks to fly. In a cove down the shore, a great blue heron stalks the shallows for food. You beach your skiff (or canoe, or kayak) on the point and walk back into the marsh. Then you hear the familiar "oak-a-lee" song of the marsh, and you follow the sound to a clump of cordgrass. Perched on a tall stalk is a male red-winged blackbird *(Agelaius phoeniceus)*.

The Chesapeake Bay's best-loved creatures are generally animals we can catch and eat, like blue crabs and rockfish. Then there are those that command our attention and affection just because they are attractive or interesting, like ospreys and herons.

The red-winged blackbird on the cordgrass stalk isn't nearly as prominent as larger birds, but he's admired because he is an essential part of any marsh scene. His jet black body with its bright red shoulder patches and buff gold chevrons underneath stands out against the greens, yellows, and browns of the marsh. His song isn't a sound of great musical beauty, but neither is it raucous like the heron's croak. It's part of the scene, a sound we recognize.

Red-winged blackbirds can be seen almost anywhere on the Bay and its tributaries, even up above the fall lines of the James, Potomac, or Susquehanna. A salt marsh in Virginia, a tidal fresh marsh in Maryland, even a river meadow in central Pennsylvania—the red-wing inhabits them all. There are thousands of these birds spread throughout the Chesapeake watershed all year 'round, although individual birds do not reside here permanently. As the winter approaches, red-wings from New Jersey north to New England begin to filter into the Chesapeake region, while our summer nesters head south.

The male of the species carries the distinguishing red shoulder patches. The female and the young are brown and insignificant-looking, with streaky breasts. They stay out of sight in the marsh while the male attracts attention with his song. He is informing anyone who is interested, birds and people alike, that this part of the marsh is his territory.

When the male bird returns in early March from wintering grounds in the Carolinas, he stakes out his territory, often the same territory as the previous year. The red-wing uses his bright badges to attract his female, and they mate sometime in April. In May the female builds a nest down close to the marsh, hidden in clumps of saltbushes, giant cordgrass, or cattails. She is solely responsible for incubating the eggs and feeding the young as well. The male would seem to have an easy life, sitting on his perch and showing off, but he does so specifically to defend the territory from other red-wings and from larger birds like marsh hawks and ospreys that stray into the area.

Most of the young fledge by sometime in July, though a few females may be raising young until August. These late broods may be the result of earlier nest destruction and renesting by the persistent females. In any case, by late summer, the family group begins to break up, leave the territory, and spread out over the countryside.

This movement as summer wanes signals a change in feeding opportunities. Red-wings of both sexes are opportunistic omnivores. They eat both plants and animal foods, depending on their needs and what is abundant at any given time. In breeding season, their need for protein is high, and a fresh crop of insects provides a rich food source both in the marshes and in farm fields nearby. As the fields are plowed, the birds will feed on grubs, caterpillars, and worms. Later on, the red-wings feast on the seeds that mature on both cultivated plants and weeds in field edges.

The marsh plants reach their peak of seed production toward late summer, and at the same time, the adult red-wings molt their feathers. This process can sometimes hinder their flying ability, so they loaf around the marshes and feed on what is locally abundant, preparing for their late-summer ritual of deserting their territories.

By September, with new feathers grown in, the birds gather into large flocks and feed heavily, especially in the big upriver marshes where the wild rice is ripe. The winter birds get by on slim pickings, mostly seeds from any sources they can find, especially bird feeders.

The fall flocks of red-wings are huge, and they give us a sense of how many of the birds summer on the Bay. Although they are spread out broadly, we always see a few in midsummer, wherever we go around the water's edge. While the females go about their work unobtrusively, the males are active and as obvious as small birds can make themselves. Watching one preside over "his" marsh is a good excuse for whiling away a summer afternoon.

AUGUST

Sea Turtles in the Bay

It just didn't look right. The shape was too small to be a boat out in the middle of Tangier Sound, but it was too big to be anything else. We had to go and look at it.

Four students and I were fishing for dinner out of the Chesapeake Bay Foundation's lodge on Great Fox Island. We picked up our lines and ran half a mile south to investigate.

It was an immense dead sea turtle. A ship must have run over it, for its head had been cut off cleanly, as had the aft quarter of its shell. Even so, the neck was some 12 inches in diameter, and the remaining shell over 6 feet long. Its flippers were intact. None of us knew much about sea turtles, so we looked it over carefully for characteristics for identification back at the lodge. Besides its size, its most striking feature was a series of lengthwise ridges along its shell.

At the lodge, the task of identifying the turtle from a field guide was easy. It was an Atlantic leatherback *(Dermochelys coriacea)*, the world's largest living reptile. This was a big one, probably weighing over 1,000 pounds.

These animals are completely pelagic—creatures of open waters—and streamlining is more important than hardness of shell. Despite their great size, they swim very well. They breed in the tropics but migrate north as far as Nova Scotia in the summer, thriving in water temperatures much too cold for other turtles to stay active. Their bodies are well insulated with fats and oils, and they can maintain their body temperatures at as much as 30 degrees higher than the water around them. The fuel that sustains these huge, active animals is surprising—jellyfish! They feed on all sorts, including the Portuguese man-of-war and our Bay's own stinging nettle. What draws them to Canada is the gigantic lion's mane jellyfish, 3 feet or more in diameter at the head, with tentacles hanging down 70 feet.

Much as we would like to have an army of leatherbacks in the Chesapeake to keep down the sea nettle population, they are uncommon here. Our turtle corpse appeared in August 1977, a summer when scientists observed several leatherbacks feeding at the mouth of the Bay. According to Dr. J.A. Musick of the Virginia Institute of Marine Science (VIMS), a large eddy formed at the Virginia Capes that summer, collecting quantities of everything that drifted in, including jellyfish.

The leatherback story illustrates the essential mystery of sea turtles. They all are long-range, open-water migrants, but they must nest on beaches, and their behavior is best known there, where they congregate. None nest in the Chesapeake, so early studies have ignored the Bay's role in their life cycles. They do, however, use our estuary, especially the Atlantic loggerhead *(Caretta caretta)*, the Atlantic green *(Chelonia mydas)*, and the Atlantic ridley *(Lepidochelys kempi)*.

Loggerheads are almost common in the lower Bay through the spring, summer, and early fall. These turtles generally weigh over 100 pounds and are colored a reddish brown. They, too, eat jellyfish but also include sponges, crabs, clams, fish, and even eelgrass in their diet. They appear to be comfortable feeding on the bottom. Before the days of sonar, commercial fishermen in the Gulf of Mexico used to look for surfacing loggerheads to mark reefs where they set their lines. In the Bay, loggerheads will sometimes take up stations on oyster shell humps and bars, and charter boat captains looking for trout will see them there every day.

Like the wandering leatherbacks, the loggerheads have an air of mystery about them. They lay their eggs on undeveloped ocean beaches from the Virginia Eastern Shore barrier islands south to the Caribbean and Central America. The tiny hatchlings are particularly difficult to trace. They crawl across the beaches from their nests and disappear from human contact for several years. Adults, on the other hand, can be marked with tags on their flippers, and extensive programs have been in operation along the coast for years.

Some particularly interesting work is being done now by VIMS researchers tracking radio-tagged loggerheads with a satellite. Early indications are that at least some of the turtles summer in the Chesapeake, migrate south close to shore as the water cools in the fall, and then swim out to the warm Gulf Stream, which carries them back up to the waters off the Virginia coast in the winter. The work continues, so more pieces of the loggerhead puzzle should turn up in the immediate future.

Although once hunted extensively for meat and eggs, all species of sea turtles are now protected by federal law as endangered. They may not be molested, and there are stiff penalties for collecting shells and other parts of dead ones. There is a better reward in studying them, anyway. Begin by reading the book *Time of the Turtle* by Jack Rudloe (see Bibliography) and send for a copy of the pamphlet *The Marine Turtles of Virginia* by Dr. Musick (see Bibliography). Keep field notes of sightings. Report any dead or stranded turtles immediately to Dr. Musick at VIMS. Incidently, some of Dr. Musick's research is being supported by the Non-Game and Endangered Species Program of the Virginia Department of Game and Inland Fisheries. Funds for the program come primarily from a checkoff donation on state income tax forms.

Sea turtles have been roaming the world's oceans for millions of years. It is a surprise to find them being tracked by satellites in a program funded by income tax refunds. If we are ingenious enough to work out these ways to study them, maybe we are wise enough to coexist with them for years to come.

A Challenging Month for Osprey Chicks

Lee and Sandy Curry, 15 teenagers, and I were headed into a salt pond in a marsh on the Patuxent, when Lee paused to look at the ospreys nesting on an old duck blind just offshore. The Currys teach at the Key School in Annapolis, and a host of lucky students get the chance to study with them outdoors each year. This time, they had a group of summer school students out in a Chesapeake

Bay Foundation canoe fleet. Sandy, the students, and I were in a little too much of a hurry to get into the pond. Lee had noticed something important enough to call us back. The young ospreys in the nest were just learning to fly.

The chicks, though only about eight weeks old, were nearly as large as their parents. They stood shakily at the edge of the blind while the parents circled nearby, calling steadily to them. First one and then the other jumped from its safe perch and flew.

It is hard for us humans who do not fly to imagine how difficult or easy it might be for a young osprey to take that daring but essential first step, alone and without direct instruction. The stakes are high—the nest is usually far enough above the water for the young bird to be injured if it falls. Worse yet, a chick after falling is wet, vulnerable, and stuck at sea level.

On the other hand, an osprey's wings are long (about a 5-foot spread) and built in part for soaring, so the young bird that spreads its wings gets lift immediately on leaving the nest. Then it can go on to learn the skills of climbing, maneuvering, and diving.

It is this last skill that presents the biggest challenge. For a time, the parents will continue to bring fish to the young birds, to keep up their strength while they learn to fish. Most parts of the Bay and its tributaries are full of small finned creatures at this time of year. Silversides, killifish, and young spot teem in the shallows. Young menhaden swarm at the surface everywhere. Ospreys are beautifully equipped to catch them. But diving on a fish is a complex, carefully coordinated set of maneuvers.

Watch an osprey dive. The bird cruises over the water, alternately soaring and flapping as it searches intently from an altitude of a hundred feet. When it spots a target, it hovers briefly to get a sense of how the fish is moving and to assess its chances. A fruitless dive is a serious waste of energy, so the bird may decide to continue soaring. But if it decides the effort is worthwhile, it folds its wings partway and plunges headlong to the water, sometimes with enough force to carry it a foot or two beneath the surface.

Because it dives headfirst, we human observers might easily conclude that it catches its prey in its hooked beak. But the osprey's beak is not a good grabbing or holding instrument. Instead, just before impact, the osprey drops its legs and sinks its talons into the fish. Rough surfaces on the underside of its feet improve its grip.

The bird is buoyant enough that it bobs to the surface almost instantly, even if its prey is large. It reaches up with those long wings and grabs some air, laboring aloft with its catch. Ten or 20 feet up, it stops to shake itself and then flies on.

Ospreys appear to make a practice of carrying their catch fore-and-aft, with one leg in front of the other, presumably to reduce the air resistance of the burden. Audubon painted one bird carrying a 3-pound gray trout this way. It is dangerous to speculate about what an osprey thinks, but the idea seems to make sense, except maybe with an eel, which is a good and nutritious meal but an aerodynamic horror.

An osprey's ordinary dive requires unerring aim and a keen sense of fish behavior. Even so, it has another fish-catching maneuver for small prey that may take even more coordination. Sometimes a bird will swoop low over the water, swing its legs forward, drive them down into the fish as it passes by, and swing them back, holding the catch as it flies away. The osprey should feel some kind of satisfaction in pulling off this trick. It's impressive.

The young birds, then, have plenty to learn, and they have to do it in less than two months. Once they are fledged, they spend much less time on the nest as they busy themselves fishing. We who have enjoyed cruising past them earlier in the summer suddenly find those nests empty. The birds are still around, and they are as active as before, but we have to watch for them in the sky and listen for their high-pitched, chirping calls.

If you haven't learned to spot an osprey at a distance on the wing, now is a good time to learn. Rule number one is to keep an eye on the sky. Soaring birds don't usually announce their presence. Ospreys soar with their wings flat, as do eagles, unlike turkey vultures and red-tailed hawks, whose wings slant upward. Unlike all these birds except the red-tails, ospreys have white bellies that will show up in the sunlight. But the red-tail's rusty brown tail feathers will show up in the light too. However, their wings are much broader than the osprey's, which are long, narrow, and crooked at the elbows. These characteristics may seem confusing, but do some watching on your own this month, and you will be surprised at how quickly you come to recognize them. Again, look for the osprey's narrow, flat wings, with crooks at the elbows, and for the white belly on a bird that seems otherwise to be dark underneath.

By late next month, this summer's young ospreys must be both proficient and well fed, for they have a big journey ahead of them. "Our" birds migrate to South America for the Southern Hemisphere's spring and summer. According to Brooke Meanley, a retired U.S. Fish and Wildlife Service biologist writing in his *Birds and Marshes of the Chesapeake Bay Country* (see Bibliography), banding studies show that Chesapeake ospreys winter primarily "in Brazil, Colombia, and Venezuela. One bird was recovered as far south as Argentina. One nestling banded at Turkey Point, Cecil County, July 2, 1954, was recovered in Brazil on September 25, 1954."

This nestling was about four months old, and it had made a migration of some 3,000 miles, fueled on fish it had caught by itself in unfamiliar waters. That is an extraordinary achievement.

Not all young ospreys make it. A substantial percentage die during their first year. Those that survive stay one or two full years in the Southern Hemisphere before returning to the Chesapeake. Apparently enough survive this challenging period to keep the Bay's population strong. Watch the young birds this month, and smile when you see them fly.

Cold Fire in the Water

Robert L. Wichterman of Lancaster, Pennsylvania, wrote me several years ago to ask about flashes of light which he and his family saw in Fairlee Creek on the upper Eastern Shore during an after-dinner walk on a summer cruise. "Walking on the beach," he said, "we noticed that as the small wavelets broke on the shoreline, there was a flash of light. Then we saw the faint outline of small fish as they swam, slightly agitating the water. Next, our kids threw sand into the water, causing flashes of light. Other persons on the beach were also throwing driftwood, and the light was brighter and more sustained.

"Later, as we motored out to our anchorage, we were able to see the light generated by the propeller's agitation of the water. As the tide ran past our anchor rode, there was a distinct, steady light. We were even able to see a few sea nettles as they undulated past our boat."

His letter was a good one for two reasons. First, he had picked an interesting subject, a puzzling phenomenon that most of us see at one time or another on the Bay. Second, because he did not know what he was looking at, he made careful observations, noting both the specific actions which brought on the light and the duration of the flashes. His descriptions made it easy for someone who wasn't there to figure out what he was seeing.

There are at least three bioluminescent creatures that light up the Chesapeake and its tributaries at night, using the same basic process as fireflies. The phenomenon is interesting, both for what it does and for the fact that it is still a mystery to scientists even after half a century of investigation. The substance that produces the light is a protein called luciferin, and it is activated by another protein, an enzyme called luciferase. The light is cold, which means that it is very efficient, in contrast with human devices like light bulbs, which release substantial quantities of heat.

Fireflies use light flashes to distinguish their own species during mating. Deep-sea fish use them for the same purpose. The reasons for bioluminescence in shallower ocean water and in estuaries are less clear, but the bioluminescent creatures in the Chesapeake do produce light, and at times they are abundant. All are simple, transparent planktonic animals that can easily be overlooked during the day.

The least obvious is *Noctiluca*, a dinoflagellate protozoan. *Noctiluca* is simple and single-celled, but it is large as unicellular organisms go, reaching a maximum diameter of ⅛ inch, though most individuals are smaller. The creature is completely dependent on water currents for travel, though its whiplike flagellum makes it rotate, which may help it capture smaller plankton for food.

Noctiluca is best seen with a low-powered microscope. It you find lit-up water, dip a jarful. If, when you look at the water under a human light, you cannot see any obvious animals, put a couple of drops on a microscope slide and look at them under low power. The creatures occur by the billion, and you are likely to find plenty of them. For a good account of watching *Noctiluca* light up both the open Bay and a tributary (the Magothy), read the chapter "The Lantern Bearers" in Gilbert Klingel's classic *The Bay* (see Bibliography).

More obvious to the naked eye are the pink comb jelly *(Beroe ovata)* and its close relative, the sea walnut *(Mnemiopsis leidyi)*. These two jellyfish reach lengths of 4 inches or so. As its name implies, the former has a pink or reddish tinge, while the latter is transparent. The pink comb jelly prefers higher salinities and thus is most common in the lower Bay, while the sea walnut is widely distributed throughout the system.

Despite the consistency of their bodies, the comb jellies are not related to our stinging nettles (which are kin to corals and anemones). Instead, they belong to a small phylum called Ctenophora (the c is silent). The name comb jelly refers to bands of cilia, tiny hairs aligned like the teeth of a comb, that run along the animals' bodies. They beat in waves, propelling the animals slowly forward. The motion is weak, so the animals are planktonic, drifting with wind and tide.

If you dip up a comb jelly, place it in a jar of water and watch it with a hand lens; you can see the "combs" beating. The creatures swim mouth forward, catching other plankton. Comb jellies are, in fact, voracious predators, capable of consuming amazingly large quantities of copepods, oyster larvae, and the like. They even eat their own kind. Predators, on the other hand, are few, but, ironically, they include sea nettles.

For now, comb jellies are just graceful, innocuous (to us) creatures that drift with the Bay's currents. They are pretty to look at by day, and they can light up the night in remarkable patterns. The lines of waves lapping on shore, the spiral of a propeller's motion, the rhythmic successive swirls from the oars of a dinghy, and the curtain of light from an anchor rode hanging in the tide—all are outlined and highlighted by *Noctiluca* and the comb jellies. They are extra delights of summer on the Bay.

What Good Are Sea Nettles?

"What use is a jellyfish to the Chesapeake?" That is a question most of us ask each summer, and with good reason. The animals are the nemeses of swimmers, board-sailors, water-skiers, and anyone else who spends time in the Bay's water. The colloquial name of jellyfish tends to change to sea nettle or stinging nettle in Virginia, but the creature is the same, *Chrysaora quinquecirrha.*

Our stinging nettle is broadly distributed through the Chesapeake. It seems to prefer middle-range salinities, so it is more abundant from Baltimore to the mouth of the York than at the extreme upper or lower ends of the Bay. Wet springs and heavy storms like tropical storm Agnes in 1972 seem to depress the population.

Sea nettles belong to the phylum Coelenterata, which includes the corals and the sea anemones. Coelenterates are primitive but highly successful. In all of them, from coral to nettle, the body is soft and jellylike, basically just a sac of digestive enzymes, with a mouth ringed by trailing arms. The arms may be long or short, and the body may secrete a hard coating, as the corals do, or remain soft. Some coelenterates feed on microscopic zooplankton, using rows of tiny waving hairs called cilia to move the food to the mouth. Most, however, are carnivorous. They have stinging cells called nematocysts on their tentacles to catch and paralyze prey like small fish. Once the prey are caught, the tentacles transfer them to the mouth. It is not uncommon to find a nettle with a small silverside "in its head."

Coelenterates that are sessile (stationary), like corals and anemones, have the body sac attached to a substrate (a reef, an oyster shell, or some other firm base), while the tentacles wave above, catching prey that pass by. Sea nettles simply reverse the plan, drifting along with the sac above and the mouth and tentacles trailing below. For all coelenterates, this body stage is called the medusa, after the mythological creature with snakes for hair. They are simple animals. The mouth serves both to take in food and to eliminate wastes. There is some sense of touch, some chemical sense (taste and smell), and some light sensitivity.

Jellyfish movements are simple and coordinated by a nerve "net" without centralized control by a brain. Swimming, though graceful, is very slow. Jellyfish are, in fact, planktonic, i.e., they drift with the wind, tide, and other currents. Most kinds of plankton are tiny, but a few are large, and jellyfish are good examples of this latter group. In fact, because they are planktonic and delicate, they tend not to occur in areas with heavy wave action, especially around beaches. Those that do are often smashed to pieces.

It is worth remembering that nettles are planktonic when choosing a place to swim from a boat. Unless they are extremely thick, it may be possible to find an area in a creek or river from which the wind and tide have carried them away.

The sting of a nettle occurs when a nematocyst senses something touching it and fires out a barb. The barb is, in effect, a

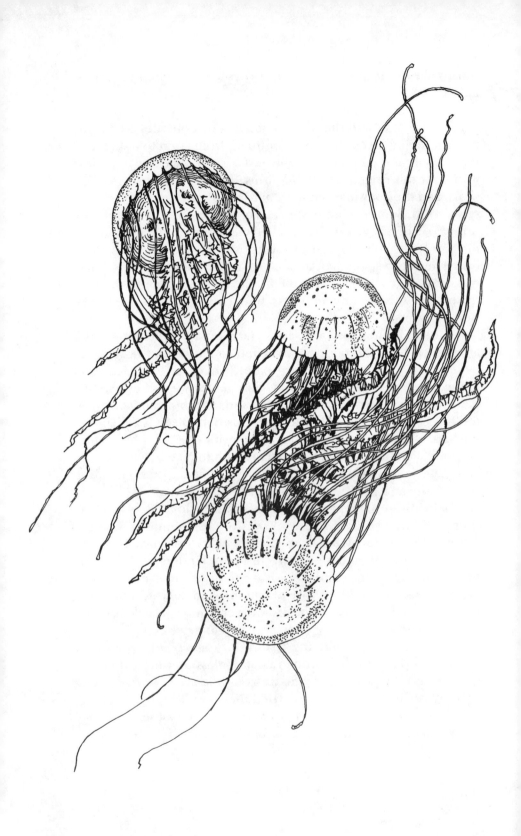

poisoned dart, with a fine filament attached to help the nettle grasp its prey. The dart is too small to penetrate thick skin, like the palms of human hands, and the filaments are too small for humans even to be aware of. But the poison, which is a protein, is something else. In most people, it causes an immediate stinging sensation, followed by a mild rash and an itch that may last 20 minutes. It is painful, but certainly not dangerous. Some people have little or no reaction. A few people experience a stronger rash with a headache, and the pain may persist for three or four hours.

First aid consists of washing the affected area, rubbing sand on it (though this has more psychological than physiological value), and applying meat tenderizer. The latter contains papain, a generalized enzyme that breaks down most proteins, so it is at least partially effective. For more serious reactions, aspirin may help. If symptoms persist for more than four hours, or go beyond a headache, see a doctor promptly.

The jellyfish system of reproduction is unusual. A number of coelenterates, and some other plants and animals, go through a process called alternation of generations. Nettle medusas reproduce sexually in late summer and early fall. Males release sperm, which are taken in by the females while feeding. Shortly after, they release larvae which swim to the bottom and attach there to live as sessile creatures called polyps. Each lives though the winter, forming the upper part of its body into a stack of disks. In spring, the disks pop off one by one (asexual reproduction). Each develops into a new medusa to haunt swimmers, skiers, and board-sailors the next summer, and then to continue the cycle. Thus there are none of the familiar nettles around in the winter.

There are, however, some other jellyfish in cold weather. The most common is the winter jellyfish (*Cyanea capillata*). It is orange in color, and it does sting, but because there are few people in the water then, it is not so much of a problem as its summer cousin. Another species that shows up throughout the year, especially in the lower Bay, is the moon jellyfish, or four-leaf clover (*Aurelia aurita*). It is large (up to 2 feet in diameter), with short 2- to 4-inch tentacles. The four-leaf clover nickname refers to the four round circles on its body that house its sex organs. The moon jellyfish is a plankton feeder, and its short tentacles are only a minimal hazard. It is more a thing of beauty than a nuisance.

Sea nettles may irritate hundreds of people, but they are not a serious enough problem to attract research money. Some work was done on them in the 1960s, but it was aimed primarily at studying the biology of the animal, and it ended without addressing the idea of controlling them. For now, all we can do is keep on buying meat tenderizer, skiing in long pants, and appreciating wet spring weather.

Monarch Butterflies in Migration

"Look! There goes another one," said Captain Dick Houghland. It was late summer, and Dick had a fishing party aboard his charter boat, *Mary Lou*, jigging trout on the Stone Rock at the mouth of the Choptank. While he worked on the Bay, he had a reputation as a superb fisherman who attracted a loyal clientele through his meticulous attention to the details of catching fish.

That particular day, as usual, he was watching wind, tide, his location on the Stone, and the signs of trout on his depth- sounder. But the powers of observation that make Dick a good fisherman also keep him interested in everything else around him when he is on the water. He was looking for trout, for sure, but he was also watching monarch butterflies *(Danaus plexippus)* migrate down the Bay.

Barn swallows and greater yellowlegs and bobolinks are all small birds that make long migrations between the Southern Hemisphere and the Northern each year. The swallows spend the summer on the Chesapeake, while the other two simply pass through. Somehow, in spite of their small size, we accept the fact that they are capable of such great migrations. But the thought that butterflies could make 1,000- and 2,000-mile migrations seems farfetched. They appear too fragile, and their seemingly erratic way of flying too slow for long hauls.

Most butterflies *are* too fragile. Their bodies are delicate, and the tiny scales on their wings are loosely attached. Any rough handling removes the scales and seriously hampers their ability to fly. There is only one truly migratory butterfly species in the world—the monarch.

These butterflies are strongly built, with tough scales firmly attached to their wings. They summer and breed all across the United States and southern Canada. In the fall, streams of them migrate south along both coasts and down the middle of the continent. Coastal flyway monarchs winter in the Florida panhandle and in southern California. Houghland was watching a small portion of the Atlantic migration, which filters through the Chesapeake, with some large concentrations stopping briefly on uninhabited islands in Tangier Sound and along the lower western shore.

For a long time, the location of the wintering grounds for the butterflies that used the midcontinent flyways were unknown to the scientific community. Their discovery in 1976 was highly publicized. Dr. Frederick Urquhart of the University of Toronto found the colonies in the mountains of north-central Mexico and wrote of his findings in a cover story for the August 1976 issue of *National Geographic* ("Found at Last: The Monarch's Winter Home").

More recently, land-use conflicts between defenders of the butterfly sanctuaries and Mexican timber interests (the Chesapeake does not have a monopoly on management problems) were described in the November 1983 issue of *Smithsonian* ("Butterfly Armies Are Now under Guard in Annual Bivouac," by Peter Menzel). Both articles provide good insight into the migratory character of monarchs and to the research that has been done on them.

Long migrations suggest that monarchs are physically tough animals. They suggest also that the butterflies can escape predators while traveling, even when large groups provide inviting targets. Monarchs are showy, with bold orange and black markings that would seem to make them easy marks for birds and other potential enemies. In fact, however, the bold markings work to their advantage. Monarch larvae feed exclusively on the leaves of milkweed plants, including common milkweed and, in freshwater marshes, swamp milkweed. Adults feed on the nectar of the flowers and are the agents that pollinate them, though they also feed on other nectars when milkweeds are not in bloom. Their relationship with these plants is so close that monarchs cannot live without them.

Milkweeds contain a poison that affects vertebrate hearts. It does not affect the butterflies, but they accumulate it in their body fluids. Any bird that eats a monarch will find out quickly that it tastes horrible. The bird is likely to vomit the monarch out rather than retain it and be damaged by the poison.

Such vomiting actually benefits monarchs as a species. A dead bird will not remember how it died, but a live one with a bad taste in its mouth will remember the bright markings of the monarch and avoid the species in the future. The bold pattern minimizes predation on the butterflies both in migration and on their home grounds.

The story of monarchs seems to be full of relationships: monarchs pollinate milkweeds; milkweeds render monarchs distasteful and poisonous to predators; the resulting safety from predators allows monarchs to make long migrations unharmed. There is one more. The monarch has a mimic, the viceroy *(Limenitis archippus)*, which is unrelated but quite similar in appearance. The viceroy is fragile, and it is not distasteful to birds, but the species derives some protection from its similarity to the bitter-tasting monarch. Birds that have learned to avoid the monarch leave the viceroy alone as well. Mimicry is not uncommon in the natural world. This case is one of the classics, well documented and well published.

Dick Houghland has left the Chesapeake to fish commercially on the Gulf of Mexico, running out of Pensacola on Florida's panhandle. The butterflies that winter in that area are the monarchs that come through the Bay in the late summer and fall. Dick smiles when he sees them and asks how the trout run was on Stone Rock.

A Nice Gestalt: Bay Marshes at Summer's End

Gene Silberhorn stood knee-deep in a marsh at the headwaters of Upper Machodoc Creek, a Potomac tributary near Dahlgren. Smoke from his almost-ever-present pipe curled around his head as he examined a smartweed plant that he had carefully dug from the black, mucky soil. "A marsh like this has a really nice gestalt," he said with a grin.

I had to admit to not knowing what *gestalt* meant, so I went straight for the dictionary as soon as I got home. The term developed in a school of psychology that originated in Germany in the early twentieth century. The *Oxford Reference Dictionary* defines it as "a perceived whole that is more than the sum of its parts." Trust the Germans to pack many layers of meaning into a single word. In my mind, I translated Gene's gestalt into "presence."

It helped to know that, for Gene, marshes do indeed have many layers of presence. He has been head of the wetlands section of the Virginia Institute of Marine Science (VIMS) since the early 1970s, so he views the Bay's marshes with the fascination of a professional botanist and the curiosity of a research program director. VIMS also performs some state agency functions, and Gene's group provides advisory services on tidal wetland permit applications, so he has a bureaucratic point of view as well. Finally, he is an avid fisherman and general naturalist, so he appreciates the contributions that marshes make to food and habitat in the Chesapeake system. A good marsh has a rich gestalt indeed for him.

Since that day, I've found gestalt to be a useful term for thinking about the Bay's marshes. Especially now, at the end of the summer, the growth of marsh plants is lush, thick with ripe seeds and colorful flowers. Plants in the seed category include smartweed, wild rice, millet, and others in the upriver freshwater marshes, and saltmarsh cordgrass and giant cordgrass in the down-river salt marshes. Flower colors range from brilliant red cardinal flower and blue pickerelweed upriver to crimson-centered white hibiscus and pink mallow at midsalinities, and sea lavender down the Bay. A host of animals from juvenile menhaden and crabs to snapping turtles, river otters, eagles, and ducks depend on them. There are many layers for us to appreciate.

One layer of presence that particularly intrigues me derives from the fact that marsh plants flourish under difficult growing conditions. They do so well in part because their soils are very fertile; but those same soils have some hostile features as well.

The fertility comes in part from the fact that rich river-borne sediments collect in the marshes. The marshes are, in fact, natural sediment traps. They also function as perpetual compost piles for the plant materials that collect in them.

But the tides that bring in rich sediments also cover the marsh soil and waterlog it. And, if the marsh is downriver, the water is salty, creating conditions that kill most plants very quickly. The Bay's marsh plants have made adaptations to deal with these problems.

Waterlogged soil creates an oxygen problem for all marsh plants. Because of the water, there is only a little oxygen in the surface layer of soil, and none below. But plant root cells need oxygen just as much as the aboveground cells do. In addition, the plant's roots need a combination of nutrients, like phosphorus and nitrogen, which they can absorb best in oxidized (oxygen-containing) forms. Some of these nutrients are by-products of the metabolism of aerobic (oxygen-using) bacteria. The interplay between plant and bacteria can be very important, and yet the bacteria cannot live in totally waterlogged soil—some natural plant toxins build up in anaerobic (oxygen-lacking) wet soils. A good example is hydrogen sulfide gas, whose rotten-egg odor is familiar to anyone who has ever slogged through a deep marsh on foot.

The solution for most marsh plants is a system of passageways in the stems which allow oxygen to diffuse to the roots. A few floating-leaved plants that grow on the water's edge of the marsh, like lily pads (yellow pond lily), even have pressurized systems that pump oxygen down to their roots. All of these systems work well enough to allow some excess oxygen to diffuse out of the roots, creating a thin layer of aerobic soil around them. If you carefully cut out a section of marsh soil with a shovel, you can see this oxygen-containing zone as a very thin gray or tan layer next to the roots, surrounded by black, sulfurous material. The aerobic zone may be splotched with a red iron sulfate which forms when hydrogen sulfide is oxidized, effectively preventing it from harming the plant. A similar process occurs with the conversion of nitrogen's ammonium compounds to the oxidized nitrate forms, allowing the plant to use them as nutrients.

Saltmarsh plants have to deal with a double whammy: waterlogged soil and salt. Salt can destroy the water balance within a plant's cells. You may remember in school soaking a carrot in a strong brine solution and having it go as limp as cooked spaghetti. The number of plants that can deal with salt is quite small, so salt marshes are much less diverse—they have far fewer species—than fresh marshes.

What saltmarsh plants like the cordgrasses can do is extract the salt that diffuses into their cells and pump it out through pores in their leaves. Run your thumb carefully down a leaf of a cordgrass plant at this time of year and then lick it. You'll taste the excreted salt and maybe even feel the grains on your tongue. The plant must use energy to pump out salt, but the soil is so rich, and the plant gets so much sunlight out on the open marsh, that it more than makes up for the loss. The opportunity for growth on the marsh soil is the reward for plants with the adaptations to deal with the problems it brings.

Places like Upper Machodoc Creek are backwaters not normally frequented by Bay boaters. For that reason, they're worth exploring, if you have a suitable craft. But in almost any boat, the gestalts of the Bay's marshes are obvious at this time of the year, from Eastern Neck Island on the Chester River to the creeks on the Severn; from Knapps Narrows at Tilghman Island to the coves on the St. Mary's at the mouth of the Potomac; from the Corrotoman on the Rappahannock to Occahannock Creek on Virginia's Eastern Shore; from the Big Salt Marsh at Poquoson to the rice marshes of the Chickahominy. Here's hoping these ideas add to your enjoyment of them.

FALL

LABOR DAY ON KINGS CREEK, just up the Choptank from Dover Bridge: It's hot, humid, even a little buggy. The plant growth in the marshes is lush. Grains on the wild rice are swelling, and the first ripe ones are shattering and falling to the ground. (See "The Wild Rice Is Ripe.") A great blue heron fishes in the shallows. My canoe rounds a bend, and a small flock of wood ducks—they are called "summer ducks" here—gets up off the water. This is no surprise. The parents nested on the creek, and the young are fledged now.

Around another bend, though, is a flock of blue-winged teal, and they tell another story. Cooling temperatures in Canada have sent them south. They are stopping over to feed on the abundant rice, smartweed (see "Smartweeds Have Much to Teach"), waterhemp, and tearthumb in the creek's marshes before pushing further south. Behind them are early mallards and black ducks, also headed south, but not as far. It may be warm enough that dragonflies are still busily hunting the marshes (see "Dragonflies: Aerial Acrobats"), and that I still have put ice water in the Thermos instead of hot coffee, but the seasons are changing.

Within another week or so, the Chesapeake's weather begins to hint of fall. A cold front drops down across the Midwest, bringing clear skies, northwest winds, and cool nights. A sweater feels good to anyone out on the water. Geese ride the winds down from their breeding grounds. Those first high flocks in late September are heart-stirring signs of fall.

But there are other, more subtle signs—like the teal—of plants and animals changing gears, getting ready for cold weather or getting ready to migrate south. Some of them are responding to cooler temperatures, some to shorter photoperiod (decreasing length of daylight). (See "Cues of the Season: Daylight and Water Temperature.")

Even in early September when days are still hot, rockfish and bluefish start chasing bait on the surface, laying on fat to help them through the winter. Gulls and terns (See "Terns: Bright Sparks of Life") will dive on the hapless bait from above, serving in the process as highly visible indicators for human fishermen. Acres of fish will feed on the surface half the day, ignoring powerboats around them. If the fish are blues, an angler dare not wash his or her hands in the water. They will keep up this activity on through October and even into November. Up the brackish rivers, the shallows cool down at night. Chain pickerel rouse themselves from their hot-weather lethargy and chase baitfish with abandon. Young-of-the-year menhaden and spot are still far up in the tidal fresh areas where the pickerel hunt, adding to the already abundant forage of killifish, silversides, anchovies, shiners, and darters. Fall is a happy time for pickerel.

With the ripening of the wild rice, red-winged blackbirds invade the upriver marshes. They are part of the sights and sounds of September. Some will stay, many will go further south.

The lower Bay salt marshes are quieter than they have been for a while. The ubiquitous willets, with their loud cries and their boldly striped wings, have left for warmer areas. But other migrants are moving through—dowitchers, sanderlings, and yellow-shafted flickers. The latter are hardly considered marsh birds, but they pass down the Bay's island chain from Poplar to Watts this month, feeding on the last of the warm-weather insects and ripe seeds from the marsh grasses.

Early September is still wildflower time in the marshes. Hibiscus is blooming in the upriver marshes; mallow, saltmarsh fleabane, sea lavender, and seaside goldenrod are down below. But all will fade this month.

By midmonth, the last two wildflowers of the year will appear. Groundsel tree *(Baccharis halimifolia)*, one of two familiar saltmarsh shrubs, will begin to put out hundreds of little cream-colored tufts (actually the plants' fruits—the flowers that came out earlier were inconspicuous). More than color, these tufts add texture to the golden tones of the early fall marsh.

As the rice begins to die upriver, yellow carpets of daisylike tickseed sunflowers *(Bidens coronata)* spring up. Old timers on the Patuxent call them "butterweed." Each of the plant's trapezoidal seeds has two awns (bristles) at the broad end. The awns catch in fur, feathers, and sweaters to travel around and disperse the species. The seeds, high in protein, are important waterfowl foods.

From now until the first frost, butterweed and the groundsel tree have an aesthetic role. With warm weather gone and cool weather here, the Bay region gets this one final set of blooming marsh flowers to remember the summer by, one last symbol of its bounty.

While these last colors in the marsh delight us, it is well to look beyond the obvious riches of the September marshes, to the drab-looking cattails and giant cordgrass that provide an important piece of habitat that is all too easy to miss. (See "Part of the Background: Cattails and Giant Cordgrass.") There is always more going on around the Bay than meets the eye.

October is obviously colder, with unsettled weather. Migrations (see "October Travelers: Ospreys and Canada Geese") and heavy feeding are both in full swing. (See "Harvesttime" and "Fall Is for Rockfish.") Anyone going afield now wears boots and carries foul weather gear, or at least a windbreaker, to wear over the sweater. Fall colors in the woods around the rivers and creeks and in the marshes make the month a particularly beautiful time to be out. (See "River Meanders.")

While these October events are highly visible, there is plenty going on beneath the water's surface as well. Oyster toadfish, generally considered one of the Chesapeake's ugliest creatures, are just finishing up the task of raising their young for the year. (See "Oyster Toadfish: A Success at Parenting.") Meanwhile, young croakers (hardheads), recently spawned out on the continental shelf in the Atlantic, are being swept into the Chesapeake by wind-driven currents (see "Croakers and Computers"), even as their relatives, spot and sea trout, are leaving the Chesapeake to winter on the continental shelf.

By November, the weather is definitely cold, sometimes even freezing. Hypothermia becomes a concern to be dealt with for any prudent person venturing out onto the water. It is time for us to put on heavy sweaters, parkas, warm hats, and gloves. Around the Bay, bird migrations are in the later stages, and falling water temperatures are slowing down the metabolisms of fish and shellfish. Winter is around the corner, but there is still a surprising amount of activity.

By this month, menhaden are coming together in massive schools to migrate out of the Chesapeake. These extraordinarily prolific fish are the target of the largest commercial fishery on the Bay (for industrial oils, animal feeds, and crab bait), but they also serve as essential forage for virtually every fish-eating predator in the Bay community. (See "Menhaden Migrations.")

Migrations of prey and predator are often intertwined. As the Chesapeake's menhaden school up and head for the Atlantic, loons arrive from the lakes of Michigan and Ontario to feed on them. These birds are very efficient underwater predators, capable of working together in flocks to herd baitfish as effectively as rockfish and bluefish. (See "Loons: Fall's Finest Fishermen?")

Loons and menhaden are relatively easy to observe for human fishermen and sharp-eyed fall cruisers, but there are much less visible events as well. Many of the Chesapeake's eels are migrating out to the Atlantic this month to spawn and then die in the Sargasso Sea. (See "The Riddle of the Eels.") Even less obvious is a significant change taking place in the phytoplankton communities, those unseen gardens of single-celled plants that drift with wind and tide. Summer species of brown and green algae are giving way to diatoms, which are shaped to take special advantage of winter circulation patterns in the Chesapeake. (See "Diatoms: Cold-Water Jewel Boxes.")

As November wears on, winter appears to tighten its grip on the Chesapeake, but there is still activity. Most of the bottom-feeding fish have departed long since for the continental shelf, so white perch have competition only from their cousins the rockfish as they move out of the creeks and coves onto the oyster bars of the rivers and the open upper Bay. (See "White Perch: A Fish for All Seasons.") At the same time, the Bay's clams and mussels continue feeding and growing in the bottom sediments. The smallest of them will provide important food for the waterfowl that are filtering into the Bay for the winter. (See "The 'Other' Mollusks.")

Fall is an important season for the Chesapeake, a culmination of summer's growth and a preparation for winter. It invites our participation. Tune into it and be part of it.

SEPTEMBER

The Wild Rice Is Ripe

On Labor Day some years ago, science teacher Suzanne Tolson, her husband Bill, and I were paddling a canoe up Rosier Creek, a Potomac tributary near Colonial Beach. We were scouting it for a Chesapeake Bay Foundation field trip that was scheduled for later in the month. The lower portion of Rosier is distinctly brackish, but the upper reaches are fresh. There we found half a dozen blue-winged teal, a noisy host of red-winged blackbirds, and some bobolinks.

With the school year about to begin, it was natural enough to think about fall coming soon, but by their presence these birds told us that it had already begun. They would stay on Rosier Creek for several weeks, but they were definitely headed south.

Long migrations are tough on small birds. They must fatten up considerably to store energy for their journey. On this day, the marsh at the head of Rosier Creek and several hundred others like it around the Chesapeake were ripe with high-energy, seed-bearing plants, especially wild rice (*Zizania aquatica*).

We usually associate wild rice with the lakes of Minnesota and Wisconsin, where it is harvested commercially, but here on the Chesapeake, our many tidal rivers and creeks offer it excellent habitat. The upper tidal reaches of virtually all the Chesapeake's big rivers give wild rice just what it needs—fertile freshwater marsh soil and plenty of current flow. In a powerful river with a big watershed like the Rappahannock or the Choptank, freshwater flow from the land is strong enough to keep incoming salt water well downstream, resulting in a long stretch of water that is considered "tidal fresh." On a smaller river like the Severn near Annapolis, pocket marshes off the side creeks form small tidal fresh marshes where rainwater flows in from well-wooded ravines with deep forest soils.

In the river environments, much of the fine silt that the current carries accumulates on the insides of curves. The outer margins of these mud banks are always underwater. Here live floating-leaved plants with buoyant stems like yellow pond lily and arrow arum. Wild rice grows behind these plants, somewhat higher in the marshes. Because it can extract the oxygen its root cells need from the water that flows over them, it can live in constantly waterlogged soil.

Wild rice is an annual growing from seed each year, but its growth rate is prodigious. It begins in late April, and by mid-May it is a couple of inches tall, looking like what it is—a grass. In late May, though, its growth rate begins to accelerate. The plant reaches 2 feet by mid-June, and 4 feet by late July, when it begins to flower. By late August, when the grains start to ripen, it will be 6 to 9 feet tall, not bad for a four-month growing season.

The grains are highly nutritious, full of protein and complex carbohydrates. They "shatter," or fall from the plant, during the first two weeks of September, though not all the plants in a given stand will be ready at the same time. The red-winged blackbirds descend on the ripe plants aggressively and grab at the seed heads, picking off grains for themselves but also shaking loose any others that are ripe, so that they fall to the marsh floor to be eaten by other birds or to sink into the mud to become next year's crop.

The Native Americans of the North Country traditionally employ a similar technique to harvest wild rice, paddling their canoes up into the marshes and shaking the rice heads over their boats so that the grains fall inside. Then they winnow them by hand to separate out the chaff. I've tried it here on the Bay, but it is a lot of work. If you decide to get out of your boat to investigate a stand of wild rice, test your footing first. The muck that it grows in is very, very soft, and it is easy to get deeply stuck.

By mid-September, nearly all of the grains have shattered, and the plants start to die. The teal, red-wings, and bobolink move on to the marshes of the South Carolina and the coastal Georgia rivers.

By the first frost here, our rice marshes, so recently very tall, will look like stubble fields of fallen-over stalks. Other seed-bearing plants like smartweeds will become the dominant foods for the waterfowl that arrive later in the fall.

Early fall is an ideal time for day trips on the Bay's tidal fresh rivers. Canoes, sea kayaks, 14- to 16-foot aluminum outboard skiffs, and powerboats to 20 feet are all appropriate for these rivers, if operated prudently. Especially good areas for exploring wild rice marshes are the Chickahominy River (off the James), the Mattaponi and Pamunkey rivers (the primary York tributaries), the Rappahannock around Port Royal, the Patuxent around Upper Marlboro, the head of the Chester, the Choptank around Denton and Tuckahoe Creek, and the Nanticoke above Vienna, including its big tributaries, Marshyhope and Broad creeks.

Smartweeds Have Much to Teach

John Wood was up to his knees in mud and marsh. A biology teacher at Loudoun Valley High School in Leesburg, Virginia, he was starting off a class's school year with a day's field study of freshwater marshes at the Mason Neck National Wildlife Refuge, on the Potomac about 8 miles below Mount Vernon. That morning, they had met Georgia Yamaki and Julie Ballinger, field guides from the Chesapeake Bay Foundation, and paddled up a creek into the marshes of the refuge in CBF's Virginia canoe fleet.

Mid-September is a great time to be at Mason Neck. The marsh is spectacular, with wild rice standing 6 to 10 feet tall, its stovebrush flower heads ripe with brown grain. At the creek's edge, big arrow arum leaves glistened in the sun, while their ripe, bulb-shaped seed heads drooped into the creek. Marsh hibiscus blossoms added splashes of white and crimson, and tickseed sunflowers shone gold in the sun.

On this day, there were blackbirds, bobolinks, and a few blue-winged teal feeding on the wild rice grains that had just dropped. Occasionally the students heard sora rails calling in the marsh, and they knew that the railbirds were there for the rice, too.

But John, Georgia, and Julie had them looking for another group of plants, small tangled stems growing around the bases of the rice stalks.

"This is smartweed *(Polygonum punctatum),*" said Georgia. "It'll make you smart if you eat it. Who needs to try some?"

"Mr. Wood. Mr. Wood does," laughed the students. John and Georgia smiled at each other. They had played out this scene together before.

"Okay," said John, "But one of you will have to eat it with me. You, Ben, take a leaf. Chew it on your front teeth and count to fifteen with me."

They never got that high. At eight, Ben yelled and spat out his leaf. Wood's eyes were watering, and he spat his out, too. "Hot stuff," he pronounced, as he passed Ben a jug of lemonade to put out the fire. "Eight-second, two-alarm smartweed. I never said it would make your brain smart, but it sure did your tongue. That's oxalic acid. It's common in a lot of plants. Even spinach has a little of it, though not usually enough to taste. Those big arrow arum seeds at your feet are full of it, even though they're very nutritious otherwise. About the only animals that can handle them are the wood ducks."

Julie asked the students to pass a smartweed plant around. She picked another plant, one with tiny, hook-shaped thorns all over its stem. "See any similarities between these two plants?" she asked.

The students examined them closely. Most had never tried to look for details on a plant stem before. After a couple of minutes, they agreed that both had short stem sections, and each section was connected to the next by a swollen leaf node, a rounded joint half again as big around as the stem itself. Even closer examination revealed a thin sheath of tissue around each node.

"Both of these plants are members of the buckwheat family," said Julie. "The one with the rough stem is called tearthumb *(Polygonum sagittatum)* because of the prickers on it. Now you know why Mr. Wood, Georgia, and I have on long pants today. The other plant is dotted smartweed *(Polygonum punctatum).*

"Look closely at the two kinds of seeds," she continued. The students did so and found them to be very similar, like small pyramids. The smartweed seeds had white outer coverings. The tearthumb seeds were slightly larger, with pink coverings. The students pinched them open and found starch oozing out. Julie assured them that the oxalic acid content was low, and several students ate them, pronouncing them mild and pleasant-tasting.

"The rice is certainly the most spectacular food plant in the marsh today," said Georgia, "But how would you rate the smartweed and tearthumb as wildlife foods?"

"Good, I guess," said a student. "There seems to be plenty of starch for energy in the winter, and there are plenty of seeds around." He waved an arm in a half-circle, pointing in the process at hundreds of thousands of smartweed and tearthumb seeds. "How are they for protein?" he asked.

"Very good," replied Georgia. "Buckwheat grains are cultivated for human food in many parts of the world. They are highly nutritious. More important, the seeds of these two plants stay attached to their stalks longer than rice grains do. In September, most of the rice shatters—that is, it ripens and falls to the marsh. It gets eaten now or it gets covered with silt. The blackbirds, soras, and early ducks like teal eat it, but most of the waterfowl migrating into the Bay won't get here till October and November, and it will be gone. But the smartweed seeds will still be around then. Diet analyses by waterfowl biologists indicate that smartweed and tearthumb seeds are very important in the winter diets of a lot of ducks."

"Diet analyses?" asked another student. "What do they do, interview ducks?"

Everybody laughed, and John Wood replied, "No, they collect stomachs and gizzards from hunters, and then they analyze the contents. Seeds, clam shell fragments, even fish bones can usually be identified under a microscope. Some important data get collected that way. When you get back to school, read the chapters entitled 'Of Ducks, Geese, and Swan' and 'The Lower James' in Brooke Meanley's *Birds and Marshes of the Chesapeake Bay Country*" (see Bibliography).

"Gee," said another student, "I never thought that there could be so much to learn about two little plants."

"That's what careful observation is all about," said John Wood. "Welcome to Biology class."

Dragonflies: Aerial Acrobats

Richard Tippett stood in a tiny salt meadow in Frog Marsh, on the St. Mary's River a mile above St. Mary's City. Around him were 20 junior high school students participating in a summer program at

St. Mary's College. They were all working on independent projects, busily studying crabs, jellyfish, silverside minnows, and marsh plants.

Richard was working especially with one student who had chosen dragonflies. He is a good hand in a salt marsh, but he had never thought much about dragonflies before. He was having a whole new world opened to him as he observed the comings and goings of two species of skimmer—the white-tailed dragonfly *(Plathemis lydia)* and the amberwing *(Perithemis tenera).*

Like barn swallows, dragonflies are worth watching as great aerial acrobats. By any measure, they are superb fliers, catching prey on the wing in a variety of habitats all over the world. More than 300 species have been observed in North America alone. Diversity of this magnitude is an indication of a good basic biological design.

One might conclude from these facts that dragonflies represent an advanced form of insect evolution. On the contrary, they are still very close to a design that has been around for 150 million years, stretching back to the age of the dinosaurs. All along, dragonflies have been among the largest of insects, though the really large ones (30-inch wingspan) have become extinct. But the big darner dragonflies still have wingspans of over $3\frac{1}{2}$ inches (compared with $1\frac{1}{2}$ inches for a large bumblebee), and the skimmers in the Bay's salt marshes are $2\frac{1}{2}$ inches across.

Dragonflies owe their flying ability to an old but apparently effective design: two pairs of large, nearly identical wings that are not coordinated directly. They swing through shallow arcs, about 40 degrees out of phase with each other, and propel the animals at speeds of up to 30 miles per hour. The wings also provide excellent maneuverability, allowing the insects to turn quickly, dart ahead, and hover; but they do not fold back, as do those of almost all other insects.

As the dragonflies have developed into great predators, their legs have become specialized. The insects can perch on plant stalks, but they cannot walk. The legs are lined with combs so that, when held together, they form baskets for scooping up prey in midair.

Huge, bulging eyes are an important part of the dragonfly's design. Dragonfly antennae are short, and their sense of smell is apparently very poor; this animal is a sight-hunter. The base of its head is jointed, allowing it to swivel, so peripheral vision is excellent, and it even has some depth perception. Distance vision is remarkable for an insect: a dragonfly can detect movement up to 40 feet away.

An insect's eye is radically different from ours. It is a bank of sensitive six-sided facets that simply register light or dark, like pixels on a black-and-white computer screen. The more facets per eye, the finer the image, like a mosaic. Some ants have fewer than 10, a housefly has 4,000; but some dragonflies have as many as 28,000. The eyes are still crude when compared with ours, but they detect movement well, since facets fire in sequence as an object moves across the dragonfly's field of view. The insect has some ability to process information from both eyes at once, allowing it to gauge distance through binocular vision.

Prey for dragonflies includes mosquitoes, gnats, and midges, which, once caught, are crushed with powerful jaws and eaten. But males spend as much time defending territories as hunting. An individual will stake out a section of marsh maybe 4 feet square and chase away any other male that encroaches upon it. If two or more species are using the area, he will chase only his own kind and disregard the others. They are not rivals for his mate, and apparently the Bay's marshes grow food enough for all.

Mating is distinctive. The male produces sperm at the tip of his abdomen and places them in a receptacle on the underside of his forward end. He grasps a willing female's head with a pair of claspers (also at his abdomen's tip), and the couple flies together for a time. Then the male perches on a plant stalk and the female, still clasped by her head, curls the tip of her abdomen forward to the receptacle to receive the sperm. Once her eggs are fertilized, depending on the species, the female may deposit them in a plant stalk, or fly low over the water and dip her abdomen into the surface film to deposit the eggs. She may lay several clutches a summer.

At this time of year, as the fall begins, the dragonflies of the Bay's rivers, creeks, and marshes will be laying their last sets of eggs and dying. Their survivors, the eggs, will hatch into aquatic larvae that will overwinter before metamorphosing into next year's adults. Indeed, some species spend several years as larvae. The white-tails and amberwings and their relatives will be around for another couple of weeks. They are big enough and active enough to be fun to watch. Get a good look. They are impressive.

Cues of the Season: Daylight and Water Temperature

It's late summer. Our ospreys are not as obvious as they were even a month ago. Their young have learned to fly and fish. The focal points of the early summer, the nests, are largely abandoned, and the birds have dispersed. Soon they will leave the Chesapeake for their other summer in Central and South America.

The shorebirds that breed in the marshes of the mid- and lower Bay, like willets and oystercatchers, are already moving south. The shorebirds that breed on the Arctic tundra, like sandpipers and plovers, are moving through on the way to the equator and beyond. So are the early waterfowl, like blue-winged teal.

In the Bay itself, fish are beginning to feed more heavily. The most obvious are the rockfish and bluefish that are becoming bolder by the day at driving schools of bait to the surface in spectacular displays of predatory frenzy. Flounder, spot, gray and speckled trout, and Spanish mackerel also are gorging themselves, though generally in less obvious ways.

Somehow these birds and fish have realized that the seasons are changing. They are picking up environmental cues and acting on them. Fall is on the way, though we humans sense it primarily in calendar pages and school reopenings. Shortly after Labor Day, the first of a series of cold fronts will blow through, with clear blue skies and cool northwest winds that will remind even city dwellers of what is ahead. Even so, we will only be catching up on what the birds and fish already know.

Late summer weather, then, poses a riddle. What specific cues are these birds and fish responding to? Air temperature is not reliable. It fluctuates too much, and there are still plenty of hot days ahead. Instead, these animals must be depending on indicators that change gradually and predictably.

For most of the birds, the cue is photoperiod, the length of daylight. Their internal biological clocks sense the shortening days, even at different latitudes. Thus "our" ospreys are noticing the change here and getting ready to head south, while "our" Canada geese, up near the Arctic Circle on the Ungava Peninsula, are getting ready to come here. The same goes for egrets, shorebirds, gulls, and terns headed south from the Chesapeake, and the other waterfowl and loons headed here from Canada.

Biological clock mechanisms have been studied by researchers for years, but they are still only poorly understood. No matter how they work, though, they are for real—extraordinary adaptations to help these birds make efficient use of widely divergent habitats that in some cases are continents apart.

For fish, the cue is the factor that dominates their lives: water temperature. Fish are cold-blooded, so their body temperatures—and thus their metabolic rates—are dependent on the water around them.

Water has a high specific heat. That phrase means that it must absorb a great deal of heat to raise its temperature 1°, or it must lose a lot to drop a degree. Thus large bodies of water change temperature only slowly, reflecting seasonal trends rather than day-to-day fluctuations. When the temperature in the open Bay begins to fall, even from the high seventies to the low seventies (F), it is a reliable indicator that the season is really changing.

Toward the end of this month, after the autumnal equinox, cold fronts will cool the shallows in the rivers and creeks, chasing upriver predators, like white perch and young rockfish, and forage fish, like menhaden, silversides, and anchovies, out to deeper water in the trenches of the ancestral Susquehanna channel in the upper Bay. As the fall proceeds and water temperatures drop further, blues, spot, trout, flounder, Spanish mackerel, and menhaden migrate inexorably down the Bay and out into the Atlantic onto the continental shelf. Hence the spectacular fall fishing each year at junction points like the Southwest Middle Grounds where the main Bay and the Potomac meet, and the Chesapeake Bay Bridge-Tunnel, between the Virginia Capes.

For us, this change of the seasons is perhaps the richest time of year. The variety of birds and fish that are present is greater now than at any other time, for there are lots of comings and goings. Because animal behavior is geared to processes that change slowly—photoperiod and water temperature—this is a long season, lasting from now until Christmas. Don't put your boat to bed yet. Go and be part of it.

Terns: Bright Sparks of Life

My daughter Kelly and I were looking for bluefish in the mouth of the Potomac on a slick calm morning. The fish were spread out, but there were plenty of them around. The largest concentrations were chasing dense schools of menhaden, and several charter boats were working around them.

We, however, found a school of 3- to 4-inch anchovies dimpling the water like raindrops. Every couple of minutes several bluefish boiled through the anchovy school, which was less obviously visible than the menhaden, so we had it all to ourselves, at least with respect to other humans, which suited us just fine. Kelly caught a couple of 6-pounders trolling around the anchovies, and three more by casting when they were breaking on the surface. I maneuvered the boat and handled the net.

Five of these blues were a gracious plenty, so we quit fishing and watched what was going on around us. It was then we realized that we and the blues weren't the only fishermen working the anchovies. There were half a dozen common terns diving on them as well. While the bluefish were certainly impressive as they herded the little silver minnows to the surface and attacked them, the terns showed great skill in hovering over the water, choosing their tiny targets, and diving unerringly onto them. They'd set their wings and plummet like stones, hitting the water with resounding splashes. Almost immediately, they'd recover, reach high with their wings, and pull up away from the river, stopping after a dozen wingbeats to shake in midair. I thought of the nickname "minner hawk" which the author John Hay attributes to tern-watchers along the Mississippi Gulf Coast. The terns' skill made even an osprey look slow and ponderous in its fishing and certainly showed up the laughing gulls that were feeding on the menhaden schools.

Intrigued with the birds and curious for more detail, I went home and reread Hay's *Spirit of Survival: A Natural and Personal History of Terns* (see Bibliography). Hay wrote that, on looking at a tern skeleton, he was most impressed with the size of the eye sockets and the large space given over to back muscles. In summer plumage, our terns have black caps which seem to hide their eyes, but those organs are large and bright, sharp enough to spot a 3-inch anchovy near the surface from an altitude of 50 feet and then keep track of it during a high-speed dive.

Back muscles are the ones that lift the bird's wings, while breast muscles supply the powerful downstrokes. The latter would seem to be more important, but terns spend a lot of time hovering

near the water, a maneuver that requires them to reach high with their wings, and they must reach high again when taking off from the water after a dive. It is at these times that those large back muscles play a key role.

Back and breast muscles drive long, narrow wings with pronounced elbows. The wings are too narrow for soaring, which sets the terns apart from their close cousins the gulls, but terns have more maneuverability. Compared to terns, gulls appear to be almost laid back, soaring for long periods and sitting on the water in flocks. Terns seem to be in constant motion, and their wings suit them well.

More than half a dozen species of tern are present on the Bay in the summer and early fall. The common, Forster's, Caspian, and least terns are the most numerous. The first two are what most of us consider "typical" terns. The Caspians, on the other hand, are larger, almost gull-sized, with blood-red bills to go with their crested black caps. The least terns are tiny and more likely to be seen on the lower Bay. Other species include the gull-billed tern, which has a stout black bill, and the royal tern, which is nearly as large as the Caspian but has a lighter orange bill. The most useful distinguishing marks of the species include bill color, tail length, and shading of gray and white on the wings. A good field guide is a big help in distinguishing them.

With a number of tern species living in the same general area, there must be some divisions of diet and habitat to keep them from competing directly with one another. While most terns feed on fish, for example, Caspians feed on smaller birds and eggs, and the gull-billed terns catch insects in flight—yet another indication of aerial ability. Forster's and common terns are very closely related, but the former, which has slightly longer legs, nests in marshes, while the latter, with shorter legs, prefers sandy beaches.

On the Chesapeake, terns breed and nest on isolated marsh islands and beaches. They don't need much land, but they do need security from predators like crows, owls, raccoons, foxes, and blacksnakes. The chain of Eastern Shore islands that stretches from Barren and Hoopers down through Smith and Tangier provides important habitat, as do isolated spots like the Hole in the Wall at the southeastern corner of Gwynn's Island and the Big Salt Marsh at Poquoson. Least terns appear to be more tolerant of people than the other species and sometimes nest relatively close to cities and towns. Even so, they need large salt marshes like the Grandview Natural Preserve at the mouth of Back River in Hampton.

The nests are casual affairs. Common terns simply scrape out a shallow depression in the sand. If a storm destroys the nest, they haven't invested a lot of labor in it; the terns move, scrape out a new one, and lay another clutch of eggs.

From their nesting colonies, the terns spread out in a broad area to feed. It is quite possible that the terns which Kelly and I watched in the mouth of the Potomac had come from the northern end of Smith or even from South Marsh Island.

Human population pressure is harder on terns than on gulls. While gulls need isolation from people at nesting time, they are opportunistic omnivores that can get by: they pick over our trash at landfills in the winter, follow farmers as they till their fields in spring, beg pieces of bread from waterfront public parks in summer, and feed on scraps from watermen's pots and nets in summer and fall. Terns are much more dependent on fish, especially small ones like anchovies and silversides. They are also susceptible to destruction of breeding habitat, especially the least terns, which lost whole colonies in the lower Bay as marshes were filled and developed before the tidal wetlands laws began to take effect in the early 1970s. They appear to be coming back slowly now, partly due to those laws and partly to good land preservation practices by local governments and private organizations like The Nature Conservancy.

In a month or so, "our" terns will head south, stringing themselves along the coast to Florida and south across the Caribbean to Central and South America. These migrations seem to pale beside the pole-to-pole trips of Arctic terns, but they are immense distances for small birds—a strong testimony to their toughness and endurance. Their long narrow wings allow them to fly into the wind with relative ease, so they can weather storms by working with them instead of fighting their way along.

For now, the terns will be active, feeding as heavily as they can to fuel up for their travels. They won't be as numerous or as obvious as gulls, and it will be easy to overlook them, but they will be there. Look for them and spend a little time watching them work. They are bright sparks of life, admirable for their toughness and skill.

Part of the Background: Cattails and Giant Cordgrass

In the richness of a Chesapeake September, we all tend to concentrate on the marshes at the peak of their year, and the birds just beginning their migrations, and the fish feeding heavily to prepare for winter. Under these circumstances, it is easy to overlook the cattails *(Typha angustifolia)* and giant cordgrass *(Spartina cynosuroides)* that grow on the shores of the upper Bay and the rivers. The rootstocks of both live from year to year, but the aboveground leaves and stalks are dying and turning brown now. Neither produces seeds of major value to waterfowl or any other wildlife, though black ducks eat some cordgrass seeds.

So there they stand, tall and tough. There are acres of them, cattail heads beginning to fluff out and cordgrass seeds falling. Up around the Susquehanna Flats, cattails grow in marshes along the shore. Further south, say on the Wye River or the upper Corrotoman, they make up the back edges of the marshes. From Eastern Neck Island and Southeast Creek on the Chester to West Point on the York, giant cordgrass grows in huge stands along the rivers. Against the marsh flowers of late summer and the fall colors of trees, both plants fade into the background. It is easy to forget they are there.

We tend to think of marsh plants in terms of food, but they have other values too. These two species provide habitat—living space—for a number of creatures in their marshes. While other plants wither and fall, these endure.

Long-billed marsh wrens, red-winged blackbirds, and black ducks have already found them useful over the summer for nesting. Most cordgrass will still have a few abandoned wren nests close by the water's edge. They are made of grass, more or less spherical, about the size of grapefruits, and built 3 to 4 feet up the stalk from the surface of the marsh.

Secretive marsh birds like rails and bitterns also have spent the summer here. From the least bitterns in the upriver marshes to the clapper rails of the Bayshore, the cattails and the cordgrasses have served as cover and safe ground for nests. Both groups of birds are shaped and colored so that they fit right in with their backgrounds. They fly very little, preferring to walk or run through the thickets of stalks. The bittern, when frightened, will stand still with its head and long beak pointing skyward, the better to merge with the strong vertical pattern of the plants around it.

Through the fall, a variety of rails and bitterns will move through the Bay country, migrating south, and they, too, will use the cattails and cordgrasses as cover. Thus the plants offer way stations—avian motels, as it were—that are nearly as essential to the birds as nesting and wintering habitat.

Only a few rails, red-wings, and wrens from northern marshes will spend the winter here, but they will find that the tall plants offer some shelter even in severe weather. The temperature in the thickets at night and on overcast days will always be a few degrees warmer than on the open marsh.

Muskrats too will use the plants. In fact, cattails and giant cordgrass probably have more year-round value for them than for any other marsh animals. With the onset of fall, the two plants offer them abundant, durable building materials with good insulating qualities. Both plants make good huts. No wonder they are also highly regarded by duck hunters for brushing duck blinds.

Cattails and cordgrasses also contribute some of the muskrats' winter food. True, the aboveground stalks are pretty hard to digest, but all during the summer the plants have been storing starch in their roots to carry them through the winter. The cattails are especially good at this task. The tender parts of the rootstocks have excellent food value, so instead of cutting the stalks off at their bases and eating the hearts, the muskrats start digging as summer ends and the weather turns cool.

In a broad expanse of marsh, it is all too easy to pay no attention to specific plant species unless they serve some obvious purpose. For opportunistic animals, however, cattails and giant cordgrass are not mere background. They are the foundations of those animals' lives. We do well to remember that ours is not the only point of view.

OCTOBER

October Travelers: Ospreys and Canada Geese

Two of the Bay's best-loved birds are traveling this month—one going and the other coming. Ospreys are migrating to South America, following their pattern of seeking endless summer. As noted above, the Canada geese are arriving.

The Chesapeake's ospreys have two summers a year, but they choose to breed here, during their Northern Hemisphere summer. Thus they spend most of their six months on the Bay nesting and raising young. Part of our affection for them lies in the fact that they tend to do this in public places: atop channel markers, on duck blinds, and in trees close to the water. Thus sailors on Whitehall Bay near Annapolis, fishermen at the Hole in the Wall by Gwynn's Island, and anyone else spending time on the water can watch the young birds grow from week to week. Ospreys appear to adapt well to the presence of man.

In late summer, the young fledged (grew feathers and began to fly) and learned to fish on their own. By now, they and their parents are headed to their Southern Hemisphere summer, in Brazil, Colombia, and Venezuela. It is remarkable, from the human frame of reference at least, that these young birds can make such flights at the age of four months, with no more than half that time as fledglings.

October, then, is a month for empty nests, and this noble but conspicuous bird becomes a rare sight. The last osprey of fall is something to take note of, a milestone in the fabric of the year. Any bird sighted here now is likely to be a straggler on its way down from New England or the Canadian Maritime Provinces.

For us, the sense of loss at the departure of the ospreys is tempered by rejoicing at the return of the Canada geese. As the introduction to Part III describes, each October there are times when low-pressure weather systems move through the Bay country. After them, the barometer shoots up, the sky turns crystal clear, the wind comes northwest, and the geese stream by high overhead all day long.

Every year, more geese summer over in the Bay region and in states just to the north. Even so, the bulk of the Chesapeake's wintering population still breeds on the tundra of the Ungava Peninsula in Quebec, especially on the shores of Ungava Bay to the east and Hudson Bay to the west. In late September and October, these are the birds that come down in the high V's, looking for familiar haunts. Fledglings migrate along with their parents. Like the young ospreys, these geese are already full-sized and strong enough for long flights.

Also like the ospreys, Canada geese seem to adapt well to man and to some of our uses of land and water. In spite of heavy human population pressure on the Bay, the goose population has increased over the last century (although as this is being written, it is lower than it has been for 20 years).

The major reasons for this increase are the mechanical grain-harvesting techniques that farmers here adopted widely after World War II—mechanical pickers leave more scrap grain in the fields than traditional methods—and the more recent practice of planting winter grains and cover crops. Geese are well suited anatomically to take advantage of these circumstances, since their legs are set far enough forward on their bodies to enable them to balance well on land. That sounds like an obvious point, but diving ducks like canvasbacks have their legs set so far back that balancing themselves on their feet for long periods is exhausting. Underwater, they are much more efficient than geese, but on land (to paraphrase the saying about fish), they are ducks out of water.

The Chesapeake is ideally set up for field-feeding geese. The Eastern Shore and much of the lower western shore are given over to productive croplands laced freely with tidal rivers and creeks. Thus the birds have abundant food on land and plenty of nearby water for roosting safely at night. They feed enthusiastically on corn, soybeans, and green cover crops, so they return to their breeding grounds each spring in better shape than before, even after harsh winters. Hence their populations increase. Sometimes, they seem almost commonplace, feeding around the Visitors' Center at the Blackwater National Wildlife Refuge below Cambridge or flying in flocks of thousands over Route 213 outside Chestertown.

October is a busy month on the Bay. There are many interesting things going on, but one of the best is standing outdoors on a clear night, listening to geese high overhead—another of the year's milestones.

Harvesttime

Vance Parks understood the richness of autumn on the Chesapeake. He spent plenty of time on the waters around his native Tangier Island, but as science department chairman at the island's school (he was one of the best teachers in Virginia), he combined a biologist's understanding with a waterman's knowledge. His ideas were worth listening to.

He always put up a batch of Norfolk spot for the winter. He'd wait until the fish got a deep gold sheen on their gray and silver backs, signaling that they had fattened up on summer's bounty. Then he would make a large catch and salt them down to help tide his family through the cold weather.

Fat, gold-colored spot are a good symbol for this time of year, but plenty of other fish are in prime condition as well. Menhaden, silversides, and bay anchovies have been feeding heavily on summer's blooms of plankton, and they too have put on weight. So have all the young-of-the-year sea trout, croakers, and rockfish that have used the Bay system as their nursery. Crabs finished their last slough of the year in mid-September, but they have continued to feed, storing up for the winter.

Summer brings a lot of life to the Bay, but that inevitably must be followed by a lot of death, and so a lot of decaying material comes to rest on the Bay's bottom. A scavenger like the blue crab has plenty to sift through, as do smaller but still important scavengers like the grass shrimp, amphipods, and sea worms that fattened Vance Parks's adult spot and the year's crop of juvenile fish.

Upriver, there is plenty more. In the tidal fresh marshes of rivers like the Rappahannock and the Choptank, there are bumper crops of nutritious seeds: wild rice, smartweed, tearthumb, rice cutgrass, arrow arum, Walter's millet, and others.

Throughout the Bay and its rivers, beds of submerged aquatic vegetation (SAV) have grown and fruited out. Around Smith and Tangier islands, the widgeon grass and eelgrass have peaked. In the Potomac and on the Susquehanna Flats, the same is true for hydrilla and wild celery. There isn't nearly as much SAV around as there used to be, a continuing cause for concern for those who struggle to restore the Chesapeake's health, but there is more than there was 15 years ago, and the plants form an important part of autumn's harvest.

Everywhere around the Bay, the tables are set with a tremendous amount and variety of food. At the same time, falling water temperatures and shorter days signal winter's approach and the need to stock up for the leaner days ahead. The fish and birds that are here for this season feed heavily, with an urgency triggered by those subtle clues.

These harvesttime feasters are a remarkably varied lot. Some are summer residents headed back out to the Atlantic. Others are just arriving from further north. Some are just passing through. A few are year-round residents. Let's look at a sampling of them.

Many of the larger fish that live in the Bay during the warm months spend the winter out on the continental shelf. Falling water temperatures alert them to winter's approach and stimulate them to feed voraciously on the menhaden and juvenile spot that are headed down the Bay by the millions. This group of fish includes gray trout, speckled trout, bluefish, flounder, Spanish mackerel, and puppy drum (young red drum), plus bottom feeders like croakers and Vance Parks's golden spot. Rockfish of all sizes join the party, and some of them will move down out of the Bay to winter off Cape Hatteras with rock that have come down from summering in New England.

The anglers who follow these fish through September, October, and November, from Annapolis and Kent Island to Tilghman and Solomons, to Crisfield and Point Lookout, to Smith Point and the Cut Channel off the Rappahannock, and then to the Chesapeake Bay Bridge-Tunnel between the Virginia Capes, will do very well indeed. They will understand as well as anyone the meaning of harvesttime.

The Bay Bridge-Tunnel plays an especially important role in this fall exodus from the Bay. It forms a valuable complex of reef habitat for prey and predator alike. Because of its location at the mouth of the Chesapeake, it is a natural intercept point to concentrate all the forage fish leaving the Bay. The big fish headed out to sea will stop off here to feed, and so will some of the fish headed down the coast, especially rockfish. Fishing for them lasts through December, sometimes right up to the first of the new year.

Not all of the Bay's harvesttime feasters are fish, however. The Chesapeake is a major wintering ground for waterfowl, and it is a natural stopover for a number of waterbirds headed further south. Fish-eating birds like cormorants and loons chase baitfish almost as efficiently as bluefish and rock, while gulls and terns wheel screaming over the melee, diving for scraps. The loons are particularly adept at working in flocks to herd menhaden. More on them next month.

Up in the marshes, the harvest is more seeds than small fish, but there are plenty of gleaners here too. From the time that the wild rice ripens in September, the upriver areas see a steady progression of bobolinks (reedbirds), sora rails, red-winged blackbirds, green- and blue-winged teal, black ducks, mallards, and other water birds moving in to pick through the litter at the edges of rivers, creeks, and guts for the tons of seeds that are the culmination of the marsh year. The SAV beds of the Potomac and Tangier Sound will also attract large numbers of waterfowl. Some, like the teal, will move on as far as Florida, the Caribbean, and even South America, while others, like the blacks and mallards, will settle in till spring.

In late September and October, Canada geese come down from their summer haunts in the far north. The harvest they seek now is scrap grain left by the combines of human farmers after their fall harvest, not the SAV that fed them 50 years ago. In November and December, some 30,000 tundra swans will join them, flying in from Canada's Arctic coast and Alaska's North Slope. They too will seek scrap grain to replace their former diet of SAV. Even though the Chesapeake's migrations of waterfowl are far lower than they used to be, the birds still form a magnificent part of the Bay community.

Last on the list of autumn reapers, but definitely not least, is us. Whether we gather what is visual, like watching a flight of geese coming in from Canada, or edible, like a baked rockfish stuffed with oysters, the banquet table is set for us too.

Our Bay still has problems that harvesttime reminds us of: swans feeding in farmers' fields instead of on the lush SAV beds they used to find here, rockfish limits at one or two per person per day instead of a coolerful, and oyster harvests a pale shadow of their former abundance, with the specter of a possible harvest closure hanging over them. Even so, this is a rich time of year for us Bay lovers, and we should enjoy it to the hilt. Perhaps what these problems do at this season is to remind us to savor each goose, or rockfish, or oyster (whether visually or on the table, or both), and never again to take them for granted, as we did in the past when the Chesapeake's bounty seemed to have no end. Savor them and be thankful for all the Bay means to us.

Fall Is for Rockfish

Twenty feet below the skiff, the tiny jig snaked its way over and around the rubble of the old Severn River railroad bridge. I could feel it move over a timber and drop. Suddenly, something ate it and darted away. I felt its power all the way down to the handle of the little spinning rod. This was not a white perch, not even a 15-incher like the one that a friend had caught here the year before.

Sure enough, after a couple of spirited minutes, a 5-pound striped bass (*Morone saxatilis*—rockfish to us here on the Bay) lay beside the boat, silver flanks and purple iridescent stripes bright in the crisp fall sunlight. It was 1988, so the Maryland season was still closed. I grabbed the leader, and the fish shook its head one more time, straightening the barbless light wire hook. A swish of its tail and it was gone. Captain Bill Pike and I grinned at each other. It was a beautiful fish.

Rockfish inspire affection. By popular acclaim, they are the premier sport and commercial species on a Bay that is rich in fish. Most of us who drop a line along the Chesapeake enjoy catching spot, croakers, gray and speckled trout, flounder, bluefish, red drum, black drum, cobia, and the other species that frequent the Bay, and the largemouth bass and channel catfish that thrive up the rivers; but somehow rock rise to the head of the class. Strong fighters on any tackle, they are beautiful and tasty. The Chesapeake has a long history of growing lots of them, and since they live in a variety of habitats, ranging from the upper rivers to the open Bay, they can be caught by at least a dozen different techniques. It should be no surprise that they are the Maryland State Fish, nor that they are highly prized in Virginia as well. Catching them consistently requires a fisherman to think the way they do, which means building an understanding not only of the fish but of every aspect of the waters in which they live. Fishing rockfish is excellent exercise in being a part of the Bay ecosystem.

One reason that rockfish are interesting is because they have a complex life cycle. By the time they mature as adults, they are using virtually all of the Chesapeake, from fresh water at or near the heads of navigation on the rivers (in fact, before the rivers were dammed, they went up the Susquehanna all the way to Sunbury, well above Harrisburg, and up the James to Lynchburg) to lower river channels, creeks, and coves, to the open Bay and the Atlantic.

Each spring, mature rock (females greater than six to eight years old and males greater than two to four years old) ascend the Chesapeake's larger rivers to spawn when water temperatures reach 55° to 60°F (12.8° to 15.6°C), generally in April and the first half of May. There are legendary stories of "rock fights" up rivers like the Choptank and the Potomac when a big female and several smaller males jostle one another to make the eggs and sperm flow from their bodies into the water.

The young fish hatch and spread out into the lower rivers, where they live in the creeks and coves, mixing with young spot, croakers, and white perch, along with silversides, anchovies, killifish, and other small fish in the Bay's rich nurseries. The juvenile rock feed voraciously (in summer, it is not uncommon to catch a 3-inch rock on a 1½-inch jig while fishing for perch). They grow fast through the fall and then winter in deep holes like the trench off Kent Island or the deep hole off Tall Timbers in the Potomac.

They spend the next several years in the Bay, feeding and growing. Often they turn up feeding with their cousins the white perch on oyster lumps in the upper Bay and in river spots like Kettle Bottom Shoals off Colonial Beach in the Potomac. In the fall, these subadult 8- to 15-inch fish school up to chase anchovies and silversides, often breaking the surface and thereby attracting clouds of gulls.

By the age of six to eight years (24 to 30 inches), most female rock mature, spawn for the first time, and migrate afterward up the Atlantic Coast to New England, or even farther. Tagged Chesapeake rock have turned up in summer as far north as the Bay of Fundy in Nova Scotia. In any given year, some 60 percent to 90 percent of the New England summer rock population is made up of Chesapeake fish.

They return in the late fall to feed around the Bay Bridge-Tunnel at the mouth of the Chesapeake and then to winter in the Bay or in the Atlantic off Cape Hatteras. In spring, they begin the cycle all over again.

That is the general outline of a rockfish year. In practice, the details are more complicated, with some big fish staying in the Chesapeake all the time, depending on water temperature, salinity, or maybe just quirks of personality. They are a source of fascination to anyone who studies them, whether angler, waterman, or biologist, though their travels make it a tricky task to manage harvests. In any case, they are wanderers whose arrivals are eagerly awaited up and down the coast.

Even with all their movements, rockfish are not offshore travelers like tuna or even bluefish; their migration routes are close to shore. Their overall body design gives a clue to their habits: they are streamlined enough for efficient swimming on long migrations, and there is plenty of oily dark muscle just under the skin to supply the motive power for those travels. (Look for it the next time you skin a fillet.) At the same time, the fish have broad tail fins that give them good acceleration, so they can lurk behind or prowl around cover such as marsh banks, rocks, bridge pilings, and other rubble (like the Severn's old railroad bridge) and ambush their prey. They will, however, also suspend off the bottom in open water to feed on free-swimming schools of forage fish like menhaden.

Their mouths are built to take a variety of prey, from grass shrimp and bloodworms to fish like silversides, menhaden, and eels. Those mouths are not huge, but they are large enough to swallow baitfish approximately one-third their own body length, with no teeth but rough-surfaced jaws to grip favorite but slippery foods like eels. Rock generally grab large prey by the head and swallow them headfirst. The fish do very well as opportunistic predators.

With plenty of food and time, rockfish grow to large sizes, over 100 pounds in rare individuals but to 50 pounds in fair numbers. The Virginia and Maryland hook and line records are both over 60 pounds, but a fish conservatively estimated at 75 to 80 pounds was caught and carefully released by Captain Ed Darwin and five clients aboard Ed's charter boat *Becky D* off Kent Island in early May 1992. (During a short and highly regulated season, it was a most unselfish, altruistic act—the fish was carrying about 8 million eggs at the time.) Many commercial fishermen who worked on the Bay in the 1950s and sixties handled fish as large.

Over the years, the Chesapeake has produced billions of rockfish, and we have caught a lot of them. Any fish this tasty and this much fun to catch is a valuable resource, and for years the supply seemed endless. Captain Fred Tilp in his classic *This Was Potomac River* refers to a haul seine catch at Sycamore Point on the Potomac in 1838 that netted 450 fish *averaging* 50 pounds apiece! Captain Dick Houghland, who for many years ran his charter boat *Mary Lou* out of Chesapeake Beach, could consistently find 100 rock per trip for his clients in the early 1970s.

Such catches, however, were misleading. By the late 1970s, Houghland and a few other good fishermen began to realize just how damaging they had been to the rock, and gradually the truth dawned on the rest of us. There were indications of other problems, like high hatch mortalities after spawning. Scientists worried that issues like water quality degradation, wetland destruction, loss of submerged aquatic vegetation, and blockages in spawning streams were depriving rockfish of much-needed habitat. Surveys of stock abundance indicated a serious decline. The fish were not endangered, but they were certainly threatened.

Maryland took strong action, closing its fishery completely in 1985, and the other Atlantic coastal states followed with stringent restrictions, all under the coordination of the Atlantic States Marine Fisheries Commission (ASMFC). About the same time, the massive interstate cleanup of the Chesapeake got underway. The cleanup, if it continues strong, will address at least some of the habitat problems over the next decade, but in the meantime, the fishing restrictions have taken the pressure off the fish.

The result is a success story. Although the ASMFC considers the stocks "recover*ing*," not "recover*ed*," rockfish are firmly on the increase. A limited fishery was reopened on the Chesapeake in 1990, designed to provide a modest harvest while allowing the stocks to continue to rebuild.

This well-loved fish seems to be able to coexist with us if given half a chance. Whether sport or commercial fishermen, we have had to adjust our thinking from wholesale to retail quantities, and to appreciate each individual fish we handle as a very special creature. Anglers live with tight limits and become increasingly sophisticated at releasing over-limit, out-of-season, undersized, or oversized fish. Most of the watermen are fishing carefully within their quotas. Violators from both groups have been prosecuted vigorously.

By and large, the fish are getting the careful stewardship they need. We still have plenty of problems here on the Bay, and big challenges remain. Still, it is a great morale-booster to know that just maybe we caught this one in time, and that we are on the way to building a great and sustainable fishery for a favorite species.

October is a traditional time for rockfishing. Early in the month, many of them are in their shallow water haunts, where artful techniques like fly-fishing and working top-water plugs are effective. As the water cools, they move out into the open Bay, where trolling and jigging become the techniques of choice. Either way, the season is something to celebrate. Caught and grilled or released with care and admiration, it's good to have our rockfish back.

River Meanders

Route 50 east from Annapolis carries hundreds of thousands of people each year across the Bay Bridge and down the Eastern Shore to Salisbury, Ocean City, and Assateague Island. For years, heavy traffic was the rule, with several backup points, of which the Bay Bridge was the best known.

The least-known was 15 miles south of Cambridge, where Route 50 constricted from four to two lanes for an old steel bridge over a narrow river with a small town on one side. Many people sitting in the traffic jams had to consult their maps to see what the town was (Vienna), and to look at the signs on the bridge to discover what river they were crossing (the Nanticoke).

The backups are mostly gone now, in summer as well as at other seasons, because the route to the ocean has been streamlined. New interchanges and bridges speed travelers on their way, and most of them cross the divided four-lane bridge high over the Nanticoke without a thought. In August, a few might notice the white-and-crimson wildflowers (marsh hibiscus) in bloom in the big marsh on the other side of the bridge, and in October they might admire the warm colors from tickseed sunflowers in the marsh and the red maple, ash, sweet gum, and black gum trees at the back edges of the marsh.

But not many look at the pattern of the town and the marsh, or see what it indicates about the way the river works. They have places to go, so it's hard for most of them to get excited about the physics of river flow, even if it has profound effects on both human and natural history. Nevertheless, the river does have a good story to tell.

Vienna is an old town built on the outside of a sweeping curve called a meander. This one is part of a long series on the Nanticoke, stretching 20 river miles from the Delaware line to Sandy Hill. Every long river entering the Bay has meanders. Obviously there is a good physical reason for their existence.

Think of the mass of water flowing in a river, even a relatively small one like the Nanticoke at Vienna. The bed is about 200 feet across, and the channel is just over 40 feet deep at maximum. The bend is a little over a mile long. Water weighs 62.5 pounds per cubic foot, plus the weight of anything dissolved (like salt—minimal at Vienna) or suspended (like sediment—usually a good bit there). The weight of that section of river is considerable, and it is, of course, connected to the rest of the water in the river.

This great mass of fluid moves back and forth in response to downstream current and tides, but it has tremendous inertia, and therefore tremendous power. Strange as it sounds, a river "works" as it flows downhill, losing energy to friction between its water and its banks. It will make any changes in elevation as gradual as possible, to make energy loss as uniform as possible. And it will remove or at least wear down obstructions that retard its flow.

The tidal portions of the Bay's rivers flow through the unconsolidated, erodible gravel, sand, clay, and mud of the coastal plain. In these media, it is relatively easy for a river to carve out a shape that fits its needs. For these rivers, that shape is a series of meanders. Like a skier taking a curving path down the face of a slope, the meanders allow these rivers to smooth out abrupt changes in elevation. These achievements are especially important as each river gathers more mass from downstream tributaries and from the water the tides bring up from the Bay. The region of heavy meandering tends not to be at the head of navigation but in the middle tidal reaches.

But curves cause friction as a river collides with its banks. The inertia of the great water masses will resist turning. To minimize the friction, the meanders tend to assume specific curve shapes that cause the least total change in direction through the whole process of bending. The curves with these geometric properties are called sine-generated curves and are similar to half-circles.

So what do these remarkable curves have to do with live creatures of the Chesapeake—people and fish and birds and marsh plants? Look at a map or a chart of a river with meanders. The insides of the curves will frequently be marked to signify marshes. Often there will be a town like Vienna on the outside of a curve.

Here is the reason for the pattern. As the river flows around the curve (in either direction, depending on tides), the water on the outside and much of the surface will accelerate, both sideways and ahead. The water on the inside will slow down. The result is a slow but powerful spiral motion that will erode the outer bank and deposit sediment on the inside. Thus the outsides of the curves are usually deep, with firm banks of heavy material like sand and gravel. The insides build shallow, fertile mud banks.

In selecting townsites, both Native Americans and European settlers looked for the outsides of curves, with firm ground for building and deep water for docking. The latter attribute doesn't mean much today, but for most of the past three and a half centuries, it was critical. Look at a map of the old steamboat ports: Walkerton on the Mattaponi, Dixie on the Piankatank, Tappahannock and Leedstown on the Rappahannock, Nottingham on the

Patuxent, Deep Landing on the Chester, Ganey's Wharf on the Choptank, Rehobeth on the Pocomoke, and, of course, Vienna. All are on the outside of meanders, and there are at least as many more. Vienna, by the way, was also an important shipbuilding town. Several Bay schooners were built there, on ways that launched the ships right down into the deep water on the curve.

The insides of the meanders, meanwhile, provide superb wildlife habitat in the form of fresh and brackish tidal marshes. The big marsh opposite Vienna is full of muskrats, juvenile and forage fish, herons, grass shrimp, and a host of other creatures. The river there has been an important nursery area for young rockfish, and it has its share of big rock as well. Eagles fish it, and a shrewd angler can find a good meal of perch and catfish. Detritus from the marsh fuels much of the lower river's food web. At this season of the year, its harvest of seed-producing plants like wild rice and smartweed is measured in tons, and its value to waterfowl arriving for the winter would be difficult to calculate.

Shipways, striped bass, marsh hibiscus, and wild rice have all owed their existence at Vienna to the big meander. Slow down and ponder that fact the next time you cross the new bridge.

Oyster Toadfish: A Success at Parenting

A couple of close friends taught me at an early age how to take an oyster toadfish *(Opsanus tau)* off a fishing line: grab the animal by the lower jaw with a pair of pliers; cut out the hook; and drop the ugly thing back overboard, saying something appropriate about how nasty it was. Oh, yes, and on the way, jab the point of the bait knife down between its eyes, in the hope of reducing the population.

Both friends are now retired Virginia clergymen of distinguished reputation and gentle manner. Stabbing anything is out of character for them, but there just didn't seem to be any use for toadfish back then, except to steal bait from proper fish like spot and croakers and trout. It is interesting to look back on that time from the perspective of a more modern ecological consciousness. One of the two friends (actually, my father) happened to read several years ago that toadfish exercise very highly developed parental skills, and he has been downright solicitous of them ever since. I won't say that he'd rather catch one than a 3-pound trout, but they certainly intrigue him.

Most of us learn about toads by catching them on hook and line. They start taking our baits when they reach the size of 3 inches or so. They can grow up to 15 inches, though anything over 12 inches is exceptional. They are ugly, or at least interesting-looking. A toad's head is wide, with brown and yellow mottled skin that is scaleless and wrinkled, with flaps hanging off it. Eyes are large and bright, and the powerful jaws are broad, with a single row of sturdy teeth on each. It is not an inviting mouth. The body is stocky, with long, soft-rayed dorsal (back) and ventral (belly) fins and a round caudal (tail) fin; the pectoral fins (on the sides behind the gills) are large and rounded. At the front of the dorsal fin and along the upper edge of each gill cover are short, poisonous spines that can cause painful punctures. Toadfish should be handled with great care.

Oyster toads range from New England to Florida, but all populations are local. Toads are not migratory, beyond moving to deep water in winter and back to shallower water in summer. Dispersal of the species even up and down the coast must have been a slow process.

The animal is a lurker and an ambush feeder. Males prefer to hide under oyster shells, in wrecks, and under any kind of bottom debris they can find. Literature written some years ago mentions that females and young toads stay in eel- and widgeon grass beds most of the summer, but the disappearance of those grasses has sent them to deeper water. In either habitat, the species' mottled color pattern helps as camouflage. Expandable color sacs in the skin (chromatophores) help individuals adjust to their surroundings, an ability they share with a number of other Bay fish. Toads feed aggressively on small oysters, clams, and various other crustaceans, small fish, worms, and decayed material. Their own flesh is reasonably tasty, but they are awkward to fillet and skin, and the yield is small, so few people ever try them.

What is most remarkable about oyster toads, beyond the variety they add to the bottom community of the Bay, is the above-mentioned system of parental care. The male stakes out a territory where he has found a den of sorts, made of shells or timber or whatever else might be lying there (a great drawing of one is on page 174 of A.J. and R.L. Lippson's *Life in the Chesapeake Bay;* see

Bibliography). He sounds a plaintive, foghornlike call to attract a female, who lays eggs upside-down on the roof of the den. Toad eggs are very large as fish eggs go (¼ inch in diameter), with adhesive disks that hold them in place. The male fertilizes them, and the young develop where they are (they are visible in the Lippson drawing) until their yolk sacs are absorbed and they are ready to swim and feed on their own.

The fact that the eggs never have a planktonic (drifting) stage further limits geographical spread of the species. The process of growing in place may take three to four weeks. The male stays on guard, leaving only occasionally to feed. Spawning takes place in the Chesapeake from April to August, so the last fry of the season don't become free-swimming until around Labor Day. After that, the male shepherds them for nearly another month. Male toads, then, are busy running nurseries from early April till early October.

It is easy to be anthropomorphic about the role reversal, but the truth is that toads don't think about such things. They have simply developed a reproductive system that works for them. Unlike many other fish species, male toads grow larger and live longer than females. In a system that relies on thorough care for a relatively small number of eggs, the larger parent is the more effective domestic.

The strategy is very different from that of fish like the Atlantic menhaden, whose females broadcast large numbers of eggs on the tides and never see them again. Judging by the menhaden and toadfish populations, both strategies do the job. It is a moot question to try to decide which is better. Each one fits its species' niche.

What is a toadfish's purpose on the Bay? That is an anthropomorphic approach, too. The fish don't have much direct value to us. They are here because they have developed a niche that gives them a good living. No amount of stabbing will make them disappear. They may have faces that only a father toad could love, but my father is right. Their success at what they do deserves respect.

Croakers and Computers

Science on the Chesapeake is complex. Sorting out the way the Bay works calls for a scientist with a broad range of interests and training, or a team of specialists who work well together, or both. Dr.

Brenda L. Norcross is a versatile biologist who has studied every-thing from natural history and physical oceanography to statistics and computers. Her Ph.D. dissertation on the Atlantic croaker *(Micropogon undulatus)*, delivered at the Virginia Institute of Marine Science (VIMS) in 1983, is a case in point.

First, though, some background. For years, croakers have puzzled Bay fishermen and scientists. Older watermen recall that during the Depression, the price of croakers was a penny a pound. A penny was bigger then, but fresh or salted hardheads were a welcome and inexpensive staple at a hungry time. Some of us who are younger remember growing up in the 1950s, fishing croakers on handlines over oyster bars from Lynnhaven to Annapolis from wooden skiffs. For us, no matter where we were, the fish were a standard feature of summer. They were fun to catch, especially the big 2- to 4-pounders that bit best at night, and they were good to eat.

But something happened to the fish of our childhood. In the late fifties, they simply disappeared. Routine young-of-the-year surveys run by VIMS failed to turn up any juveniles. Watermen around the Bay's mouth caught a handful of big fish each spring, but that would be all. For over 15 years, they were "out of sight, out of mind."

Suddenly, in 1975, there were young "pinhead" croakers everywhere. Sure enough, by 1977 there were lots of 1½- to 2-pound croakers around. But 1977 also brought a hard freeze, followed by sporadic cold weather in the winter of 1978. Once again, the bottom fell out of the young-of-the-year surveys.

It turns out that the croaker is near the northern edge of its geographic range in the Chesapeake, and the timing of its spawning season makes it vulnerable to cold water. The fish have returned off and on since then, including a big run in 1991 and 1992, but fluctuating populations will be the rule for the foreseeable future.

The Atlantic croaker belongs to the family Sciaenidae—the drums—which includes Norfolk spot, gray trout (weakfish), speck-led (spotted sea) trout, red drum (channel bass), and black drum. The family's value for both food and sport is substantial all along the Atlantic and Gulf coasts.

Most of the sciaenids spawn in the spring and early summer (e.g., gray and speckled trout, black drum) or in the winter (spot). The warm water spawners appear to drop their eggs in the open lower Bay or just outside it in the nearshore waters of the continental shelf. The spot spawn farther offshore, where the water is cold but the temperature is stable.

Croakers have a different calendar. They spawn now. The adults spawn, in fact, over a long period in late summer and fall on the shelf and in the lower portion of large estuaries. Then they spend the winter offshore. The juveniles move up into the estuaries for the winter. This is the same basic scheme that the spot follow, but the croakers are four to six months ahead of them. On the Gulf and the southern Atlantic coasts, this timing is fine. The young fish spend the winter in warm water with plenty of food.

Here, however, winter water temperatures in the tributaries and the upper Bay can fluctuate widely. Remember that the temperature of a large water mass like the ocean or the lower Bay changes very slowly, even if air temperatures change rapidly. But smaller water volumes, like those of the upper Bay and tributaries like the Piankatank or the Choptank, can change more rapidly. A quick hard freeze or a prolonged cold spell can drop tributary temperatures below the tolerance levels of young croakers. Even a heavy spawn can be completely wiped out.

Croakers are prolific fish. An individual female can produce well over 100,000 eggs, so a small spawning population can produce a large year class under favorable conditions. But even a heavy spawn from a large adult population can be decimated by cold weather. Hence the widely fluctuating population levels.

In general, it is not difficult to correlate cold winters with poor croaker fishing and mild ones with full fish boxes. Croakers are, however, important commercial and sport fish, so estimating their population status accurately from year to year is essential for state fishery biologists developing harvest regulations. Hence the need for a more precise predictive technique.

Dr. Norcross began her study with a detailed life history of the croaker. She used it to identify points at which survival is strongly influenced by environmental factors like temperature. An important part of this process was finding accurate sources of data. Fortunately, VIMS had 30 years of monthly trawl net catch data for stations from the mouth of the Bay up into the York River, as well as daily winter temperatures at its main pier at Gloucester Point. The Norfolk airport supplied data for offshore winds.

With the numbers in hand, Norcross divided the life history into sections called submodels in order to evaluate the influence of each environmental factor. Using a big VIMS computer and a statistical technique called regression analysis, she evaluated first the effects of summer and fall wind patterns, which govern the size of the warm bottom water area where the croakers can spawn. The winds also drive the currents that transport the larvae either off the continental shelf into the open sea or up into the Chesapeake's nursery grounds.

The wind conditions (direction, strength, and duration) were combined into a single index number. When the index for each year was compared statistically with fall recruitment figures (the number of young fish surviving to enter the Bay) for that year, Norcross found good correlation in nearly two-thirds of the cases, an indication that her analysis was on the right track.

Next, she worked out an index for winter temperatures and found correlation in about three-fourths of the years. When she combined the two indices, she found good correlation in 90 percent of the cases. It is worth noting, though, that she had usable summer wind data for only 11 years, which did not allow her to verify her model over as broad a span of time as she would have liked.

For the croaker, the size of a given year class does not necessarily reflect the number of spawning adults that produced it. That is, recruitment of juveniles to the Bay is affected more by environmental factors than by the number of spawners in any given year. But stock size does have some effect, especially in years when size of the class is very small. Norcross added an index based on commercial landings of market-sized adult croakers for Virginia and North Carolina (which appear to form a single spawning stock on the shelf) and found that her model now correlated with over 95 percent of her data. As a final check, she "hindcast" recruitment for 1982-83, for which she had data, but which was not a part of her model. The model's prediction was for a very strong year class, which was verified by VIMS trawl catch data. The exact size predicted was incorrect, but the actual data were within the confidence limits of the prediction.

Several points about Norcross's study stand out. First, the model described a succession of factors that operated in sequence, each one affecting the result produced by the previous one. Second, several factors were important only when they occurred at the extreme ends of their ranges, e.g., low winter temperatures and spawning stock sizes. Third, Norcross's analysis began with an examination of the most obvious factors, like temperature. Then she progressively added other variables and adjusted her model until it described her data with a high degree of accuracy. Finally, wind gauges and nets and days on the water were essential to her study. If VIMS had not been operating routine surveys for all those years, her work would have been impossible. But the artful statistical methods and the massive VIMS computer were just as essential, because they allowed her to analyze a problem with several variables and assess the effects of each.

These tools add an important advantage for scientists working on a system as complex as the Chesapeake. For us laymen, they provide elegant explanations of complicated processes that we usually see only in fleeting glimpses.

It would be great to be able to say that we are close to working out models like this one for every species of fish in the Bay. Unfortunately, that level of sophistication is still a long way off. Each model takes a great deal of work. Even so, one by one they are being developed, with team approaches that combine field observations with physical and climatological data and with statistical analysis. A model for the Bay's blue crab is being worked out by a team whose members come from VIMS, Old Dominion University, and the Horn Point Environmental Laboratory of the University of Maryland. Such studies and the understanding they bring are not only essential for sound fishery management, but fascinating as well. We observers of the Bay can look forward to deeper insight in the years to come.

NOVEMBER

Menhaden Migrations

As noted in October's sketch "Harvesttime," most of the Chesapeake's summer population of menhaden are headed out to their wintering grounds. Juveniles no longer dimple the surface of shallow flats in the creeks. Anglers' depth-sounders no longer show great blobs on the screens as they go over 10-foot-deep schools. Pound net fishermen down the Bay catch fewer of them to freeze for next year's crab bait. And the Reedville purse seine fleet finds itself working farther down the Bay and more often outside in the Atlantic. Finally, some of the fish boat crews call it a season and go home for deer season on the Northern Neck. Most years, a few boats head south to Beaufort, North Carolina, to fish into December.

Sometimes these crews make good money in this fall fishery. The menhaden are there in tremendous numbers. But the vagaries of weather affect the fishes' migrations. An early, cold winter like that of 1977 can shut the fishery down prematurely. Gales can keep the boats tied up for days on end, even when the fish are there. Despite these handicaps, the men usually enjoy themselves. John Frye covers this fall fishery well in *The Men All Singing: The Story of Menhaden Fishing* (see Bibliography).

When the profits are there, watermen can do quite a bit of effective fieldwork for the scientific community. Years of intensive fishing effort have given the menhaden industry a good overall picture of the fishes' movements. The first menhaden down the coast in the fall are the ones moving out of the open waters of the Chesapeake. They tend to be two- to four-year-old fish measuring 10 to 12 inches. After them come larger, older fish from Delaware Bay, New Jersey, New York, and New England.

There is a limit, however, to the amount of information that can be gotten from the fishery itself. More precise data are needed for managing it. A smart scientist listens to fish boat captains, and to crewmen and spotter pilots, too. And smart fishermen listen to scientists. Together they can get a lot of work done.

Following adult fish in their travels is usually done by tagging. This most easily yields results with species like rockfish that are caught by anglers on hook and line or handled individually by watermen. But menhaden come aboard by the tens of thousands, drawn from the net through a hose by a pump. A menhaden tagging study would require an ingenious tagging and recovery system and a large sample of tagged fish to ensure a statistically useful number of returns.

Several researchers have worked out a way to inject numbered, stainless steel tags into the menhadens' body cavities with tagging guns. The fish are then released. Tagged fish that the purse seiners take are cooked and pressed for oil right along with the rest of the catch. Magnets, placed at various points in the processing plants, pick up tags out of the resulting loose scrap as it is processed into fish meal. William R. Nicholson and his associates of the National Marine Fisheries Service Laboratory at Beaufort worked with commercial purse-seiners to tag over a million adult and juvenile menhaden from Florida to New York in the late 1960s and the early 1970s. His results were published in the September 1978 issue (Vol. I, No. 3) of *Estuaries,* the Journal of the Estuarine Research Federation.

Mortality from this tagging system is apparently variable and sometimes large; still, Nicholson got over 10 percent return on his tags, and a clear picture of the migration emerged. Fish tagged in a specific area were never caught south of that area, except in the fall fishery in Beaufort. The longer the period between tagging and recapture, the further north the tags were recovered. Thus, fish tagged in the Chesapeake turned up in plants as far north as Gloucester, Massachusetts, and Portland, Maine, as many as six years after tagging; but slightly over 20 percent of the recoveries came from plants at Beaufort during the fall. This basic pattern of northward migration by older fish holds for the menhaden tagged in the other areas as well.

Menhaden spawn primarily along the coast over the continental shelf. Greatest activity appears to be in winter south of Cape Hatteras, but some spawning occurs throughout the year as far north as New England. The juveniles, of varying sizes depending on when they hatch, move into the estuaries for their first summer. The estuaries thus are critical to the species' life cycle. The Chesapeake is probably the most valuable of these nurseries, but that statement will come as no surprise to anyone who has spent time up the Bay's tidal creeks in July and August.

While the juvenile fish move into the rivers and creeks, most adults stay in the mainstems of the estuaries or migrate up the coast, with the oldest, largest fish moving furthest north in the summer. Then, as temperatures drop, they head back down the coast in waves. In the early winter, off the Cape Lookout–Cape Fear area, they disappear. No one knows exactly where they go, which probably means that they disperse into deeper water. In the late winter and early spring, they return to the surface of inshore waters, school up in groups of like age and size, and head back up the coast.

Patterns of fish migration are fascinating and useful, but there are always exceptions without explanations. It is not unheard of for an angler on the Severn River above Annapolis to catch a nice pickerel in December and find a fresh 5-inch menhaden in its belly. Some years, large schools stay up one or another of the Bay's rivers all winter. The reasons are known only to the fish. Perhaps they do it just to keep good watermen and scientists humble.

Loons: Fall's Finest Fishermen?

It was a late fall Saturday 20 years ago. Captain Wallace Lewis, the legendary Reedville charter skipper, and several of his friends were going out aboard his *Hiawatha* to look for late-season rockfish in the mouth of the Potomac. He invited me along, and I accepted with pleasure.

The day was chilly, but I spent a lot of it up on *Hiawatha*'s fly bridge with a pair of binoculars, looking for fish. The pickings were slim, but at last I saw what I thought we were looking for a half-mile away: gulls diving and water boiling as baitfish found themselves trapped from above and below. I yelled down to the cabin in great excitement, and Captain Wallace pushed the big boat's throttles forward. Something in his face, though, told me that he didn't quite share my excitement.

We got to the scene in a matter of minutes, and the reasons for the skipper's reserve quickly showed themselves. A dozen common loons (*Gavia immer*) surfaced with satisfied looks on their faces. They had been driving the bait, not rockfish, and it was clear that they were just as effective at this tactic as a school of rock would have been. Their strong legs, set well back on their heavy, streamlined bodies, made them both fast and maneuverable underwater.

At the time, I didn't know that the Chesapeake even had loons, much less that they could drive bait so well, but Captain Wallace was certainly familiar with them. In his gracious way, he said, "I didn't want to disappoint you, but I was afraid that those gulls were diving on loons. There are a lot of 'em out here at this time of year." He was right. We saw over a hundred that day. All were in winter plumage, with white throats and breasts, and gray-brown backs.

It was highly appropriate to be introduced to the Chesapeake's loons by Wallace Lewis. In addition to his chartering skills, he is one of the finest menhaden captains ever to work the Bay, and, indeed, the Atlantic. It is no accident that he saw a lot of loons during his commercial fishing career. Those little forage fish are the main reason that the birds come here in the fall, according to preliminary data compiled over the past three years by Dr. Paul R. Spitzer, a research ornithologist.

Loons are as well loved and well studied in summer by people on North Country lakes as ospreys are by us here, but there is remarkably little known about their migrations or winter behavior. As far as we know now, the loons that spend fall and spring here come from the Great Lakes area and parts of Ontario. When they leave those warm-weather habitats, they appear to head for the nearest salt water with abundant food and minimal ice. The Chesapeake meets those requirements.

The birds need plenty of food to prepare for winter. They are recovering from breeding, raising their young, and making a long migration. In addition, they molt in January and February, so they will be flightless for a period of a month or more and thus limited in their ability to search for food. They need to pack in the calories during October and November.

Menhaden are rich in oil and protein (which is why we humans fish them so intensively). The young-of-the-year, now 3 to 4 inches long, are ideal loon food. The Chesapeake's rivers and creeks serve as vast menhaden nurseries each summer, and observers of those waterways are familiar with the cat's-paw patterns the young fish make as they feed near the surface on summer evenings. As the weather cools in the fall, they head out of the creeks and come together in massive schools in the lower rivers.

For loons intent on stocking up for the winter, these dense schools are excellent targets, just as they are for rockfish and blues, and for the gulls that pick scraps from everybody. Paul Spitzer calls these occasions "banquets" and theorizes that the loons literally follow the menhaden on their one- to two-month progress from the river mouths out to the main Bay and down to the Atlantic.

During the banquet season, Spitzer has come across some huge concentrations of loons, as many as 700 or more in the mouth of the Choptank in mid-November and over 600 off Coles Point in the Potomac a week later. On two occasions in December, he has found over 1,000 loons during three-hour searches in the open Chesapeake off Mobjack Bay and the mouth of the York River.

As winter comes, the menhaden swim out onto the continental shelf and down off the North Carolina coast, where they move offshore, disperse, and go into deep water until late February and March. The loons from the Chesapeake follow them down to the vicinity of Wilmington and Harker's Island, where enough other species of fish spend the winter on the shelf to tide the birds through their flightless molting period.

For anyone accustomed to thinking of loons as solitary creatures of remote northern lakes, this social behavior on the Bay appears out of character, but loons have presumably been following these behavior patterns for thousands of years. We just haven't been watching them long enough in enough different seasons.

Paul Spitzer believes that the Chesapeake has major importance for North America's loons. He estimates that at least 6,000 of them spend the fall here, with a lesser number in the spring. He has committed himself to a long-term research project to work out the details of their movements. His research will give us new insights into the behavior of these beautiful birds while they are here on the Bay.

The Riddle of the Eels

Armistead Saffer stood at the edge of a backwater at the head of Occupacia Creek, a tidal tributary of the Rappahannock, and beamed his flashlight into the clear brown water. A hundred 3-inch-long elvers were swimming back and forth, getting ready to climb the wet rocks at the sides of the spillway leading up into Hunter's Mill Lake. He stared at them and shook his head, knowing that these juvenile eels were a year old and several thousand miles from their birthplace. (At least that is what his well-respected science teacher had told him.)

Douglas Burke lives on the south bank of the James in Richmond, about 5 miles upriver from its fall line and 120 feet uphill from its banks. An intermittent stream runs through his back yard. One year, he was clearing brush beside it and found several large eels (2 to 3 feet long) buried in the mud. He, too, looked at them and marveled.

The Bay is full of American eels *(Anguilla rostrata)*: in open waters, tributaries like the Rappahannock, subtributaries like Occupacia, ponds like Hunter's Mill, and even upland streams like Douglas Burke's. Eels tend to be nocturnal, and most people here consider them ugly, slimy things, so they do not attract much attention—with one exception: Commercial watermen harvest them by the ton, partially for crab bait, but primarily for export to Northern Europe (see Larry Chowning's excellent *Harvesting the Chesapeake*). There, their tasty flesh is considered the finest of seafoods.

Some commercial eel fishermen are still working the Bay this month. It is not easy work, the world economic climate can depress the market, and competition from other countries is intense. The only watermen still at it are the specialists, the best professionals. But they are in the high season, potting the "silver eels" on their way out of the Bay. Most rivers have at least one or two boats working.

Those who harvest eels become fascinated by them. Their complex behavior patterns are remarkable. The story that Armistead had heard in school is widely accepted, with good reason, but it is recent knowledge. The European eel *(A. anguilla)*, a close relative of the American, has been a source of food and curiosity for centuries. It has also been a source of mystery. Most early naturalists had interesting theories, like the idea that eels were born spontaneously from mud. In midspring, elvers turned up in streams, but the most persistent efforts to find developmental stages failed.

This failure seems especially strange since adults and their habits came to be well known, especially to commercial and sport-fishermen in Europe. They knew, for example, that eels are tough and adaptable, able to live for surprisingly long periods in mud or out of water, as long as they don't dry out. (Their skins, it turns out, are richly supplied with blood vessels, allowing them to absorb oxygen directly from the air.)

They knew that eels are slow growers, with life spans up to 15 years. If an area is overfished, it can take years to recover.

Eels can be found in lakes at elevations above 3,000 feet. (They have even been found to make short migrations overland, mostly at night to avoid drying out.) In the fall, some eels undergo remarkable changes. Their heads and pectoral fins become pointed, and their eyes enlarge. They change color from yellowish brown with dirty white bellies ("yellow eels") to metallic silver with black backs. These are "silver eels," rich in fat and the most favored as food for humans. They themselves cease eating and move downriver toward the sea. None return.

For years, naturalists tried unsuccessfully to decipher the mysteries of the eel's life cycle. Meanwhile, in 1846, a German scientist caught an unknown fish in the Mediterranean. It was tiny, flat, and clear. He named it *Leucocephalus brevirostris*, placed it in a jar of alcohol, and described it in a scientific journal. Then everyone forgot it. But around the turn of the century, two Italian naturalists caught some more and kept them in a tank. Imagine their excitement when the tiny fish metamorphosed into elvers, unmistakably juvenile eels. Since then, the flat larval stage has been called the leucocephalus.

The stage was set now. In 1904, a Danish biologist, Johannes Schmidt, caught a leucocephalus off the Faroe Islands, in the North Atlantic. He sensed that he was onto something, so he began towing his plankton nets further south. For the next two years, he caught leucocephali by the hundreds.

Such research, however, was painstaking and costly, and Schmidt had little funding. When he could not afford to pay for an expedition with his own vessel, he talked steamship captains into towing nets for him. Over a space of 15 years, he pieced his data together into a working picture of the eel's life history. (There is a good account of his work in the 1981 Yearbook issue of the commercial fishing magazine *National Fisherman*. See also "Journey to the Sea" and "Return" in Rachel Carson's *Under the Sea Wind;* see Bibliography.)

There are still some discrepancies, but the basic story is this: the silver eels leave the ponds, lakes, streams, rivers, and estuaries in the fall for the open ocean. There they head for the Sargasso Sea, southeast of Bermuda, reaching it by spring. They spawn at an unknown but considerable depth, then die.

Eel larvae develop at sea and are carried by ocean currents to North America and Europe. The two species differ only in the number of vertebrae, and their spawning ranges appear to overlap. Just how they sort themselves out is still a mystery, though the North American larvae spend a year at sea, while the European larvae spend three.

In either case, by the time they reach their respective continents and change into elvers, they are about 3 inches long. That spring, they ascend the rivers, to places like the Hunter's Mill Lake spillway, and amaze and delight people like Armistead Saffer. Johannes Schmidt unlocked a wonderful puzzle.

Diatoms: Cold-Water Jewel Boxes

The water is getting colder, and the days are getting shorter. From the upper rivers to the open Bay, plants are responding to the change. Cordgrasses in the salt marshes have turned from gold to brown. In the fresh marshes, pickerelweed has withered away, and the wild rice has fallen over to become part of the stubble on the surface of the marsh. Many of the perennial plants like cattails have reabsorbed nutrients from their leaves and stored starch in their root systems. The annuals like millet and smartweed have left heavy crops of seeds.

In the open waters, most groups of phytoplankton (those microscopic plants that live in the upper layers and drift with the currents) are decreasing as the cooling water slows their metabolism. One group, however, is just building up. The Chesapeake's diatoms reach high concentrations in the fall and drop only a little through the winter.

Diatoms are the dominant group of phytoplankton for much of the Chesapeake's year, and they make major contributions of food and oxygen to the Bay's waters. They comprise a group of algae called Bacillariophyta, all microscopic and either unicellular (single-celled) or colonial (single cells attached together). There is a large group of benthic (bottom-dwelling) diatoms in the Bay, but even more are planktonic. In numbers and tonnage, these drifting diatoms are stunningly abundant. Concentrations can run to 10 million cells per liter (about a quart) of water.

Diatoms are best known for their frustules, cell walls of silica. The walls are made in two halves, with one fitting over the other. Silica is a common element in sand and quartz. We humans extract it mechanically from these minerals to make glass. Diatoms extract it physiologically from river water and Bay water, somewhat in the way that oysters and crabs extract calcium. Then they secrete it into all sorts of complex shapes in the frustules. A.J. Lippson, in her *Environmental Atlas of the Potomac Estuary* (see Bibliography), likens them to "intricately carved glass jewel boxes." Ladies and gentlemen interested in natural history during England's Edwardian period made a hobby of collecting diatoms, looking at them under microscopes and marvelling at their designs.

The shapes are wonderful to look at, but recent and current research is directed more to how diatoms fit into the Chesapeake system. Their siliceous frustules raise particularly interesting questions. They offer the diatoms both advantages and disadvantages.

All phytoplankton, diatoms included, have two basic needs: nutrients and sunlight. Sunlight is needed at least part of the time to photosynthesize food, so they must spend a significant portion of their lives (a day to a week or more, depending on temperature) in the upper levels of the water.

But they need nutrients too, essential building blocks. Because phytoplankton can bloom to dense concentrations, they can use up dissolved nutrients very quickly. A stationary alga cell suspended in

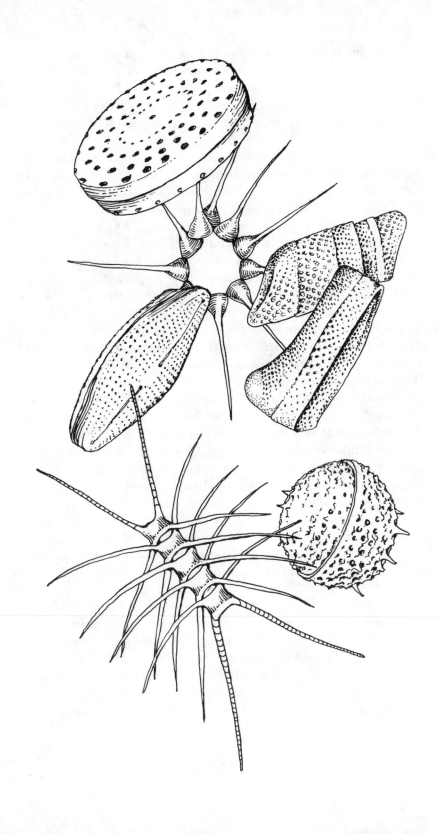

the water can easily run out of them. By sinking, the cell can come into contact with more water and thus increase the nutrients available to it. Sometimes there is an advantage in sinking all the way to the bottom, where nutrients collect. But sinking takes the cell away from sunlight, so it needs a way to get back to the surface too.

Silica is relatively dense, giving diatoms the potential to sink. But the diatom community has developed a strategy to rise to the surface again. Some species develop frustules that are broad, flat disks. Others build complex arrays of ribs, folds, horns, and spines, all of which tend to slow their sinking rates. The basic result is a group of plants that sink slowly in still water but rise to the surface with turbulent water.

A key part of the strategy is the diatoms' ability to grow well at lower water temperatures than most phytoplankton. Their populations are highest in fall, winter, and spring, when periodic stormy weather keeps the water stirred up. In the summer, when the Bay tends to stratify, with little mixing taking place between surface and deep water, the diatom community yields its dominance to the mobile dinoflagellates. For the rest of the year, however, the diatoms depend on sinking to provide them with nutrients, and on turbulence in the Chesapeake's relatively shallow waters to bring them back to the sunlight.

Studying the roles of diatoms in the Bay system brings together an elegant array of scientific disciplines. Physics and mathematics (calculus and statistics together) attempt to describe the transport mechanisms of turbulence and thus of cell movement. Sophisticated biochemical techniques offer insight into nutrient uptake and release. Both laboratory and field studies provide data on grazing by zooplankton such as copepods and fish larvae. Computer modelling gives a sense of the ways the community responds to environmental alterations due to man's activities and varying weather patterns.

This kind of systems approach will gradually uncover general principles to make the Bay easier to understand and manage. It is quite different from Edwardian collecting, exciting because it is close to the heart of understanding the Chesapeake system, and unsettling because it is enormously complex. For now, though, just think of all those jewel boxes drifting back into the light every time it storms this fall.

White Perch: A Fish for All Seasons

There were at least two things you could say about my Uncle Froggy de Bordenave: He loved fishing for white perch, and he loved eating them. The rest of the family went out to bottom fish for spot and hardheads, a more traditional catch on the Virginia side of the lower Potomac around Sandy Point.

Froggy, however, had a cottage on the Yeocomico River upriver of Lynch's Point, so his point of view was different. He would clamp his shiny black 4-hp Martin onto his skiff, chug up to the widgeon grass beds off Mundy Point, and anchor. Then he would cast a peeler crab–baited bottom rig underhanded into the bare sandy patches of open water scattered throughout the grass beds and wait for the perch. They were big and dark-colored, and they ran hard when hooked. He'd pick up a dozen for dinner and chug home.

Uncle Froggy's love for perch put him in the minority on the lower Potomac. Like many Virginians, the rest of the family said they preferred eating spot. Froggy just laughed, and told them they didn't know what they were missing. He would have found a lot of sympathetic company, however, up the Potomac around Colonial Beach, or up the Bay in Maryland towns like Rock Hall, where perch are more abundant and their taste more appreciated.

Perch are upper tidal river fish, generally preferring salinities from zero (fresh water) to about half that of seawater. Since the Upper Bay is the tidal Susquehanna, the biggest river flowing into the Chesapeake, perch are plentiful there. The Potomac near our house at Sandy Point, on the other hand, is too salty for perch to be comfortable most of the time.

Tidal rivers are rich places, but they change continuously. Saltwater inflow varies with the tides, which are influenced by the moon and the wind. At the same time, varying rainfall patterns affect the inflow of fresh water from the rivers' watersheds. The balance between salt and fresh shifts constantly over the course of a year.

Even though they stay out of the lower Potomac and the lower Bay, white perch adapt well to salinity changes within what is actually a broader range than most fish can tolerate, and thus they are able to enjoy the rivers' abundant food. They are omnivorous and remarkably predatory, eating grass shrimp, seaworms, small clams, and minnows, or whatever is abundant at the moment.

The white perch has an equally broad temperature tolerance, living in river systems from upper South Carolina to the Canadian Maritime Provinces, plus ponds, lakes in New England, and Lakes Erie and Ontario. This characteristic is helpful to the perch that live among the temperature variations that exist on the Bay, because the fish are active nearly the whole year, becoming dormant only in the very coldest weather. My friend and "perch professor," Bill Pike, fishes them from early March until ice and snow drive him off the water in the dead of winter.

White perch spawn in the spring at very low salinities and at water temperatures of 50° to 60°F, about the same temperature as the spawn of its close cousin, the rockfish. However, most perch spawn even further upstream where water tends to warm more quickly, so they are generally a week or two earlier than rockfish. Especially favored perch spawning areas on the Chesapeake include the Rappahannock just below Fredericksburg, the Potomac between Chain Bridge and Little Falls, and the Susquehanna above Havre de Grace.

After the spawn, young of the year stay upriver for the summer, foraging in shallow backwaters, while adults spread out downriver, hanging around old wharves and bridge pilings and, where dissolved oxygen is good, over oyster bars. A river may have several populations living in different habitats at the same time. As fall approaches and the water cools, more of them head out to open water.

By the time the fall rockfish season closes in Maryland, white perch are the only game in town for Bay anglers. Many people put their boats away, but a few savvy fishermen like Bill Pike stay out there. They know how much fun perch are to catch on light tackle, and how especially good they taste when taken from cold water.

Bay-wide, white perch are valuable for both sport and commercial fisheries. Virginia's perch fisheries are localized in the upper tidal portions of the big western shore rivers where harvest pressure is relatively light. Commercial landings of perch average about one-fifth of Maryland's catch, and recreational pressure is even less. White perch are definitely an underharvested and underappreciated resource in Virginia.

In Maryland, annual commercial landings varied generally from 500,000 to 1 million pounds prior to imposition of the striped bass moratorium at the beginning of 1985. Then catches declined below 500,000 pounds because of restrictions on areas, seasons, and gear that were designed to reduce by-catch (incidental harvest) of rockfish. Commercial perch fishermen shifted from gill nets to fyke nets, which catch fewer rockfish and permit live release of any that turn up.

The recreational harvest was estimated to be roughly equal to the commercial harvest in the 1970s and the early eighties. The fish are a major resource in the upper Bay for shore anglers at Fort Smallwood on the Patapsco near Baltimore, small boat fishermen launching at Sandy Point State Park by the Bay Bridge, and charter boats running out of Rock Hall, the Magothy, and Middle River. Because the fish live in so many different kinds of habitat, it is possible to fish for them in an interesting variety of ways.

One of the problems, however, for a good-tasting panfish that congregates in schools is that people tend to measure angling success in wholesale quantities. It's one thing to bring home a couple of dozen perch but quite another to take a coolerful. Reproduction in most of the Bay's rivers appears to have been reasonably strong in the past few years, so the recreational and commercial fisheries are expected to hold up, at least in the short run. There is much that is still not known, though, about the relationship between white perch production and harvest. The Maryland Department of Natural Resources is beginning to formulate a management plan designed to keep catches within sustainable levels. We don't want perch to go through a decline like rockfish.

Perch deserve to be harvested with wisdom and appreciation. Uncle Froggy had the right idea.

The "Other" Mollusks

Clams in the Chesapeake are not widely known. Two different species, the softshell clam or manno (*Mya arenaria*) and the hard clam (*Mercenaria mercenaria*), are harvested commercially, but most of the catch is shipped outside the Bay. Mannoes grow best up the

Bay, and hard clams down, so people in different sections of Bay country have different pictures of what the word *clam* means. To confuse the situation more, there are several other species of clams and the closely related mussels that are not harvested by man to any great extent. Even so, these relatively unknown mollusks play important roles in their own communities.

Whenever Joe and Ilia Fehrer paddle their canoe on the upper Pocomoke (which is often), they always keep their eyes out for shells on the banks. The river's freshwater clams (*Unio* spp.) are food for otters and raccoons, who carry them up onto the banks to pry or bite them open. Unio clams are also called freshwater mussels. They live in loose mud, and they taste like it, so they have little value as food for humans. But they once were harvested across the eastern United States for their pearly inner shells, which were cut into buttons. Plastics put an end to the trade, and now the animals are back to the relative safety of obscurity. The freshwater sections of most of the Bay's tidal rivers grow them.

In the low- and medium-salinity sections of the rivers lives the brackish-water clam (*Rangia cuneata*). The animal lives in both sand and mud, and it tends to take on the taste of the bottom area in which it is living. Sometimes that is clean sand, in which case the clam has a good taste. River-wise humans gather these with quiet smiles, steam them, and eat them with relish. Most of the Rangia clams, though, live in mud and so have little to fear from man. Seagulls take to them, however. They pick up larger clams, fly aloft, and drop them onto hard surfaces to crack them. The bayside parking lot of the Westinghouse Oceanic Division research laboratory, at the western end of the Bay Bridge, is littered with fragments of Rangia shells.

This clam is to be admired for its adaptability. It lives well in low salinities, and it can tolerate turbid water that would suffocate other clams. When tropical storm Agnes hit the Chesapeake in June 1972, it drastically lowered the salinity of the whole system and poured in millions of tons of sediment. Many of the Bay's clams died, but the conditions that killed them spread the Rangia clams into places where they had not lived before. That winter, waterfowl returning to the Bay from Canada found wrecked aquatic vegetation and clam bars, but they also found beds teeming with small Rangias. Over the next couple of winters, the Rangia population grew, and the clams became a staple in the diets of several water-fowl, especially canvasback ducks and whistling (tundra) swans.

Waterfowl swallow small clams whole and grind them up in their gizzards. In addition to the canvasbacks and swans, diving ducks like scoters and oldsquaws consider clams and small mussels staple foods. Two particularly important species are *Macoma balthica*, a small, soft-shelled clam that lives best at medium and high salinities, and *Ischadium recurvum*, the hooked mussel, which lives in the same salinities and attaches to firm substrates like oyster shells and pilings. In warm weather, both species are also important to bottom-feeding fish, especially spot and croakers, who dig them out and swallow them wholesale. Open the intestinal tract of a big spot from the lower Bay, and chances are there will be enough shell fragments in there to pave a road. It is remarkable that the fragments don't damage the intestines as they pass through.

One other mollusk deserves mention, and that is the ribbed mussel *(Modiolus demissus)*, which often lives half-buried in the banks of salt marshes. This animal filters food from the water at high tide and closes tightly as the water drops, to avoid drying out.

A mussel attaches to its substrate by a bundle of strong threads called a byssus. The threads are made of keratin, a tough protein fiber which also occurs in human hair. Byssal threads are so tough that, in Brittany, fishermen's wives used to knit their husbands' work gloves from those of the blue mussel *(Mytulis edulis)*, a relative of the ribbed mussel much esteemed for its flavor and native to Europe and New England. *Modiolus* will never support a great market, but it is edible and worth gathering for steaming. Anyone who does so will realize just how strong the byssus is. The ribbed mussel is most important in the Bay as a favored winter food for raccoons living around the salt marshes.

The Chesapeake's most sporting clam is the stout razor *(Tagelus plebius)*. Digging it is a pursuit that expends more calories than the digger gets from eating it. Stout razors live in sand or firm mud. One can harvest them from the shallow flats where they live by looking for holes on the surface and then digging into the burrows below. This is most easily done when low tide uncovers the flats. It sounds simple—no equipment needed. But stout razors are tricky. They are generally 12 to 18 inches deep to begin with, and they can dig fast. The digger, then, kneels on the mud and begins digging with one hand down into the burrow. With luck, it will be possible to get three or four fingers around the clam and, with gentle pressure, force it to release its hold on the mud. But sometimes the digger can get only a couple of fingers onto the clam—not enough to pull with. And sometimes a clam will just keep on digging, leaving its pursuer up to the armpit in the hole, fingers grasping only watery mud. Stout razors live in medium and high salinities on flats around the salt marshes of places like Tangier Sound, Gwynn's Island, and Poquoson. Digging them means getting wet and muddy, so it is best done in a bathing suit in warm weather. But that means greenhead fly season. It is painful to have one arm stuck down a burrow while half a dozen greenheads go to work on your back. Digging stout razor clams requires a sense of humor.

One serious caution: there may be shell fragments with sharp corners buried among the burrows. Moving a hand suddenly could cause a deep cut that might require stitches. So, before digging, check a flat carefully for broken shells. In any case, digging stout razors will cause small nicks in the fingers. It is a good idea to rub these with a thin coating of antibacterial ointment to minimize infection and speed healing.

After all this, stout razors are often gritty. Put them into a pan of fresh Bay water with a cup of cornmeal and set them in the shade for an hour or so. Then steam them and eat them with melted butter. They are an aesthetic exercise from start to finish, but that is the way a sporting proposition should be.

In the end, many of the Chesapeake's clams live their lives with minimal human interference. They are, however, vital members of the Bay community. Consider, for example, what a ribbed mussel is worth in late November to a hungry raccoon trying to keep its body temperature up on a cold night, or a *Macoma* clam to a young canvasback duck exhausted by its migration from the Saskatchewan prairies. Studying a less well known member of the Bay community is often a good window to understanding it better.

WINTER

GENE JETT, who for many years owned a marina on the Little Wicomico at Smith Point, used to say he fished rockfish "till the weather shut in after Christmas." That was in the days before strict rockfish seasons, but the weather does begin to shut in now. Some years it does so sooner and harder than others.

Any way you figure it, though, there are always some basic changes in the Bay around the first of the year. The weather turns cold and stays that way. A lot of creatures that had been intermittently active, like rockfish and crabs, become almost completely dormant in the warmest and most stable environment they can find, usually the deep trenches in the open Bay and at the mouths of the big rivers. (See January's "Crabs in Winter.") Every cold-blooded animal from seaworm and barnacle to white perch and even the ubiquitous killifish (see January's "Killifish Are Tough") slows down. Oysters feed through December, till Gene's "shut-in" time, but then the water temperature closes them down, too.

Historically, early winter was a time to celebrate the Chesapeake's oysters. They are in such deep trouble now, though, that the most appropriate response to the season is to think about how much of a role they play in the way the Bay works. (See December's "How Oysters Eat, and What They Mean to the Bay.")

Only warm-blooded animals—the birds like swans (see December's "Swan Time"), geese, ducks, herons, and eagles (see February's "Eagles Nesting"); and the mammals like muskrats (see December's "Muskrats and Winter Marshes"), river otters (see February's "Otters Are Busy Now"), and raccoons—are still active. For most of the Bay's residents, this is a time for sleep, a time when life is unobtrusive.

For those of us who love to explore the Bay, it is a time to be conservative, a time to respect the dangers of hypothermia and limit our travels on the water to carefully planned, unambitious trips with wide safety margins. It is a good time to read and think, to learn about subjects like the Chesapeake's origins and what was here before this Bay (see December's "Miocene Fossils: Putting Bay Time into Perspective"), to find a good place for quiet walks beside the water, and to contemplate the Bay landscape stripped to its bare bones (see January's "Winter's Extra-Low Tides").

For those who love to walk, winter is an especially good time to study the Chesapeake's wonderful collection of waterfowl. Like the oysters, they were once thought to be inexhaustible and are now in trouble, but there are still enough around to make them one of winter's finest features. (See January's "Waterfowl Joys and Sorrows" and February's "Sea Ducks Relish Winter on the Chesapeake.")

Winter is also a time for death. Phytoplankton and zooplankton populations drop to their lowest levels of the year, and in the process they give the Bay its clearest water. Cold temperatures slow their metabolism, and thus their rates of growth and reproduction.

Many of the zooplankton are tiny crustaceans with short life spans—copepods and water fleas. As the water temperature drops, the time between generations becomes longer. Adults die, and their young are slow to replace them. There are several species that die off almost completely in winter and are replaced by other species more amenable to low temperatures. Even so, the overall concentration of zooplankton declines sharply.

As these creatures die, they sink to the bottom. This process goes on constantly throughout the year as generation succeeds generation; but especially as the temperature drops, the surface layers literally rain dead plankton. Since zooplankton graze heavily on phytoplankton, this rain indirectly includes much of the fall's phytoplankton production. Thus, by early winter, much of the food in the open waters of the Bay and its tributaries has found its way to the bottom.

Along the shores, the marsh plants have already died, each species in its own fashion. Wild rice, for example, is an annual. All the rice plants died in the fall, and now most of the stalks are matted brown stubble. Dotted smartweed and tearthumb, the rice's neighbors in the fresh marshes, have died also. Pickerelweed, arrow arum, yellow pond lily, and cattails are perennial, so their rootstocks are alive under the mud, but their leaves and stalks are dead and decaying. In the salt marshes, all the significant plants are perennial; hence their soil-holding power. But all the cordgrasses' leaves and stalks are dead brown now, and the saltbushes have dropped their leaves.

Winter rains, winds, snow, and ice break the dead plants and stalks down into small pieces in the process called weathering. Fresh marshes turn into bare mud banks with some ragged patches of stubble. By mid-March, even that is gone. Saltmarsh plants break down much more slowly, but they too show the effects of winter weather. Cordgrass marshes, for example, look particularly battered after heavy snowfalls.

But death leads to regeneration. The Chesapeake's biotic community does not waste much. Metabolisms are slow on the Bay's bottom now, but the benthic invertebrates have all winter to ruminate on the tiny corpses that have descended upon them. As the fragments sink into the mud, seaworms eat their way through them. The undigested and partially digested material they leave behind is colonized by bacteria which break it all the way down to inorganic nutrients like phosphates and nitrates. The worms become valuable fish food. The nutrients, like broad compost piles, build up over the winter and are resuspended in the surface layers when spring weather and overturn stir up the bottom. Once back to the surface, they become the building blocks for the new year's first plankton blooms.

While the worms move through the bottom mud, other invertebrates filter and sort scraps of dead zooplankton, putting them to similar uses. The scraps are essential food for oysters, clams, sea squirts, anemones, barnacles, amphipods, and mud crabs. All these animals return undigested and partially digested material to the bottom, for bacteria to colonize and decompose. If the bottom water gets too cold for the invertebrate community to feed, the material simply stays on the bottom till temperatures rise. Thus the invertebrates have abundant food on into spring, while nutrients build up for phytoplankton.

The marshes too assure regeneration. Last year's rice plants left behind many grains. Some fed blackbirds and teal, but some are still in the mud, waiting to germinate in spring. The fertility of the mud will be ensured by the composting piles of last year's stalks. Winter weather also assures that a significant percentage of last year's leaf and stalk production will end up out in the marsh guts, creeks, and rivers as a vegetable soup of tiny particles of decayed plant material. This will fuel major zooplankton blooms in early spring, just in time to feed juvenile spot, striped bass, and other fish.

Winter is important to the Bay system. (See "Cold Water Brings a Quiet Season.") Cold weather's harshness lays the groundwork for warm weather's bounty.

DECEMBER

How Oysters Eat, and What They Mean to the Bay

It is hard to empathize with an oyster. Not that we never have the chance. Shucking them and eating them on the half shell give us plenty of opportunity to examine the animals. But their body plans are so different from ours that it is difficult sometimes to remember that they share the basic processes of life with us. How do oysters eat? It is easy enough to forget that they eat at all.

An oyster on the half shell is a mass of gray and tan tissue. There is no feature there that resembles anything human, as there is in a bird or a fish or even a crab. In the center is a muscle, the adductor, used to close the shell and hold it shut. Around the adductor is a large, rounded digestive sac that may, on close examination, show some fluids circulating. And there are gills, four flat layers of tissue that lie in a long curve beside the digestive sac, forming a band between it and the shell. Tiny ridges radiate across the gills from sac to shell. This much is visible at a raw bar.

But the system that fattens the oyster enough to get it to the raw bar is remarkably complex. The animal is an intricate system of pumps and filters. It is capable of straining 50 gallons of water a day, all the while discriminating between what is edible and what is not, ingesting what is, and discarding the rest. Heavy sedimentation of its bed can choke it, though it can deal with some suspended mud particles and reject them.

The central part of the gill system is a coordinated group of ciliae, tiny hairs on the gill surface that wiggle in concert. Some of them set up the currents that bring water and suspended particles in between an oyster's two shells as they are opened slightly. Other ciliae capture light organic particles in the water, while heavier inorganic particles fall into the troughs between the gill ridges.

"Organic particles" is a very general term. For the oyster, it refers to phytoplankton, bacteria, and detritus (decayed but once alive material). Phytoplankton appear to be the most nutritious and therefore the most desirable food. "Inorganic particles" means the fine mud that is usually suspended in the water close to the bottom over oyster beds. When these particles fall into the gill troughs, mucous glands stick them together in globs called pseudofeces, which are carried by the water currents to the edge of the shell and dumped out.

The lighter food particles, meanwhile, are carried from ridge to ridge toward the top of the oyster. The sorting system is not perfect, so some sediment is carried, too, but most of it is eliminated.

Near the top of the oyster are two pairs of palps, folds of tissue like the gills but smaller. They cover the mouth. The palps have ridges and ciliae too, but they also have chemoreceptors which can taste food. Further sorting occurs here. The ciliae sweep food toward the mouth, but the troughs between the ridges are wide, and any particles whose taste the oyster does not like will be allowed to fall into them, to be coated with mucus and swept out. When a preferred particle comes across, the oyster can close off the troughs, allowing the food to pass to the mouth. By this time, the food is caught in strings of mucus, which may be wound into the mouth and the digestive sac by the *crystalline style*, a protein rod that rotates in the sac.

Some food is broken down and absorbed on the crystalline style and the inner surface of the digestive sac. But with water passing through the oyster in huge quantities, it is all too easy for food and digestive enzymes to be carried out and lost. Thus much of the digestion is done by special cells that engulf the food, digest it within their cell membranes, and pass proteins, sugars, and fats on to other cells that need them.

For a filter feeder, summer should be a prime time, since the water is thick with phytoplankton and other oyster food. In fact, however, it is a hard time for oysters. They are spawning for most of it (a big effort, since a prime female may produce 10 million to 100 million eggs in a summer), and, toward the end of the season, dissolved oxygen levels in their waters are often low. Spawning and low oxygen cause them stress, especially on the deeper bars.

Fall brings relief, as the dissolved oxygen levels at the bottom increase. Though temperatures fall slowly from September to January, the water is the warmest at the bottom, where the oysters are. They can feed down to a temperature of about 5°C (41°F), which means that, in all but the coldest winters, they are feeding right through December. There is plenty of food—algae, leftover detritus from summer, and debris from the fall bloom of zooplankton. With the metabolic demands of egg and sperm production at low levels, the oysters can use most of their food to fill out and fatten up. Cold weather helps keep them firm.

They will cease feeding when the winter really shuts in, and live on their reserves of fat, glycogen (animal starch), and protein. Quality of meat will drop slowly till spring. The drop will not be enough to make them unappetizing, but they will not be as plump then as they are now. It is a happy coincidence that just as the weather gets chilly and our bodies start needing sturdy food like oyster stew, scalloped oysters, and a dozen on the half shell, the oysters themselves are in prime eating condition.

The oyster's eating system is well adapted to concentrating food, even in a poor environment. Thus it is no wonder that a rich estuary like the Chesapeake has produced so many of them. For literally thousands of years, from the Early Woodland Native Americans through European settlement and up to the mid-1980s, the Bay's oysters have been its most valuable seafood resource.

The last hundred years, however, have shown an inexorable decline. Today, they are in grave crisis, with harvests a shocking 1 percent—*a hundredfold decrease*—of what they were at the end of the nineteenth century. Imagine what a contraction like that means to the business people in the industry, from watermen to packing-house operators and employees. Imagine the broader economic and social impacts on the towns around the Bay, and the increased pressure on other fisheries, especially for crabs, as watermen look for other sources of income.

It is not only watermen who have lost out. It is all of us, and not just in the fact that what few oysters we still have are expensive. Max Chambers, who operates the Flomax oyster hatchery on the lower Eastern Shore, likens a Chesapeake with too few oysters to a big pasture without enough cows: there isn't enough grazing, so the grasses get out of hand. Oysters not only "graze down" phytoplankton (at a time when the Bay's high nutrient levels are growing more tonnage of the tiny plants than ever before), they also package suspended sediment particles into larger sticky pseudofeces which settle to the bottom, as explained above. Scientists estimate that, a hundred years ago, a volume equal to all the water in the Bay circulated through the oyster population every four days. That filtering capacity is all but gone—current estimates are that the process now takes over *400* days.

The other loss is "live bottom," the diverse community of living things that grows up on an oyster reef (or "rock"). Worms, sponges, anemones, barnacles, and shrimplike amphipods all find hard oyster shells to be excellent habitat. Small fish like silversides and bottom feeders like white perch, spot, and croakers find these rocks to be virtual storehouses of food. They in turn attract larger fish like trout, rockfish, bluefish, and drum, and other large predators like us. It is no accident that most good bottom fishermen know what an oyster rock looks like on their sonar sets; but they are finding to their dismay that these live bottom areas are becoming fewer and smaller.

What has happened? How could we have lost something as valuable as our oysters, in spite of state programs to save them? The loss is the result of a combination of factors, some subtle and some not so subtle. Low oxygen is one. Oysters don't need as much as fish and crabs, but they do need some, and they can't move when conditions get bad. Likewise, they can't get out of the way of silt, and while they can handle a limited amount, they suffocate all too easily under a heavy coating. Spat (very young oysters) are particularly susceptible to suffocation. Silt has become an insidious pollutant in the Chesapeake, an unwanted but copious by-product of all the changes we make to the face of its watershed.

In times of less silt, strong, healthy populations of spat settled on existing oyster rocks and built up these rocks faster than silt could cover them. Heavy overharvesting reduced both the height of the rocks and the brood stock for spat production, a double whammy that drastically reduced the Bay's natural oyster reproduction. Even shell and seed plantings by state programs and private growers were not enough to reverse the decline.

The stage was set for two mysterious diseases, MSX and Dermo. The former decimated beds in the high-salinity parts of the Bay in the 1960s and gradually worked its way up-Bay and up the rivers, advancing in dry years when salinities rose. Droughts in 1980, '81, '85, '86, '87, and '88 allowed it to spread like wildfire through both Virginia and Maryland, sparing only the farthest-up-river bars like those above the Route 301 bridge on the Potomac and around the Bay Bridge on the mainstem. What beds MSX did not kill, Dermo has infected, and it is tolerant of lower salinities than MSX, so the wetter summers of 1990 and 1991 did not deter it at all.

The diseases are stubborn adversaries. Nearly four decades of research on Delaware Bay (where MSX has also wreaked havoc) and three decades on the Chesapeake have revealed remarkably little about the life cycles of the disease organisms or ways to avoid their impact by establishing wild populations of disease-resistant oysters.

The picture is bleak, but it is *not* barren. Necessity has fostered ingenuity. Some private growers are producing limited quantities of excellent oysters by using experimental techniques like growing hatchery-reared spat in trays suspended off the bottom. The Chesapeake *can* still produce the fat, tasty oysters for which it is famous. The issue is how to rebuild the wild oyster stocks.

It is time for tough choices, like whether or not to close the fishery; this would give the surviving oysters, which presumably have some resistance to the diseases, a chance to propagate and repopulate without interference. Other questions involve how much of a role aquaculture can play, and whether it should be practiced by private growers in Maryland, which has strongly favored its public fishery instead. How much money can the states put up to pay watermen to help rebuild the oyster rocks into high reefs? How much money should be invested in research on MSX and Dermo, especially at a time when money is tight?

State agencies, watermen, research scientists, and conservation organizations together are debating these questions. That debate is fierce at times, because the choices are so tough, but it must continue until a workable plan is developed and put into practice.

Two things are sure: first, our love of oysters continues, especially at this time of year when they are at their best, and the Bay can produce a limited number of them for us as long as we allow harvesting; second, there will be no quick or easy answers to restoring the stocks. We can only hope that the former continues long enough to make us persevere through the latter. A Chesapeake without its oysters is not a healthy Bay.

Swan Time

You can almost set your fall calendar by them. They're not quite as precise as ospreys in March, but they're close. Sometime shortly after November 15, a cold front will sweep through the Bay country. That night, if you listen carefully, you'll hear them—tundra swans (*Cygnus columbianus*, formerly known as whistling swans) flying in for the winter. They'll sound at first like geese, but the honks are higher-pitched and more quavery, with the even-higher-pitched "wheeps" of the young birds (cygnets) mixed in.

Over the next few days, small groups will filter into the Bay, heading to the Blackwater National Wildlife Refuge on the Eastern Shore near Cambridge, or to the mouth of the Rappahannock River, Back Bay near Virginia Beach, or Lake Mattamuskeet in North Carolina.

More small groups will arrive, and then a week later, after another cold front, a day will come when the big birds pour onto the Bay, a continuous stream of flocks ranging in size from 10 to 100 birds. They'll sleep a lot for a day or two and then settle into their winter routines.

The swans have a right to be tired; they've flown nearly non-stop some 1,500 miles from the North Dakota prairie pothole country. Even with the tailwinds behind the fronts, it's a long haul.

The swans typically spend the last half of October and the first half of November resting and feeding in North Dakota, where the pothole marshes make a good halfway point. Their summer breeding grounds are the tundra of the Canadian Arctic coast, the North Slope of Alaska, and the Bering Straits. Most of the birds from the Bering Straits (about 40,000) go down the Pacific flyway to the

Sacramento River delta, but those from the other breeding grounds, another 30,000 or so, come to the Atlantic. It's an amazingly long migration by any measure, but it's especially remarkable that the cygnets make the trip at the age of five months.

If we could interview the adult birds, we'd find that most have returned to the same places they wintered last year. These migrations have been going on for thousands of years, so there must be some long family traditions involved. That's speculation, of course, but we know an amazing amount about what has been going on for the past 20 years because of a remarkable research program at the Johns Hopkins University.

Dr. William J. L. Sladen and his associates have banded several thousand swans with colored, numbered, plastic neck collars. These are in addition to the U.S. Fish and Wildlife Service leg bands that all marked birds must carry. A few birds tagged by Dr. Sladen have also carried tiny radio transmitters.

Both the neck collars and the transmitters fall off in time (the former in several years, the latter within a couple of months), but in the meantime, they yield large quantities of data. The great value of the collars is that they can be read with a 20× to 45× spotting scope. Thus the birds need not be recaptured and handled for researchers to gather data on their travels. It also means that lay people can help with the data collecting, and a number of Bay region residents have gotten involved as amateur observers.

Sladen and his associates have been able to work out many of the details of when swans migrate, under what conditions, and where. The original work was supported in part by the U.S. Air Force, which is interested in bird/aircraft strike hazards. A 20-pound swan flying at 40 miles an hour can do as much damage to a plane as a cannonball. Sladen's data help pilots in the eastern United States avoid routes and altitudes frequented by the swans during migration times (early November and late March).

The neck collar sightings carried out here on the Bay, at Lake Mattamuskeet, along the bird's migration routes in the Midwest, and on the Arctic tundra have provided details on where individuals go. These data give us a remarkable look into the private world of the tundra swan, demonstrating that they are indeed creatures of habit. In addition to using the same wintering grounds year after year, they breed in the same areas of the tundra each spring.

Why do the swans make such a long trek back and forth across the continent? We can only speculate, but a large part of the answer may be that the wintertime Chesapeake is the closest coastal body of water that provides plenty of food and reasonably ice-free conditions. Birds from the Canadian Arctic and Alaska's North Slope come this way because they have a migration corridor that provides them with the waterways—prairie potholes and the Great Lakes—they need for feeding and safe roosting at night.

In the end, it is probably the Bay's creeks, coves, and shallow flats that bring the birds to us. The swan's traditional foods are small shellfish, especially the small soft-shelled clam *Macoma balthica*, and the rootstocks, tubers, and seeds of submerged aquatic vegetation. Up through the 1960s, there was plenty of both to keep the swans well fed.

During the period in which Dr. Sladen has studied the swans, there have been shifts in their wintering patterns. The reasons are all too familiar. The acreage of Bay grasses has declined drastically. Even though there have been recent rebounds in some areas, there is still much less than there was 25 years ago.

Without this staple food, the swans return to their traditional haunts, feed on clams for a short period, and move on. They are big, warm-blooded creatures who need lots of food to keep up their body temperatures, even with their swansdown parkas on. There simply aren't enough small clams in a river like the Severn, near Annapolis, to hold them for any length of time. Twenty years ago, 2,000 swans wintered there, feeding on huge grassy beds of redhead pondweed (*Potamogeton perfoliatus*). But the grass is gone. Now a few birds (maybe several dozen) drop in for a week at most before moving on.

Fortunately, we haven't lost our swans to other regions, yet. As creatures of habit, they keep coming to the Bay and are at least somewhat adaptable. As the grasses disappeared, they began to move into farm fields to feed with the Canada geese. Early in the year, they forage for scrap grain, and later they graze on cover crops. National wildlife refuges like Blackwater and Mattamuskeet, which are managed for waterfowl, also hold thousands.

A few flocks settle in around communities where people put out corn for them, like Hillsmere Shores on the South River near Annapolis. Feeding swans is a big responsibility. Anyone who begins must continue every day, and a flock of 30 birds can go through half a ton of corn a month. Nevertheless, corn is addictive to swans, and swans in turn to people, so many residents feed the flocks year after year. It should be no surprise that neck collar studies show these birds to be the same individuals each winter.

Thanks to the birds' adaptability, the Bay's winter swan population is still strong. We can only hope that if we reverse the decline in water quality, the grasses will continue to come back, and the birds will return to some of their old haunts on the rivers. (The farmers wouldn't mind. Swans can cause significant crop depredation, and their big feet compact soil.)

Tundra swans are spectacular citizens of winter on the Chesapeake. We have good opportunities to enjoy watching them, and we have a responsibility to them as well as to ourselves to make the Bay a place worth returning to each winter.

Muskrats and Winter Marshes

My daughter Kelly and her friend Stacey were rowing a small boat around a salt pond on the Severn above Annapolis one summer day. Kelly noticed some sprigs of cordgrass floating on the surface near a pocket marsh. "Look," she said, "A muskrat has been here." "Huh?" said Stacey. "How do you know?" "See?" said Kelly, "They've all been bitten off." Sure enough, each stalk had been cut at a 45-degree angle near the base. "You mean they eat grass?" asked Stacy. "That's weird." "It is not. Haven't you ever chewed a grass stem?" queried Kelly. She rowed over to the marsh, pulled several stems of grass out from their bases, and peeled them down to their tender parts. Stacey screwed up her courage and took a bite. "Hey, that's good," she said. "It tastes like celery, but salty and sweet at the same time. Maybe muskrats aren't so weird after all."

Muskrats are the Chesapeake's most abundant aquatic mammals. The species (*Ondatra zibethicus*) breaks down into 16 subspecies that range over most of North America. The animals are rodents, related to moles, mice, beavers, and squirrels. Muskrats measure 10 to 16 inches long, with 5 to 7 inches of scaly, nearly hairless tail. Weight for adults in the Bay is 2 to 3 pounds, with males being slightly heavier than females. The animal's coat color generally ranges from rusty red-brown to nearly black, though

several color mutations are known. Soft, dense fur grows under long, glossy guard hairs. Muskrats swim well, chugging across the surface by kicking their webbed hind feet and diving when necessary to feed or to avoid danger. In general, they are most active at night.

At the front of a muskrat's upper and lower jaws are paired, sharp incisor teeth (hence the neat cuts on Kelly and Stacey's cordgrass sprigs) with rows of molars behind for chewing plant food thoroughly. The animals primarily eat the tender parts of submerged vegetation and marsh plants. In the Chesapeake region, their major foods are narrowleaf cattail in freshwater marshes and a bulrush, Olney threesquare *(Scirpus americanus)*, in brackish marshes. As noted by Kelly and Stacey, they also eat a good deal of saltmarsh cordgrass. Locally, this diet opens up hundreds of thousands of marshland acres to muskrats, especially the broad threesquare marshes of Dorchester County below Cambridge on the Eastern Shore. In addition, the large meander curves on major rivers offer brackish marshes with communities of cattails, bulrushes, and cordgrasses growing side by side.

With so much food available, muskrats are highly prolific. They produce litters through most of the year, though the peak period is March to September. Females bear two to five young per litter and can produce three litters a year. Kit mortality is high. Over half of a litter may die in the first year from disease or predation. Adult mortality is high too. Predators include marsh hawks, raccoons, foxes, and man. Maximum life span in the wild appears to be four years, but the average is one or two. Muskrats grow fast, breed fast, and die fast.

It is easy to get a feel for the muskrat's life-style in warm weather. Kelly and Stacey were exploring Ray's Pond in August, and the cordgrass was still green and growing. Now it is winter: the grass is dead, at least aboveground; the water is very cold; and the marshes are iced over part of the time. Muskrats are especially interesting now because they are one of the few species on the Bay that are active in winter.

Their major strategy for cold weather is to build shelters. On the rivers and creeks, some muskrats dig burrows into the banks. On the open marshes, they build lodges. These are 4 to 6 feet in diameter and 2 to 3 feet high, usually rounded or oval, with one or two chambers inside and a couple of exits to leads cut through the marsh. Materials come from whatever plants are readily available, and the lodges are reasonably well insulated. Often a system of short leads will connect the lodge with several feed huts, smaller and simpler shelters close to food supplies where a muskrat can get out of the weather to eat.

Winter food foraging on the Bay requires a change in behavior because there are no tender shoots to eat. Instead, the muskrats concentrate on digging into the marsh peat for the starchy rootstocks of cattails and bulrushes. A very hard freeze can make digging difficult, so the animals will dive below whatever ice is present and burrow into marsh banks from the side to find food. Finally, if necessary, they will switch to animal foods like clams, grass shrimp, and killifish.

Shelter building and resourceful ways of feeding are important behavioral strategies. Muskrats also have a physiological one: their coats grow denser and glossier in winter, increasing their insulating and water-repelling qualities. While it is possible for a muskrat to stay in the water too long and get wet through to the skin, the animal usually avoids this situation by using its shelter and lead system to minimize exposure.

For us, it is difficult to understand how a warm-blooded mammal can live in an aquatic habitat in the dead of winter. The lessons are clear—the food value in the stalk hearts and rootstocks of marsh plants is remarkably high; the huts provide snug housing; and muskrat fur is a very efficient insulation system. There is plenty to admire in this little rodent.

Miocene Fossils: Putting Bay Time into Perspective

Brent Heath climbed out of his canoe, bent over, and felt around on the bottom like a big raccoon. Grinning, he straightened up with a huge scallop shell and a chunk of coral in his hands. We were on Dragon Run at the headwaters of the Piankatank, near the Route 17 bridge at Saluda.

The Dragon is fresh, a dark-water stream winding through a long, narrow cypress swamp. Nothing like that scallop or the coral lives there today, for these creatures predate the Chesapeake Bay. The two fossils hark back to a very different time, perhaps 10 million years ago, when this part of the world was covered by warm, shallow, coastal seas. That was the Miocene Epoch in geologic time, a period that began about 25 million years ago and ended about 10 million years ago.

The present Chesapeake Bay seems to us as if it has been here forever. Yet we know that it is only about 15,000 years old, formed when the Atlantic Ocean flooded the mouth of the Susquehanna River system at the end of the last ice age. Several other bays preceded the present one, as earlier glaciers came and went, causing sea level to drop and rise over the past million years (the Pleistocene Epoch).

The Miocene Epoch predates even the glaciers by many, many years, but certain features of the region were already recognizable even then. The coastal plain had already formed, as the snows and the rains and the sunshine gradually weathered the Blue Ridge and Appalachian mountains, sending huge quantities of sand, gravel, and mud down the ancestors of our modern rivers. Thus, the eastern margin of the continent was already made up of these loose sediments, beginning around the present sites of Richmond, Fredericksburg, Washington, Baltimore, and Havre de Grace.

At times, sea level was low, and the coastal plain was exposed all the way to the edge of the continental shelf. At other times, like during the Miocene Epoch, the ocean covered virtually all of it. We can only imagine that the area was much like today's Atlantic Coast of Florida, Georgia, and South Carolina, with barrier beaches, shallow bays, and a relatively warm climate.

It's amazing to find out what lived in these warm seas. There were Brent Heath's big scallops and corals, plus porpoises, whales, oysters, sea turtles, rays, sharks, and other assorted fish, as well as crustaceans and mollusks, both large and small. Their fossils are littered along beaches near Miocene outcrops on the Bayshore and the tributaries.

For over 10 million years, these creatures lived and died by the millions, and plankton lived and died by the trillions. It is difficult to comprehend those numbers in any but an intellectual sense. The upshot, though, was that as they died and sank, they were buried in layers of seabed sediment several hundred feet deep. The estuaries that have developed in the past million years (including the present Chesapeake) have covered them over with more sediments, so the fossils of these Miocene creatures lie under much of our Bay region.

As noted above, the Pleistocene Epoch has seen several ice ages come and go, with glaciers advancing and retreating and attendant sea level fall and rise. When the sea level has been low in the periods during ice ages, the rivers in this area have run rapidly down to the edge of the continental shelf and out into the Atlantic, cutting deeply through the soft sediments of the coastal plain.

This downcutting is the mechanism that has produced the high bluffs that occur in spots along the Bay's main stem and rivers. Not all of these bluffs contain Miocene deposits, but many of them do. The most famous are the Calvert Cliffs and the nearby Scientists Cliffs along the Bayshore in southern Maryland, which may be the largest exposed deposit of Miocene fossils in the world. Large deposits also exist on the Potomac below Colonial Beach. There are interesting smaller deposits on most of the Bay's rivers, including Brent Heath's vein on Dragon Run; scattered outcrops on Wilton Creek (about 10 miles downstream on the Piankatank); and the Boston Cliffs (which are less than 30 feet high) on the Choptank River above Cambridge.

These spots offer an intriguing look into a time which is otherwise very difficult to imagine. They are good points of interest for cruising people and small boat explorers who learn to recognize them in the Bay's creeks and rivers. However, wave action erodes the bases of the cliffs, both large and small, and chunks fall off from time to time. Climbing them is extremely dangerous.

There are several excellent resources from which to learn about the Bay region's Miocene deposits and how to study them. The best is the Calvert Marine Museum in Solomons, at the mouth of the Patuxent. It has superb exhibits of Miocene fossils and can provide information on some ways to explore the Calvert Cliffs safely. A trip to the museum makes a good wintertime weekend outing. Both Westmoreland State Park in Virginia and Calvert Cliffs State Park in Maryland have good seasonal programs. Finally, A.J. and R. L. Lippson's *Life in the Chesapeake Bay* (see Bibliography) has a good chapter on Miocene fossils. Make use of these resources, and they will give you a whole new perspective on the Chesapeake.

JANUARY

Crabs in Winter

Cold water slows down even our feisty blue crabs. Like most of the Chesapeake's other creatures, they are cold-blooded. That is, their body temperatures are the same as or close to the temperature of the water around them. When that water is warm, the rate of metabolic activity in their bodies is high, and they are active. At lower temperatures, their metabolism slows down, and so does their level of activity.

Fish and crabs go through a winter season of inactivity that we call dormancy. Most of the fish that remain in the Chesapeake system seek out deep holes in the Bay and its tributaries where bottom water is a degree or two warmer than at the surface. That slight temperature differential gives them just enough body heat for limited movement and feeding. Crabs, by contrast, bury themselves in the mud, "tucked in for the winter," as William W. Warner puts it in *Beautiful Swimmers.* The bottom sediment, whether sand or mud, or a combination, acts literally as a blanket, insulating the crabs from sudden drops in water temperature that could kill them. They are efficient diggers, using their walking legs and swimming paddles to work their way in. They are able to burrow as deep as 6 to 12 inches, depending on bottom composition, if they sense a cold snap coming on. For most of us humans, they are out of sight, out of mind.

But think for a minute what this behavior means for the Chesapeake: a veritable carpet of crabs on the Bay bottom. By the roughest sort of estimate, I would guess that there are at least 300 million crabs buried in the Chesapeake and its tributaries.

Over the past 50 years, scientists have worked out their basic cold-water distribution patterns. In general, jimmies (mature males) head for deeper water as temperatures drop during the fall, burrowing into the deep trenches and holes of the Bay's ancestral Susquehanna River channel in 50 to 140 feet of water in both Maryland and Virginia. Sooks (mature females), by contrast, seek out the high salinities in the lower Bay. Many of them are carrying sperm packets (from summer matings) that will allow them to develop and spawn eggs the following summer, and those eggs need salty water to hatch properly. (More on their winter behavior shortly.) Immature crabs of all sizes bury themselves wherever winter overtakes them. They may be tiny individuals from the last hatch of the year, digging into channel edges as they ride the Bay's bottom currents upstream, or they may be half-grown and buried in a cove of a tributary like the Corrotoman or the Corsica.

The Chesapeake's research community may have worked out the general distribution of wintering crabs, but the real students of their behavior are the watermen who dredge them in Virginia from early December to late March. Despite often nasty working conditions in the Chesapeake's widest-open waters in its coldest months, the best of the dredgers become fascinated with their quarry. "At first, I just needed a job," says Lonnie Moore, arguably the best crab dredger on Tangier Island, and certainly one of the best on the Bay. "But the challenge pulls me back every year. I can't stop." Moore and his big deadrise workboat *Loni Carol II* work most of the year running field trips for the Chesapeake Bay Foundation's Port Isobel Island education center near Tangier, but he takes off two months each winter to "look the bottom over."

This kind of addictive curiosity is the major ingredient of successful winter crabbing. "Looking around," bird-dogging every possible patch of crabs, is the theme that comes up over and over in conversations about dredging. Moore covers literally all the mainstem of Virginia's portion of the Bay, from Cape Henry to Smith Point. Also important are a sense of history, of how crabs have reacted to weather changes from year to year, plus the willingness to work hard and good boat-handling skills.

"It's a brain game," says Moore. Crabs don't feed, but they move up and down in the bottom, from just under the surface to a foot down, which is too deep for the dredges to catch them. William Warner points out that dormancy is relative, not total. "The crabs toss and turn nervously in their beds on the bottom. Although they seldom get out of bed and pace the floor, so to speak, they do expend considerable energy changing position, digging in and digging out, trying to outsmart winter's caprices." Moore tells of days in January when he covered a particular piece of bottom and caught very few. Then a thaw came. He went back to the same spot and loaded the dredges. Then a cold front came through, and the crabs disappeared again deeper into the bottom.

Winter dredging has always been a controversial fishery, since its primary targets are the mature sooks that will spawn later in the year. Since he works for a conservation organization, Lonnie Moore is acutely aware of the criticism. He feels, with some justification, that dredging puts no more pressure on the crabs than the intensive potting that goes on in both Maryland and Virginia as the sooks head south in the fall.

He feels even more strongly, however, that the Chesapeake's crab stocks *are* being heavily exploited, in *all* fisheries. As watermen work bigger, faster boats with sophisticated electronics and more pots or larger dredges, there is more pressure on the crabs than ever before. The result is sometimes even more work for less money. "Last winter," he says, "we were catching a limit [75 bushels] and getting 6 dollars per bushel. Then crabs got scarce, and 50 bushels each brought 12 dollars. It was better for us *and* better for the crabs. Personally, I'd like to see a 50-bushel limit, and I'd like to see it built into an overall Chesapeake Bay crab management plan that covers *all* fisheries, both commercial and recreational, in Virginia and Maryland. There's no sense in doing any of it unless we look at the big picture. And crabs are too important to all of us to ruin them."

Moore is interested in the long pull, in a sustainable fishery. He wants to keep dredging—and studying winter crab behavior—for many years. "Just when you think you've got 'em figured out," he says, "those old crabs will prove you wrong. They're fascinating."

Killifish Are Tough

Don Baugh works for the Chesapeake Bay Foundation. Some winters, he spends time every day chopping ice around the foundation's piers and workboats. Several years ago, he found a killifish trapped in a chunk of ice. The fish hadn't been there long enough to freeze, but its body temperature was very low. Don thawed the ice gently and put the fish back into the creek. It swam away.

The killifish's name drives from a Dutch word, *kill*, meaning brook, but they are often referred to as bull minnows. They may be the most abundant group of inshore fish in the whole Chesapeake system. There are four widely distributed species: the sheepshead minnow *(Cyprinodon variegatus)*, the common killifish or mummichog *(Fundulus hetroclitus)*, the banded killifish *(F. diaphanus)*, and the striped killifish *(F. majalis)*.

Sheepshead minnows, 1 to 2 inches long, have short, deep, rounded bodies with wide vertical blotches and, in summer, orange-tinted fins. They are common in very shallow water at the heads of marsh guts and pools. The other species frequent these areas too, but they are more usually found in large numbers along the edges of open water and around bulkheads and dock pilings. In fact, there are few stretches of shoreline anywhere in the Bay and its rivers that do not hold some of them in warm weather. At midrange salinities (5 to 15 parts per thousand, or 15 to 50 percent that of seawater), a minnow seine pulled along a marsh bank will catch all three.

The mummichog is the stockiest. Females are dull olive on the back, with dusky silver flanks. Most have thin, dark vertical bars. Banded killifish are slimmer, and the males have distinct iridescent bars. Striped killifish are silvery, with dark backs and a few dark, vertical bars. Large females develop horizontal stripes. Maximum size for the first two species is about 4 inches, but some female striped killifish grow to 7 inches.

One of summer's best delights is pulling a minnow seine in the shallows and finding it full of bull minnows. These are great fish for children to play with, as long as they first wet their hands to avoid wiping off the fishes' protective mucous coating. The creatures are quite hardy and can take a lot of gentle handling. They also keep well in simple aquaria.

This hardiness, in fact, is part of the reason they are so wide-spread and so important to the estuary. Like raccoons and crows and seagulls, killifish are tough and adaptable opportunists. They can live in a broad variety of environmental conditions and can eat a number of different foods. They are not active now, compared to their summer level, but at a time when other fish have left the Bay or lie dormant in the deep holes, killifish are still moving around and still come up into the shallows on warm, sunny days.

They seem to do equally well in summer, even when the sun heats their mud flats, marsh pools, and guts above 90°F, driving much of the water's oxygen out of solution and causing evaporation that can raise salinity levels. Despite these stresses, shoals of min-nows go about their business.

"Business" in summer is breeding and feeding and avoiding predators. The ability to live well in very shallow water accomplishes the last task for some. Breeding runs from May to September, with the peak in the first three months. Male mummichogs are particu-larly colorful at that time. Food includes marsh detritus and mos-quito larvae. The mouths of all the species are well adapted for the latter food, with the lower jaws protruding below the uppers for easy surface feeding. The fish also do well as scavengers, as anyone who has ever looked into the water around a charter boat dock where fish are cleaned can attest.

Killifish have no direct value to man, but their indirect value is substantial. Because of their great numbers, they are important forage for most inshore predatory fish, from channel catfish and largemouth bass up the rivers to summer flounder on down the Bay. Because of their tolerance to cold, they are the primary winter food of chain pickerel and yellow perch, which also are moderately active then. Because of their hardiness and broad appeal to preda-tory fish, they are widely used as bait by anglers.

It is easy to overlook killifish, but they are important links in the Chesapeake's food web. By any measure, they are pillars of the Bay community.

Winter's Extra-Low Tides

Dr. William Dodge retired from his medical practice in Albany, New York, in the early 1950s. He and his wife, Helen, moved to a small farm at the mouth of Taskmaker's Creek, just south of Smith Point and the mouth of the Potomac on the Northern Neck. He loved his land there, with its sweeping view of the broad open waters, and he walked the beach every morning until his death in the early 1980s.

Dr. Dodge saw in detail how the seasons change and how one year is different from another. One of his favorite times of year was January, when a heavy winter storm would be followed by a calm, clear, diamond-bright day with exceptionally low tides. He loved to take up his walking stick and inspect the sand and mud flats uncovered by the receding waters.

January is often a month of storms. When a strong northeaster moves up the coast, it drops snow on the Bay country while its winds push large volumes of water in through the Virginia Capes. As a result, tides rise to abnormal highs. But after the storm passes, a strong high-pressure system—a tall mound of cold, clear air—drops down from Canada. The pent-up high water from the storm rushes back out to the ocean, pushed by the northwest winds on the leading edge of the fair weather system.

After the winds subside, the high atmospheric pressure pushes down on the surface of the Bay, keeping the water relatively low even when the tide rises. With low tides, many of the shallow areas that are normally underwater are exposed. It's as if some of the Chesapeake's bare bones are showing.

Wintertime tides produce several interesting ecological effects, all related to water's high specific heat and the fact that water increases in volume as its temperature falls from 4°C (39.2°F) toward freezing at 0°C (32°F). Because of the high specific heat, deep water habitat changes only very slowly, but temperatures can fluctuate considerably in the shallows. Water changes volume as it freezes and thaws, and ice crystals forming or dissolving can actually cause mechanical destruction of the cells of living plants and animals. Death usually results.

Low tides expose some shellfish to the air. Clams in shallow flats and oysters and mussels in the marsh banks are sometimes killed if low tides coincide with especially cold nights and days. A more serious problem occurs on shallow bars. The low tides reduce the volume of water over these bars and thus reduce the water's capacity to buffer extreme temperatures. Oysters on these bars can be killed, as can any crabs buried in the mud around them. Most fish will have left these areas, but a prolonged freeze can kill any that may be trapped there.

Low water and low temperatures can have positive effects, too. The tides expose new clam flats and bars to shoreline foragers like raccoons and to shallow-water feeders like tundra swans. Many a morning, Dr. Dodge found coon tracks leading out to the flats at the mouth of Taskmaker's Creek. The tracks usually ended at a crater where the coon had dug a breakfast of *Macoma* clams. The low water concentrates minnows like killifish in relatively small areas where otters can catch them more easily. It allows sea ducks to reach bottom feeding areas with less effort. And it opens new areas for gulls, who forage for whatever turns up. All these animals are warm-blooded. The colder it gets, the more food they need. Extra-low winter tides offer them much-needed feeding opportunities in areas they would not have access to otherwise.

There is another advantage to cold weather and low tides. The very combination that subjects marsh bank oysters and mussels to destruction also breaks up the dead grasses on that bank. The warm-weather food web in any tidal creek is heavily dependent upon detritus from the previous year's marsh plants. Freezing and thawing can break up granite, so it certainly does a good job on cordgrasses. The low tides that reduce the water's temperature-buffering capacity around marsh banks allow the cold nights and the sunny days to work on the marsh plants. The root systems stay alive, but the aboveground parts of the plants are ground and broken by the changing temperatures of the water in and around them. Soon enough, spring rains will sweep away the bits into the creeks, to feed the host of zooplankton, grass shrimp, and small fish that will need them come spring and summer.

Winter is severe, but the Chesapeake has adjusted to it and needs it. Dr. Dodge understood that fact and took great joy in his low tide explorations.

Waterfowl Joys and Sorrows

Twenty-eight species of ducks, geese, and swans spend some part of their year on the Chesapeake and its tidal tributaries. Most of them use the Bay as winter habitat. In this cold season when most other residents of our region are dormant or inactive, they provide a rich and diverse tapestry of life to anyone who troubles to look. Winter may force us to curtail fishing, crabbing, and sailing, but it also gives us waterfowl. For centuries, the birds have been among the Bay's best-loved creatures.

Almost all of our waterfowl spend the summer far away, in places like the tundra of Alaska's North Slope (tundra swans), the prairie pothole marshes of Canada and the upper Midwest (most ducks, e.g., canvasback, scaup, pintail, widgeon), the tundra and muskeg on the east side of Hudson Bay (most of "our" Canada geese), and the lake marshes of Newfoundland, Nova Scotia, and New Brunswick ("our" black ducks). Now why would a species set up such a complex life cycle, with a 1,000- to 4,000-mile migration every six months? The answer lies in the birds' diets. Very young waterfowl need large quantities of protein-rich food, and insects are an excellent source. Summer in northern latitudes is short, but insect populations are very high (as anyone who has dealt with Alaskan mosquitoes can tell you).

At summer's end, harsh weather drives the birds south to areas where they can find warmer temperatures with plenty of food. Some ducks, like green- and blue-winged teal, fly all the way to Central America, but many come to the shallow estuaries of the Atlantic coast to feed on their submerged aquatic vegetation and small shellfish and to live in their marshes and swamps.

Waterfowl are creatures of habit. They use the same wintering and breeding grounds each year. Hence their migration patterns are generally stable and predictable. For thousands of years, North America's ducks, geese, and swans have followed these patterns and prospered. Historians on the Chesapeake say that in the last century, the birds were so numerous that they "darkened the skies."

But no more. In the past hundred years, waterfowl numbers have declined dramatically. Here on the Chesapeake, commercial hunting in the late nineteenth and early twentieth centuries started the problem, with millions of birds harvested and shipped to market. That practice was made illegal years ago, but the birds have also lost both food sources and habitat as our submerged vegetation has declined and wetlands have been disturbed by human activities. The waterfowl that breed in the Canadian prairie potholes have lost many ponds and lakes as that land has been drained and plowed to raise wheat. Reductions in good habitat have been exacerbated by periods of bad weather, especially on the breeding grounds where drought can dry up what potholes remain or, in most northern latitudes (like Quebec's Ungava Peninsula, where most of the Chesapeake's wintering Canada geese breed), where cold, wet summers can disrupt nesting and brood development. Finally, for some species, recreational hunting has been a problem.

It's the old story—a combination of human factors work together to cause major declines and compromise a species' resilience to periodic spells of bad weather conditions. Populations of canvasbacks, greater and lesser scaup, blue-winged teal, black ducks, and pintails are all at very low points throughout their ranges, and the number of Canada geese in the Chesapeake has dropped by over half in the past 20 years.

Fortunately, there are extensive management programs in place to deal with the problems. U.S. federal and state government agencies form a coordinated network that works closely with their counterparts in Canada to control harvests and improve habitat. That relationship has been formalized in the North American Waterfowl Management Plan, whose goal is to return the birds' populations to the levels of the early 1970s. Another important element in the restoration effort is the ongoing work of Ducks Unlimited and the Delta Waterfowl Foundation to restore and preserve nesting habitat in Canada and, to a lesser extent, in the United States. Here on the Chesapeake, Easton's Waterfowl Festival, Inc., has pumped hundreds of thousands of dollars into the projects of Ducks Unlimited and Delta, as well as into local efforts like those of Chesapeake Wildlife Heritage, also based in Easton.

An important part of the interstate Chesapeake Bay restoration program focuses on living resources, including everything from submerged vegetation and fish to waterfowl. Thus a strong team of state agencies and the U.S. Fish and Wildlife Service has pulled together a comprehensive Chesapeake Bay Waterfowl Policy and Management Plan that summarizes existing knowledge and programs. It also describes specific plans for waterfowl research and management, with special emphasis on restoration of habitat and food sources.

Implementation of this plan is very much a part of the Chesapeake Bay cleanup. Fairfax H. Settle, a retired Virginia waterfowl and game biologist who helped develop the plan, summed up the situation well: "It all gets back to water quality. What's good for the rockfish and the crab is good for the duck, the goose, and the swan."

The Chesapeake's waterfowl need all the appreciation and support they can get. Ask your state wildlife agency how you can help. If you get cabin fever this winter, spend some time with the birds. Get a copy of the plan (see Bibliography) and read it for the background it gives you on the birds. Then go see them. Put on a pair of boots, a warm coat, a hat, and gloves. Fill a Thermos with something hot, pack a pair of binoculars and a field guide, and visit some of the areas where waterfowl congregate. In general, any of the Bay's national wildlife refuges, the state and county parks on the tidal rivers and the open Bay, and picnic areas beside bridges over the rivers are good places to view waterfowl. See the section on winter walks in *Exploring the Chesapeake in Small Boats* (see Bibliography) for some specific suggestions.

The Bay's waterfowl give a rich dimension to our winters. Enjoy them.

FEBRUARY

Eagles Nesting

Rod and Lucy Coggin were paddling a canoe along the shore of her family's farm on the lower Potomac. A mature bald eagle was soaring over them. Presently another appeared. It swooped down onto the first bird, and they locked talons. Then, with wings outstretched, they whirled down like a double-bladed helicopter toward a tall loblolly pine. Just above the tree, they parted and went their separate ways. Rod and Lucy watched in amazement and delight.

This eagle behavior pattern is a spectacular recognition and mating display. It is quite a rare sight, at least for human observers. But being around eagles is not rare at all for Rod and Lucy. The Potomac has a number of successful nests. Midwinter counts for the whole Bay region have increased substantially in the past 20 years. The eagle population on the Bay is rising.

The bald eagle is still an endangered species. It is still intolerant of disturbances by man. People still shoot eagles, for a variety of reasons (none good, or legal). But since EPA's ban on DDT in 1972, the population has been rising steadily. The lowest year on record was 1962, when 59 breeding pairs on the Bay produced 0.2 young per nest (12 eaglets). In the past 10 years, nesting success has been solidly better than 1.0 per nest, and the total number of nesting pairs approaches 300.

The birds are grouped primarily along the rivers, and each major river system on the Bay has several nests. Heaviest concentrations occur at the U.S. Army's Aberdeen Proving Ground at the head of the Bay, along Virginia's big western shore rivers, and in the huge marsh country of Dorchester County, on Maryland's Eastern Shore. Recommended public places to watch eagles include Blackwater National Wildlife Refuge near Cambridge; Eastern Neck Island National Wildlife Refuge at the mouth of the Chester near Rock Hall; Patuxent River Park at Croom, near Upper Marlboro; Mason Neck National Wildlife Refuge, on the Virginia side of the Potomac below Mount Vernon; Caledon Natural Area on the Virginia side of the Potomac above the Route 301 bridge; Westmoreland State Park, on the Potomac between Colonial Beach and Montross; the Colonial Parkway on the York near Williamsburg; the Jamestown Parkway; the James River Plantations, especially Shirley, Berkeley, Westover, and Evelynton; and Hog Island State Wildlife Management Area near Surry on the south bank of the James.

Seeing an eagle takes a little practice. Sometimes it is possible to go down the Wildlife Drive at Blackwater and find a mature adult, dark brown with white head and tail, sitting unconcernedly in a dead tree 50 feet from the road. More often, though, the bird will be soaring some distance away, and the white head and tail may not show up. In fact, immature eagles do not show white. They are dark brown with a few flecks of white all over, and they stay more or less that way for at least their first four years. It is easy to confuse them with turkey vultures.

There are, however, several field marks that are useful for identifying eagles even several hundred yards away. First, the only other large dark hawk-type soaring birds commonly in the area are the turkey vulture, the black vulture, and the osprey. Of these, only the eagle and the osprey soar with their wings flat. The vultures' wings slant upward (the shape is called dihedral).

The osprey has a white belly, where the eagle's is dark, and the osprey's shorter wings (4½-foot spread) curve backward at the elbows. The eagle's wings are longer (6-foot spread), straighter, and narrower than those of the vultures (5½- and 5-foot spreads respectively). The eagle's head is much larger and longer than those of the other birds. On a clear day, sunlight will highlight the white tail of a mature eagle soaring.

Eagles in the Bay tend to roost in tall trees, often loblolly pines. From them and while soaring, the birds watch their territories and hunt food. Stories of stealing from ospreys or eating carrion are true, at least sometimes. The birds are big, and, while powerful, are not as quick as ospreys. Thus they feed shrewdly. Fish, especially catfish, carp, and eels, are their most common food, though recent surveys show a marked increase in bird remains around nests. Eagles in the Bay feed occasionally on mammals, like muskrats and rabbits, and on turtles. It is thought that most birds and mammals caught are sick or wounded.

There is evidence that the Chesapeake is important habitat not only to local nesting birds but to others up and down the Atlantic Coast. Local nesters tend to be nonmigratory and occupied with nesting and raising young most of the year. They're on their nests in late fall, repairing them and lining them to lay eggs and begin incubating this month. The eggs hatch in mid- to late March, and young are fledged in June. They stay around their parents till late summer. Then they go out on their own in the early fall, and the parents start a new cycle all over again.

Florida's large population, meanwhile, lays eggs earlier, in November, and some young birds wander up to the Chesapeake the following summer, as will some nonbreeding adults. Birds from New England, where eggs are laid in May and June, will come down for the winter. It appears that most members of every population of eagles on the East Coast use the Chesapeake at some point in their lives. There are spots on the James, the Rappahannock, and the Potomac where eagles congregate at certain times during these movements, and counts can run over 30 birds in a 2-acre area, a remarkable sight to be sure.

Eagle watching is a good activity any time of year. Remember, though, the birds do not tolerate disturbance well, especially now when they are nesting. Enough disruption will cause them to abandon the nest, usually for good. They are best appreciated from a distance. Watching them can be done from the shoulders of public roads, which means having a warm car close by to ease the February chill. A pair of binoculars is useful. Just watch the sky and be patient. The eagles are there.

Otters Are Busy Now

Dave and Pat Carpenter own the Poquoson Marina, down below Yorktown near the mouth of the Poquoson River. It's a big marina, and icy winters mean trouble for boats and pilings. But Dave and Pat like ice, because they can watch the otters play on it. The animals seem to spend more time around the marina then, or maybe they just show themselves more in the daytime. They fish around the pilings and appear to delight in sliding across the ice.

The Chesapeake has a healthy population of otters. In fact, the river otter *(Lutra canadensis)* is widely distributed in North America, except for the most Arctic sections of Alaska and Canada and the extreme parts of the southwest United States. On the Chesapeake, every river system has at least one family, from the hardwood swamp streams of the upper Pocomoke and the Presqu'ile National Wildlife Refuge on the James to the river marshes of the York and the Gunpowder, and the Bayshore marshes of Tangier Sound.

Otters may be widely distributed, but there are not a lot of them. They are carnivores, feeding at the top of the food web, and there simply is not as much for them to eat as there is for herbivores like muskrats or for opportunistic omnivores like raccoons and opossums. So like their kin, the other species of otters around the world and minks and weasels, river otters are secretive, elusive creatures that hunt large territories. Depending on where they live, otters will mark out 5 miles of stream bank or 50 miles of coastal marsh and beach. Working a large area ensures that no part of it will be overfished, and an animal constantly on the move is likely to stay out of the way of potential enemies.

The river otter is smaller than its well-publicized and endangered cousin, the sea otter of the Pacific Coast. Males grow to about 4 feet in length, two-thirds head and body and one-third tail. Maximum weight is 25 pounds (as opposed to 80 for the sea otter). Females are slightly smaller.

The animal's feet are webbed, with hair on the soles. The coat is rich brown, with long, glossy guard hairs over thick fur. The belly is lighter in color, and hair about the face is gray. The animal is well equipped for life in the water, even in the coldest weather.

The otter's body is long and sleek, with a flat head and muzzle. In the water, where it counts most, the animal is well streamlined. It swims with its forelegs tucked against its chest, oscillating the after part of its body from side to side and steering with its thick, muscular tail. Often the hind legs are tucked up against the body, but the animal can use them for extra bursts of speed. The otter's backbone appears to be particularly flexible, allowing for extraordinary maneuverability either at play or at the serious business of fishing.

Otters eat a variety of food, with diet depending on habitat. They eat primarily fish and shellfish, but will also eat young muskrats, birds, and frogs. In Britain, they have long been despised and hunted as destroyers of trout and salmon, as any reader of Izaak Walton's *Compleat Angler* knows. But like trout and salmon, the predatory fish that live in the Bay are fast, agile, and hard to catch, and so make up only a minor part of the otters' diet. Wild creatures must expend energy to catch food, and if they expend more calories in the catching than the eating, they starve. The net amount of energy gained is what counts to them. Hence it pays otters to concentrate on food that is relatively easy to catch.

On the Chesapeake, this means small inshore species like killifish, juvenile spot, and mullet, although they have been known to catch fish as large as a carp in some of the tributaries. One soft-crabber on Virginia's Northern Neck reports that otters visit his peeler traps regularly, looking for the fish that swim into them. When this happens, he finds a fish head left on top of a trap. Only when the traps have no fish will an otter take a crab.

Otters appear to mate for life, and they usually breed late in the winter, though some breeding takes place in every month of the year. Young are born in every month of the year also, but there is survival advantage in having them born in the spring, with summer's warm temperatures and more abundant food to aid in their slow development. To this end, a bitch otter bred in the summer or fall is able to hold the fertilized egg until late winter before it attaches itself to the wall of her uterus and the embryo begins to develop. This remarkable process, rare but not unique to otters, is called delayed implantation. The young, one to five in a litter, stay with their mother for about a year. The dog otter stays away when the cubs are newly born, but there is evidence that he takes part in their rearing later in the year.

The dog maintains a large territory, while the bitch and young hold a smaller one within it. They hunt parts of the territory each night, moving on to other parts the next night. Somewhere in each territory, though, there is a well-hidden den, usually in a dense thicket. The animals are wanderers, but they are also creatures of habit. They use the same trails over and over.

Early morning is a good time to see otters, but the best way to begin is to look for signs and trails first. On a firm beach, tracks can be useful. The animal leaves a peculiar, stretched-out track pattern as it lopes along (the result of its distinctive body shape). But the most reliable signs are piles of scat (droppings), especially fish scales and bones. (Otters eat their fish whole and somehow manage to pass the scales and bones without giving themselves ulcers.)

Otters have anal scent glands that they use with droppings to mark their territories, and the scents may vary enough to be useful to them in recognition of each other. Thus the places where they drop their scats become important parts of their territories. In these places and along their trails, they will also tear up and leave piles of vegetation which they have marked with scent.

A few otters have been partially domesticated. They have received a lot of publicity, especially in Britain, in Gavin Maxwell's *Ring of Bright Water* and Philip Wayre's *The River People*. But both Maxwell and Wayre are careful to point out the difficulties and dangers of keeping them. Otters are wild, and that is part of their appeal. They are perhaps the wildest, most elusive, and secretive creatures on the Chesapeake. They certainly see more of us than we do of them. Watching them play on the ice in February is one of the year's best thrills.

Sea Ducks Relish Winter on the Chesapeake

The open Chesapeake Bay is not a hospitable place in February. Most of the month is bitter cold. Strong winds and snowstorms are always possibilities. On the surface of the Bay, only crab-dredgers and hard-clammers (in Virginia), a few oystermen, and commercial shipping interests are active. Most animals are absent or dormant.

It is a surprise, then, in this otherwise desolate scene, to find a group of ducks who seem to thrive on February's freezing temperatures and nasty weather.

These waterfowl include the oldsquaw and three species of scoter: black, surf, and white-winged. The four are related, they are all adapted to cold open waters, and they make remarkably long migrations to spend the winter here on the Chesapeake.

The birds' summer breeding grounds are particularly striking to the imagination. The oldsquaws that winter, say, around Hacketts Bar off Annapolis, may have come from the tundra of Alaska's North Slope, Canada's Arctic coast, or Greenland. Black scoters around Great Fox Island in Tangier Sound have come from ponds in the forests of western Alaska, Labrador, and Newfoundland. Surf scoters around Smith Point Light and off the Bayshore of the Northern Neck have come from glacial lakes in Alaska and northern Canada. White-winged scoters off Lynnhaven, around the Bay Bridge-Tunnel, have likewise come from lakes in Alaska and Canada, though a few may breed as far south as North Dakota. All of these areas produce heavy summer crops of aquatic insects whose larvae provide essential protein sources for the fast-growing ducklings.

If insect hatches in the high Arctic summer provide one essential dimension to the lives of these sea ducks, the Chesapeake's relatively shallow and at least generally ice-free waters with (historically) broad expanses of "live bottom" oyster rocks give them the other. The shallow waters (the average depth of the Bay is 21 feet) mean that they do not have to dive great distances to pick up food. The abundance of life on the bottom of this rich estuary provides them with a rich food source, mostly mussels and other small shellfish that live attached to oysters.

Each of the four sea duck species differs slightly in food preferences, but it is easy enough to draw some general observations about their way of life. They are heavily insulated against cold water, they dive to catch their food from the bottom, and they are capable of crushing shellfish as they eat them. Let's look at each set of features in turn.

Body heat conservation is a critical element in the sea ducks' design. All four species have compact, stocky bodies to minimize surface area through which to lose warmth. Plenty of downy under-

feathers provide insulation and are covered by tough outer feathers that act as foul weather gear. The birds "waterproof" these surface feathers by preening, or rubbing the edges of their bills over themselves. This grooming behavior keeps the feathers properly arranged and allows the ducks to pick up oil from the preen glands at the bases of their tails and spread it as additional waterproofing on the feathers.

The major design feature for diving is placement of the legs far back on the body, a characteristic which these sea ducks share with other diving waterfowl, like loons and cormorants. It gives them great power underwater. In addition, the oldsquaw and the white-winged scoter use their wings for propulsion underwater, and the other two scoters open them slightly to steer. The oldsquaw is the champion diver, capable of reaching depths in excess of 150 feet, though such dives are undertaken only in extreme need. It is very much to all four species' advantage to conserve energy by diving only short distances whenever possible.

Once the birds dive to the bottom, their stout bills allow them to nibble and tug at mussels and barnacles they find on oyster rocks and to root in the bottom for small clams. Once food articles are dislodged, the birds can swallow them and crush them in their muscular gizzards. They may also eat worms, small crabs, grass shrimp, and other tiny crustaceans that they find in the oyster communities.

Sea ducks have been coming to the Chesapeake for thousands of years. For most of that time, the Bay offered them extensive oyster rocks with plenty of food. As water quality in the Bay began to decline earlier in this century, other waterfowl species like canvasback began to lose submerged aquatic vegetation upon which they depend, but the sea ducks still had plenty of oyster bottom and clam beds. Now the precipitous decline of the Chesapeake's oyster stocks is taking one source of food away from these birds.

The sea ducks are not yet in crisis; their numbers have declined only slowly in the past 20 years. Still, there is concern for them, and any efforts we are able to mount to restore our Bay's oysters will benefit them greatly. The oldsquaw and the scoters are tough, competent ducks. Any bird that thrives on the open Chesapeake in February deserves respect.

Cold Water Brings a Quiet Season

"February is the longest month," growled Bill Pike as he looked out on a cold, gray day and an iced-up Severn River. In his retirement, Bill normally fishes every day, but this month breaks his routine.

Winter temperatures force most of the Bay's creatures into inactivity or dormancy. Cold-blooded animals, whose body temperatures are basically dependent on that of their environment, are most susceptible to the season. As water temperatures drop in late fall and early winter, they seek out the warmest habitat they can find where temperatures are stable. In general, the most comfortable place to be is in deep water.

Cold water can hold gasses in solution at higher concentrations than can warm water. This property means that oxygen concentrations are higher in winter than in summer. As water temperatures in the Bay and its tributaries drop in the fall, the cooling surface waters, which are well-oxygenated from contact with the air, increase in density and sink to the bottom, bringing up deep water and allowing it to be reoxygenated. Stormy weather, with winds and rain, add more oxygen. Summertime oxygen concentrations are low in the deep waters of the Bay and some of its tributaries, but now they are much higher.

Thus these deep waters are stable, relatively warm, and well oxygenated, so they represent the best February fish habitat in the system for most species. Many of the fish that winter in the Chesapeake can be found in these areas, especially forage like anchovies and silversides, and larger species like rockfish.

Although February is hard on Bill Pike, his favorite fish— white perch—can be caught in deep holes on a number of rivers and creeks right through the month, so he does get out when the weather is decent. But anyone seeking bluefish, trout, spot, croakers, or flounder is out of luck. With the onset of cold weather, these species head for an even more stable environment than the Bay— the Atlantic Ocean. They winter offshore out on the continental shelf, returning to the Chesapeake's rich feeding grounds when the weather warms up. Most menhaden, which are major forage for blues and trout, also head for the ocean, though a few schools will stay in deep holes in the Bay.

Some other cold-blooded animals are dormant this month. In late fall, as we have seen, crabs seek out holes and channels, where they bury into the bottom mud. Snapping turtles and diamondback terrapins hibernate in the mud too. Shellfish like oysters and clams may continue to feed through a mild winter, but their food intake slows down with their metabolism. There is less food available to them anyway, since plankton populations are low now (which also results in winter's characteristically clear water).

By late February, the Bay region usually experiences a thaw, and creatures begin to stir. Crocuses bloom to remind us humans that spring will come. Experienced bird-watchers know that bald eagles have finished their nest repairs and are laying eggs. Bill Pike starts to fish a deep hole where yellow perch have schooled up for the winter. Even though the fish are nearly a month away from spawning, their bodies are swelling with milt and roe, so they are feeding at least sporadically. February may be long, but it doesn't last forever. By the end of the month, Bill is smiling again.

BIBLIOGRAPHY

Burgess, Robert H. *Chesapeake Circle*. Cambridge, Md.: Cornell Maritime Press, 1965.

————. *This Was Chesapeake Bay*. Centreville, Md.: Tidewater Publishers, 1963.

Burgess, Robert H. and H. Graham Wood. *Steamboats Out of Baltimore*. Cambridge, Md.: Tidewater Publishers, 1968.

Carr, Archie. *Handbook of Turtles*. Ithaca, N.Y.: Cornell University Press, 1952.

Carson, Rachel. *Under the Sea Wind: A Naturalist's Picture of Ocean Life*. New York: Oxford University Press, Inc., 1952.

Chesapeake Bay Waterfowl Policy & Management Plan, available from the Communications Office, EPA Chesapeake Bay Program, 410 Severn Avenue, Annapolis, Md. 21403.

Chowning, Larry. *Harvesting the Chesapeake: Tools and Traditions*. Centreville, Md.: Tidewater Publishers, 1990.

Cownose ray information: Write the Sea Grant Advisory Service, Virginia Institute of Marine Science, Gloucester Point, Va. 23062, for prices of the pamphlets: "Biology & Identification of Rays in the Chesapeake Bay," by Joseph V. Smith and J.V. Merriner; "Cleaning & Preparing the Cownosed Ray"; "Handle with Care: Mid-Atlantic Marine Animals That Demand Your Respect," by Jon Lucy.

Ernst, Carl H. and Roger W. Barbor. *Turtles of the United States*. Lexington: University of Kentucky Press, 1972.

Frye, John. *The Men All Singing: The Story of Menhaden Fishing*. Virginia Beach, Va.: The Donning Company, Publishers, 1978.

Gibbons, Euell. *Stalking the Blue-Eyed Scallop*. New York: David McKay Co., 1963.

————. *Stalking the Wild Asparagus*. New York: David McKay Co., 1961.

Hay, John. *Spirit of Survival: A Natural and Personal History of Terns*. New York: E.P. Dutton & Co., Inc., 1974.

Horton, Tom. *Bay Country*. Baltimore: The Johns Hopkins University Press, 1988.

Horton, Tom, and Wm E. Eichbaum. *Turning the Tide: Saving the Chesapeake Bay*. Washington, D.C.: Island Press, 1991.

Klingel, Gilbert. *The Bay*. Baltimore: The Johns Hopkins University Press, 1986.

Lippson. A.J., ed. *Environmental Atlas of the Potomac Estuary*. Baltimore: The Johns Hopkins University Press, 1979.

Lippson, A.J., and R. L. Lippson. *Life in the Chesapeake Bay*. Baltimore: The Johns Hopkins University Press, 1984.

McClane, A.J. *A Guide to the Freshwater Fishes of North America*. New York: Holt, Rinehart, & Winston, 1974.

———. *A Guide to the Saltwater Fishes of North America*. New York: Holt, Rinehart, & Winston, 1975.

Meanley, Brooke. *Birds and Marshes of the Chesapeake Bay Country*. Centreville, Md.: Tidewater Publishers, 1975.

Musick, J.A. "The Marine Turtles of Virginia." Write the Sea Grant Advisory Service, Virginia Institute of Marine Science, Gloucester Point, Va. 23062, for the price of the pamphlet.

Penrod, Ken. *Fishing the Tidal Potomac River*. Beltsville, Md.: PPC Publishing, 1989.

———. *Tidewater Bass Fishing*. Beltsville, Md.: PPC Publishing, 1991.

Robbins, Chandler S., Bertel Bruun, and Herbert S. Zim. *Birds of North America*. New York: Golden Press, 1966.

Rudloe, Jack. *Time of the Turtle*. New York : Alfred A. Knopf, 1979.

Schubel, Jerry. *The Living Chesapeake*. Baltimore: The Johns Hopkins University Press, 1982.

Silberhorn, Gene M. *Common Marsh Plants of the Mid-Atlantic Coast*. Baltimore: The Johns Hopkins University Press, 1982.

Snediker, Quentin, and Ann Jensen. *Chesapeake Bay Schooners*. Centreville, Md.: Tidewater Publishers, 1992.

Tilp, Frederick. *This Was Potomac River*. Privately published in 1978, available from the Chesapeake Bay Foundation, 162 Prince George Street, Annapolis, Md. 21401.

Walters, Keith. *Chesapeake Stripers*. Bozman, Md.: Aerie House, 1990.

Warner, William W. *Beautiful Swimmers: Watermen, Crabs, and the Chesapeake Bay*. Boston: Atlantic-Little, Brown, 1976.

White, Christopher P. *Chesapeake Bay: Nature of the Estuary, A Field Guide*. Centreville, Md.: Tidewater Publishers, 1989.

Williams, John Page. Jr. *Exploring the Chesapeake in Small Boats*. Centreville, Md.: Tidewater Publishers, 1992.

INDEX

Chromatophore, 156
Chumming, 71
Clam, 32, 51, 126, 175, 176, 185,
198, 207, 220, 222; freshwater,
177; hard, 176, 177; *Macoma*,
178, 179, 194, 208; *Rangia*,
177; soft-shelled, 75, 176; stout
razor, 178, 179
Coastal plain, 154, 199, 200
Cobia, 71, 73
Cockerell Creek, Great Wicomico
R., Va., 81
Coelenterata, 111
Coggin, Lucy, 212
Coggin, Rod, 212
Coles Point, Potomac R., Va.,
167
Colombia, 38, 143
Colonial Beach, Potomac R., Va.,
174, 200
Colonial Parkway, Williamsburg,
Va., 213
Connecticut R., 14, 30
Conowingo Dam, Susquehanna
R., Md., 29
Continental shelf, 5, 12, 14, 15,
20, 42, 64, 65, 88, 89, 125, 126,
136, 146, 160, 161, 165, 167,
199, 200, 221
Copepod, 10, 11, 21, 22, 23, 24,
57, 65, 74, 110, 184
Coral, 198, 199
Cordgrass, 118, 142, 185, 195,
197, 208; giant, 117, 125, 141;
saltmarsh, 22, 46, 117, 197
Coriolis forces, 41
Cormorant, double-crested, 11,
18, 19, 147, 220
Corning, N.Y., 14
Corrotoman River, Rappahan-
nock R., Va., 76, 119, 141
Covington, Va., 28

Crab: blue, 4, 5, 9,12, 16, 23, 26,
32, 42, 48, 51, *61*, 64, 67, 68,
69, 70, 78, 87, 88, 89, 117, 145,
161, 183, 189, 201, 202, 203,
208, 216, 220, 222; fiddler, 44;
horseshoe, 49, 50, 51; mud,
48, 67, 185
Crappie, 94
Crayfish, 36, 78
Crisfield, Md., 43, 48, 146
Croaker, Atlantic, 48, 64, 66, 125,
145, 146, 149, 158, 159, 160,
161, 178, 190
Curry, Lee, 105, 106
Curry, Sandy, 105, 106
Cut Channel (Rappahannock
Shoal Channel), Va., 147
Cypress, bald, 38

D
Dahlgren, Va., 116
Darter, 124
Darwin, Capt. Ed, 151
deBordenave, Rev. E.A.
("Froggy"), 174, 176
Deep Landing, Chester R., Md.,
155
Delaware Bay, 18, 89, 91
Delaware R., 30
Delta Waterfowl Foundation, 210
Denton, Md., 130
Detritus, 10, 16, 23, 42, 74, 155,
188, 206, 208
Diatom, 26, 74, 91, 126, 170, 171,
172, 173
Diet analysis, 132
Dinoflagellate, 109
Dixie, Piankatank R., Va., 154
Dodge, Helen, 206
Dodge, Dr. William, 206, 207, 208
Dorchester Co., Md., 197, 213
Dornin, Bob, 55, 56